I WILL SURVIVE

The African-American Guide
to Healing from Sexual Assault and Abuse

I WILL SURVIVE

The African-American Guide
to Healing from Sexual Assault and Abuse

LORI S. ROBINSON
foreword by **Julia A. Boyd**

I WILL SURVIVE:
The African-American Guide to Healing from Sexual Assault and Abuse

Copyright © 2002 by Lori S. Robinson
Foreword Copyright © 2002 by Julia A. Boyd

Published by Seal Press
An Imprint of Avalon Publishing Group Incorporated
161 William St., 16th Floor
New York, NY 10038

Library of Congress Cataloging-in-Publication Data is available.

ISBN 1-58005-080-8

9 8 7 6 5 4 3 2 1

Designed by Shona McCarthy

Printed in the United States of America
Distributed by Publishers Group West

ACKNOWLEDGMENTS

All praises to the Most High! When I stop to think about the trauma I endured and what I have accomplished in the seven years since, I am overwhelmed. I give thanks for the miraculous healing power of God.

The night I was raped, the first person I called was my sister, Leah. Leah, you have nurtured and supported me for as long as I can remember. You are a natural, gifted healer. Without you, I would not be where I am today. Thank you for taking me in, leading me into a spirituality that sustains me, and ministering to me for so long.

"This will just bring us closer together," said my new boyfriend when I told him by phone that I had been raped the night before. It is difficult to imagine a man being more supportive in such a time of crisis than was Ollie A. Johnson III, now my husband. Ollie, I am constantly amazed by your love, patience, gentleness, and support. Not only has my healing been a challenge for both of us, I am well aware that writing this book has required a major sacrifice on both our parts. Thank you for everything. I love you more than words can say.

Many people set the stage for my healing in the days and weeks after my assault. Thank you to my childhood friends and my Spelman friends for your encouragement, prayers, comfort, and laughter. Special thanks to Askhari Johnson-Hodari, who made me feel safe and who was the first person to encourage me to write about what happened. Thanks also to my boss at the time, George Curry, for your support, including unlimited leave. And thanks to the *Emerge* staff who supported me in those early days: Victoria Valentine, Sherri Roberts-Lumpkin, Alayna Gaines, and Flo Purnell.

Of course, professional healers have played a significant role in my healing process. Thank you to my therapist, Rev. Dr. Atiba Vidato-Haupt. Toward the end of wrtiting this book, acupuncturist extraordinaire Sharon Rojas helped me push through to completion. Thanks for your generous support.

Sometimes family isn't blood. TaRessa Stovall, has gone above and beyond the call of duty to help me heal and to get me through the writing of this book. TaRessa, I don't believe I would have achieved this without your encouragement, your prodding, and your advice to put the book down when I had re-traumatized myself. Thank you for adopting me as your spiritual daughter. And a big shout out to our short-lived writers' group. It was just what I needed to get going.

I must thank my two favorite editors in the world. Leah Latimer helped me get organized for and actually start writing this book, and she came through for me in the end, commenting on several chapters. Leah, your assistance was crucial. Thank you. Marcia Davis edited my article about rape that appeared in *Emerge*. Marcia, I have learned so much from you. Thank you for encouraging me to do the story and for forcing it out of me when I couldn't get it done by myself. That article was the catalyst for this book.

Thank you to the information specialists at the National Sexual Violence Resource Center for your help with statistics.

Thanks to everyone who read chapters for me, including Susan Newman, TaRessa, and Ollie, who read the entire manuscript.

This project has been a family effort in many ways. Mom, thanks for tying up so many loose ends while I was overseas, for the optimistic gene, and for working so hard to keep me whole. To both my parents, thank you for your financial support. Lord knows where I would have worked if not for the generosity and kindness of my aunt and uncle, Eloise and Benjamin Woods. Thank you for the rent-free office. And special thanks to my cousins, Kelvin Woods and Benjamin Woods, Jr., for your technical assistance.

There is certainly no shortage of patience at Seal Press. I have worked with many editors there, and it has been a pleasure working with all of you. Thank you for your compassionate approach and for supporting this project. Thanks also to Jessica Roncker for your hard work on the resources section.

Thanks to the dozens of experts and several survivors I interviewed, there are many important messages in this book that can contribute to a healthier, safer, more joyful world for all of us. To each reader, thank you for your role, however great or small, in the healing of an individual, a neighborhood, our nation. Much love to you.

To the ancestors sexually violated during and after slavery, when the political, economic and social structure of the United States supported their victimization.

To the girls, boys, women and men who have been sexually assaulted or abused and have not yet found the help they deserve.

To the lightworkers—professionals and volunteers—who are committed to helping survivors heal.

To my hero, Ida B. Wells-Barnett.

Author's Note

- Throughout *I Will Survive,* I have used male and female pronouns interchangeably to refer to survivors. I have used female pronouns most often simply because far more women and girls are victims of sexual assault and abuse than boys and men. I am not overlooking the victimization of males—this book is for them as much as it is for women. I have also used male and female pronouns interchangeably when referring to professionals in various fields. In no case does this mean that the job can be done only by people of the gender referenced.

- In most instances, contact information for resources such as organizations, books, and hotlines that are mentioned in the text appears in the resource section in the back of the book.

- In referring to the many types of sexual violations, organizations, and experts, use a range of terms that vary in definition. In *I Will Survive,* I use "sexual violence," sexual assault," and "sexual victimization" as comprehensive terms covering all types of sexual violation, including completed or attempted penetration with a body part or object, fondling, and oral sexual acts. "Rape" is used to refer to a sexual violation that includes penetration. "Child sexual abuse" encompasses any completed or attempted sexual violation of a child, including showing a girl or boy sexual images, photographing a child for pornography, and any inappropriate physical contact. "Sexual abuse," when referring to adults, can mean sexual violations that happen in the context of relationships or sexual victimization in general.

CONTENTS

PART II: SURVIVORS' STORIES OF HEALING

FOREWORD

It's been a long time coming, and it's way overdue, but it's here now and let us say a resounding thanks. *I Will Survive* by Lori S. Robinson is the first definitive book for Black women and men that addresses not only the devastation and trauma of being sexually assaulted, but the power of emotional healing. Using her own story as a backdrop, Robinson takes us on a step-by-step journey of healing. Yes, sexual violence is emotionally traumatizing, yes, the legal system is confusing, and no, sad but true, we don't always get the support we want or need in times of crisis; however, Robinson continues to remind us throughout the book that while the journey may be rocky, our destination is what's most important. *I Will Survive* gives us permission to take care of ourselves while acknowledging and validating the difficulty we may experience in needing support from others.

I read *I Will Survive* twice: once straight through from beginning to end as a body of knowledge, and, the second time, skipping around to different chapters for quick reference-guide information. Both times I felt I had gained supportive information and useful techniques for putting one's life back together after the trauma of sexual assault.

Robinson meticulously walks us through the medical maze of a physical exam and evidence gathering in the first chapter, "Your Physical Health." The medical procedures are physically invasive, she warns us; however, they are necessary in order to ensure our physical well-being.

The candor and directness that Robinson uses to describe the legal system in "The Pursuit of Justice" is equally refreshing and insightful. In my experience working with sexual assault survivors, the process of taking legal action terrifies many people because they don't know what, if anything, they can expect in terms of justice. Robinson clearly spells out the differences in legal definitions, types of litigation, and methods of punishment, and she points out that whatever option we choose, we deserve and can get support in our pursuit of justice.

"Emotional Recovery" is not business as usual; we're not super-human, we're human, and with that distinction comes the ownership of feelings. Robinson reminds us that a violation of the body often involves a violation of the spirit, and having loving, supportive family and friends around is the best medicine. The speed at which our emotions move up and down, burying themselves deep underground and then rising to the surface, can seem like the roller-coaster ride from hell. Talking to a therapist, a family member, a close friend, a journal, or a spiritual advisor—someone who won't judge what we say or how we feel—can remind us we're not alone.

I found myself drawn over and over again to Chapters 6 and 7, "Reflections on the Spirit: A Discussion with Two Womanist Preachers" and "Prayers: Tools for Spiritual Healing." The wisdom, inspiration, and hope infused in these two chapters is truly a balm to a weary spirit. Our faith is such a large part of who we are as a people and community. By adding these two chapters, Robinson helps us draw comfort from knowing that the spirit, however we choose to define it, is and will always be with us. Listening (I truly felt as if I were hearing instead of reading this conversation) to the conversation between the women ministers was spiritually enriching. They confirmed that sexual assault of any kind is never our fault, and that it's not some form of vengeful punishment for the ways we've chosen to live our lives.

Chapter 10, "Responding to Oppression: Attitudes and Solutions in the Black Community," offers some excellent answers to the question "How did we get to this place of violence directed toward each other?" Robinson takes a hard look at the routine sexual victimization of Black women throughout our history in the United States. This chapter also gives powerful examples of various groups within our community that are actively standing up against sexual victimization.

As I read the section, "Survivors' Stories of Healing," I truly felt my heart swell with pride at the survivors' courage, hope, and determination. While emotionally wrenching, each story held a gem of hope about the ability to survive.

In this beautifully written, factual, and well-grounded book, Lori S. Robinson has given a long overdue voice to Black survivors everywhere.

JULIA A. BOYD
October 2002

INTRODUCTION

African-American women are raped at a higher rate than White women, and are less likely to report it.[1] We have suffered in silence far too long.

Rape is not sex. It is a crime of violence. A perpetrator forces the contact of sexual body parts. It leaves you angry, ashamed, terrified, and traumatized. Though it changes you forever, you do not have to live with those feelings for the rest of your life. I should know.

On May 15, 1995, two men ran up behind me as I approached my apartment building, and one of them pointed a gun at my head. In the hour that followed, I was blindfolded, gagged, tied facedown to my bed, and raped by both.

On the first anniversary of my assault—and each anniversary since—I celebrated my life and my healing. I journeyed so far so fast toward wellness and peace because of my therapist, my boyfriend (now husband), supportive family and friends, and divine healing. That's not to say I don't still face challenges from the attack. But what was done to me no longer has power over me.

There are no easy paths, no quick fixes, for this journey. Confronting the emotional, spiritual, and sometimes physical scars of sexual violation can be a difficult, exhausting exercise. It can take years, even decades. Yet, no matter what happened to you, it is possible to become emotionally, mentally, and spiritually strong and healthy.

No race, ethnic group, or economic class is spared from sexual violence or the myths and misinformation that complicate the healing process for survivors. But in addition to our higher victimization rate, African Americans are less likely to get the help we need to heal.[2] What's more, our community is burdened by a centuries-long history of sexual victimization and other violent abuses that continue to make the issue even more complex for us.

Discussions of the victimization of Black women are sometimes interpreted as being anti-Black men. Historically, Black men have been characterized as sexual predators. For decades after slavery ended, false reports of the rape of White women resulted in the torture and violent murder of Black men.[3] In recent decades, studies have shown that Black men are disproportionately incarcerated for sexual assault, and are given longer sentences than White men.[4] Unfortunately, these realities have led to a common misperception that Black women who speak out about being raped are just like those White women up through the era of the civil rights movement— trying to bring the Black man down.

Because of the pain of past and contemporary racial injustice, we live in the midst of a distorted reality with its attendant myths. First is the myth of the Black rapist terrorizing White women. Historically, interracial rape occurred frequently, but most perpetrators were not Black men. From slavery's end through the first two-thirds of the twentieth century, no southern White man was convicted of the rape or attempted rape of a Black woman, leading the National Commission on the Causes and Prevention of Violence to state in 1969 that "white males have long had nearly institutionalized access to Negro women with relatively little fear of being reported."[5] Anyone who knows anything about American history knows that Black men were victims of racist brutality, but Black women's brutalization by White men is frequently overlooked.

Fast forward to today: Most rapists in the United States are

White, educated, middle-class men.[6] And the vast majority of rapists victimize someone of their own race.[7]

The second myth under which we operate is that women often falsely accuse men of rape. In actuality, false reports of rape are quite rare. The figure often used by sexual violence experts for estimating falsified reports is 2 percent, about the same rate as other crimes.[8]

The tendency to think Black women falsely accuse Black men of rape also comes from a misunderstanding of what rape is and why it happens. The following passage accurately describes how I felt when I was assaulted:

> *A torturer puts his victim in a position of helplessness, makes clear to his victim that he is utterly at the torturer's mercy, breaks his will by humiliating and degrading him, and finally inflicts pain on him, usually to the most tender parts of the body. A rapist duplicates these acts.*[9]

This scenario can happen between a husband and wife, boyfriend and girlfriend, co-workers, strangers, adults, children—virtually any combination of people. In two-thirds of cases, rape is committed by someone the victim knows.[10] And with 7 percent of offenders armed, it is less likely to involve a weapon than any other violent crime.[11] Even if a woman goes home alone with a man she just met, that arguably poor decision does not mean she has forfeited her right not to have sex. Rapists rape because they want to gain power over someone else and because they are capable of disregarding someone else's rights and wishes.

Because I was raped by strangers with a weapon, no one ever accused me of lying or suggested that I wanted it to happen. It is time for the Black community to honestly examine the issue of sexual violence so that survivors of incest, marital rape, date rape, and acquaintance rape are treated with the same compassion and sensitivity I was.

African-American anti-rape efforts are not anti-Black men. They are pro-Black people. Black men as well as Black women have much to gain from ridding our communities of sexual violence, both as potential victims and as loved ones and friends of survivors. When Black girls and boys are sexually abused, it can cause lifelong emotional problems and make them more vulnerable to abuse as adults. When Black adults are sexually assaulted, it can impede their ability to function at home, at work, and in the community. Sexual abuse or assault can hamper any survivor's ability to have healthy relationships. Sexual victimization can be the catalyst for the mildest to the most severe dysfunctions, such as low self-esteem, substance abuse, and depression.

For the purposes of this book, I have had to narrow my focus to healing, risk reduction and anti-violence organizing for adults, as well as some information for adult caretakers of child sexual abuse victims. I wish I had the time and space to address sexual violence even more comprehensively, particularly in environments with significant African-American populations. I would have liked to provide victims in the military with information about the separate criminal justice system they must navigate. And I would have liked to address the prevalence of rape in prisons. The sexual abuse of women prisoners, primarily by male employees, and male prisoners, primarily by other prisoners, is an often-ignored crisis. In most of the reports and studies of sexual violence, the rape of prisoners isn't considered. Couple that with decreasing resources for rehabilitation and you can't help but wonder if the criminal justice system is in a way contributing to the problem of sexual violence rather than making our communities safer.

Hopefully, as organizations, schools, churches, and mosques address sexual violence, these and other topics will be covered in their discussions and activism. I am confident that once more African Americans have a factual understanding of this issue and how comprehensively it affects our communities, we will make anti-rape efforts a priority.

Sexual assault and abuse is nothing new, and it is certainly not unique to African Americans or the United States. Not only is it a phenomenon found in societies throughout the world, it is used as a political tool and an act of war. During the Bosnia-Herzegovina conflict in the 1990s, soldiers conducted mass rapes of Muslim women as part of an "ethnic cleansing" campaign.[12] One European Community fact-finding team estimated that 20,000 women had been raped in less than a year.[13] In Peru, security forces have punished civilian women perceived to be sympathetic to opposition forces by raping them.[14] Before and during World War II, an estimated 80,000 to 200,000 women, primarily Korean, were forced into sexual slavery in military brothels for Japanese soldiers.[15]

I've written *I Will Survive* not because African Americans are the only people affected by sexual violence, but because we are uniquely affected. Sometimes people are more comfortable working on their own challenges in culturally specific ways.

I hope survivors of all ethnicities and races benefit from reading this book. *I Will Survive* is for everyone concerned about the tragedy of sexual assault and abuse. Whether or not you have been directly touched by sexual violence, it is an issue that affects you. Incest, date rape, marital rape, stranger rape, and other types of victimization are happening in your community, no matter where you live.

I hope parents, educators, health care professionals, community groups, youth organizations, churches, mosques, and rape crisis centers will find *I Will Survive* an effective tool in the escalating struggle against sexual assault and abuse. I included the historical foundation for the sexual victimization of African Americans in order for you to better understand its contemporary reality. Through reading this book you will learn to broaden honest dialogue in your community and engage in anti-rape activism in ways large and small. You'll become aware of resources available for the reduction of the risk of sexual assault.

I Will Survive was also written for the family and friends of survivors. Your loved one needs you now more than ever. I urge you to use this book to become the best supporter you can be. People often don't know what to say or do to support survivors. Sometimes they opt to do nothing. It is not uncommon for the people a victim depends on for help to cause more harm than good with hurtful or dismissive words. You will learn how to help your loved one access needed resources and how you can effectively assist in the recovery process. You will also come to realize that you are a victim too. You will go through some of the same emotions as the survivor. You will be encouraged to get the support you need as well.

Most importantly, this book is for my fellow survivors. I offer you comfort, encouragement, and empowerment. I have provided information to help guide you through physical, emotional, and spiritual healing, as well as the criminal justice system. You will understand that the violation you suffered was not your fault, and that you are not alone. You will read the stories of survivors who have triumphed in their healing process. You will learn what to expect and how to get the services and resources you need for your own healing.

I decided to write *I Will Survive* because I want other Black victims of sexual violence to become survivors too. I want your pain to cease. I want you to thrive. I want our community to be healthy, to be safe, and to flourish.

Peace, courage, strength, and blessings,
Lori S. Robinson

Notes

[1] Rennison, Callie Marie. *Criminal Victimization in the United States, 1999: Statistical Tables* (Washington, D.C.: U.S. Department of Justice, Office of Justice Programs, January 2001); White, Aaronette. "I Am Because We Are: Combined Race and Gender Political Consciousness Among African American Women and Men Anti-Rape Activists," *Women's Studies International Forum* 24, no. 1 (2001), 12-13; White, Aaronette M. "Talking Feminist, Talking Black: Micromobilization

Process in a Collective Protest Against Rape," *Gender & Society* 13, no. 1 (February 1999), 97.

2 White, "I Am Because We Are," 12-13.

3 Davis, Angela Y. *Women, Race and Class* (New York: Random House, 1981), 183-184.

4 White, Aaronette. Interview by author. Bowie, Md.

5 White, Deborah Gray. *Ar'n't I a Woman? Female Slaves in the Plantation South* (New York: W.W. Norton and Company, 1985), 164.

6 Lindquist, Scott. *The Date Rape Prevention Book: The Essential Guide for Girls and Women* (Naperville, Ill.: Sourcebooks, 2000), 52; Federal Bureau of Investigation. *Crime in the United States 2000* (Washington, D.C.: Government Printing Office, 2001), Table 44; Benedict, Helen. *Recovery: How to Survive Sexual Assault for Women, Men, Teenagers, Their Friends and Families* (New York: Columbia University Press, 1994), 9.

7 Rennison, *Criminal Victimization in the United States, 1999.*

8 White, "Talking Feminist, Talking Black," 97.

9 Benedict, 5-6.

10 Rennison, Callie. *National Crime Victimization Survey: Criminal Victimization 2001* (Washington, D.C.: U.S. Department of Justice, Office of Justice Programs, September 2002), 8.

11 *Ibid.*

12 Equality Now. "Bosnia-Herzegovina: Mass Rape, Forced Pregnancy, Genocide," *Women's Action Update* (April 1994).

13 Lewin, Tamar. "The Balkans Rapes: A Legal Test for the Outraged," *New York Times* (15 January 1993).

14 Human Rights Watch. "Rape as a Weapon of War and a Tool of Political Repression," *The Human Rights Watch Global Report on Women's Human Rights* in Human Rights Watch website [cited 2 August 2002]; available at www.hrw.org.

15 Soh, Chunghee Sarah. "The Comfort Women Project" in Online @ SFSU website [cited 2 August 2002]; available at online.sfsu.edu/~soh/comfortwomen.html.

PART I
THE ROAD TO HEALING

CHAPTER 1
YOUR PHYSICAL HEALTH

Sexual assault is a trauma commonly followed by long-term emotional recovery. Fortunately, the same is rarely true for physical recovery. Several studies show that few rape survivors sustain serious physical wounds, with estimates as low as 5 percent and less than 1 percent requiring hospitalization.[1]

Still, it's perfectly logical to be concerned about the effect of an assault on your physical well-being. It's likely that by the time you read this, weeks or months will have passed since your assault, but you may still have questions about physical health issues. Since much of this chapter deals with the medical concerns and procedures that immediately follow an assault, you may want to skip to the section on preventative treatment, or you may find that little of the information covered here is relevant for you. If you did seek emergency medical treatment after being assaulted, this chapter will give you a better understanding of all that your examination and treatment entailed. Also included here is information for adult caretakers of children who are known or suspected victims of sexual abuse.

Why Go to the Hospital

Even if your injuries don't seem serious, it is important to be examined by a health care professional as soon as possible. You might have

3

internal injuries of which you are not aware. You may also need testing and treatment for sexually transmitted diseases and pregnancy prevention.

Another crucial reason to go to an emergency room is for the purpose of collecting medical evidence in a forensic exam, also called a rape kit exam. In order for a comprehensive examination to be conducted, it must take place within thirty-six hours of the assault because forensic evidence deteriorates quickly from the body. If you get examined within seventy-two hours, there will likely still be some evidence that can be collected.[2] Even if you haven't yet decided to pursue criminal or civil charges against the assailant, it's better to have evidence collected than to be without that potentially decisive proof should your case make it to trial.

The purpose of a post-assault examination extends beyond medical care and evidence collection. "It's to try to empower the survivor in some way to start the healing process," says Elaine Martin, a sexual assault nurse examiner at the Child and Adolescent Sexual Abuse Resource Center in San Francisco. "It is important that they come in and they start the healing process, whatever that means. And we help them find out what that means."

Unfortunately, few are aware of Martin's philosophy. In one national survey, only 17 percent of survivors had a medical exam after being assaulted.[3] Since rape is believed to be the United States's most underreported crime, the actual proportion of women and men survivors who seek treatment could be even lower.[4]

For many people, going to the hospital means being in a safe, secure place. It can also represent a first act of self-care and control in a healing journey. And in practical terms, health professionals will care for you in a way that others can't. Don't let a lack of health insurance or money keep you from the hospital. Government or law enforcement funds usually cover the cost of the exam.

Some people opt to go without treatment for fear they will have to press charges against their assailant, not always an easy decision to make. But that shouldn't keep you away either. You cannot be forced to report a sexual assault to the police.[5] The only exceptions are cases of vulnerable elderly victims or minors, for which reporting is required.[6]

Even if the police know who the rapist is, it is unlikely that a criminal prosecution would happen without your support. If you haven't yet decided if you want to report the crime to the police, the evidence can be stored temporarily. Your attending health care professional should let you know how much time you have before your evidence will be thrown away.

Survivors who were under the influence of alcohol or drugs when the assault occurred might think they won't be believed, or that they will be judged or blamed for the assault. Getting drunk or high doesn't make you responsible for something someone else did to you, and it doesn't make you less deserving of medical care than anyone else. Hospital workers will examine you regardless of your condition.

Many survivors simply figure an exam won't help anything. "A lot of people think, 'It was just me and him there. No one's going to believe me. There's nothing I can do.' But there is. There's a lot you can do. And there are things that we can document and show," says Martin.

Through a rape kit exam, injuries are documented, sometimes even those not visible with the naked eye. Specimens of DNA-containing matter, such as body fluids and hair, are analyzed in a crime laboratory and later matched with suspects. During consensual sex, the human body naturally undergoes certain physiological changes that prevent common rape-related genital injuries, so trained health professionals can identify wounds typically sustained only during assaults.

The evidence collected in a forensic exam can be the key to the arrest and prosecution of a perpetrator. "I sat in on one rape case this summer and it was just hands down," says Kim Hutchinson, a forensic nurse examiner in Winston-Salem, North Carolina. The suspect said that he didn't have sex with this girl and she said he [raped her], and the DNA evidence was 99.9 percent [conclusive] that it was his semen found."

Should you decide not to go through with an examination before or even after it has begun, you will not be forced to continue.[7] Martin actually recalls advising one woman against being examined because without needed psychiatric attention first, her healing process would be hindered. The survivor returned to complete the exam, once she was more stable, within seventy-two hours.

It may take all the courage and energy you can muster, but it is important for your well-being, peace of mind, and possibly your legal case to get examined as soon as possible after being assaulted. If you cannot work up to it, honor your decision and don't beat up on yourself. Each person must do what is best for her own total wellness.

Rape Crisis Centers

Decades ago, it was all too common for hospital workers to snicker, voice disbelief, rush through exams, or otherwise treat patients insensitively. The people who were supposed to help made a bad situation worse.

It can still happen, but treatment and the attitudes of the people who give it are better than ever before. Broad-ranging developments, including advances in technology and emerging health careers, have evolved into an improved support system for survivors. And just as important, many health care providers have become aware of the unique needs of survivors.

One innovation deserves much of the credit for this progress. In the early 1970s, rape crisis centers were created to struggle against sexual violence and to empower women in healing and risk reduction.[8] Today more than nine hundred centers nationally provide a range of services.[9]

No matter where in the United States you live, there is probably a rape crisis center nearby that provides services such as a telephone hotline, counseling, community education programs, and self-defense classes.

If you're considering a hospital visit, rape crisis centers usually provide another useful service: Victim advocates or patient advocates, as they are commonly known, will accompany you. They provide emotional and practical support, such as helping to fill out forms, explaining procedures, or even telling your family what's happened if you feel unable to do so.

"We also speak [on survivors'] behalf, because sometimes at the hospital they can almost get railroaded for things that they really don't want to do. They're not aware of their rights," says Felicia McGruder, program director of the Rosa Parks Sexual Assault Crisis Center in Los Angeles. McGruder gives the example of seeing police try to coerce a minor into telling who her assailant was when she didn't want to. "The survivor has just been through a traumatic event and she really doesn't need to worry about that."

Advocates serve another vital purpose, making sure patients get all the information necessary to make informed decisions about their health. Despite dramatic improvements in health care, not every medical professional provides ideal treatment. According to a report in *Annals of Emergency Medicine*, a seven-year study revealed that only 34 percent of rape survivors who got emergency room care received or were prescribed the medication recommended by the Centers for Disease Control and Prevention for treating sexually transmitted diseases.[10]

Advocates also help with less overt problems, such as cultural communication gaps or racial bias. A victim advocate can serve as a buffer when there is tension or miscommunication between a patient and a clinician.

Health Care Professionals

Another development growing out of the rape crisis movement promises to revolutionize physical exams. Originating in the late

1970s, sexual assault nurse examiners (SANEs) are registered nurses specially trained to collect physical, legal evidence and testify in court proceedings as expert witnesses.[11]

SANEs are taught to treat patients with nonjudgmental sensitivity and dignity, notoriously absent from the bedside manner of emergency room doctors in decades past. They also help alleviate logistical concerns.

Survivors sometimes experience long waits while doctors handle life-threatening medical emergencies first. If your area has a SANE program, it's unlikely that your wait will be long because its nurses are on-call twenty-four hours a day for sexual assault cases only.[12] SANE exams often last up to three hours, longer than a traditional emergency room doctor's exam. SANEs have fewer patients than emergency department physicians, so they can afford to devote more time and detail to each individual.

That attention to detail may help you in the legal arena. One prosecutor says few of her cases handled by SANE nurses make it to trial because the evidence is so strong that defendants usually plea bargain, preventing survivors from having to testify.[13] One Wisconsin SANE program reported a 100 percent conviction rate when a SANE testified in a criminal case during a three-and-a half year period.[14]

If you decide to get a physical exam, ask the hospital if a forensic nurse is available, or call your local rape crisis center to find out which hospital in your area has a SANE program.

It's not known exactly how many hospitals use SANEs, although estimates are low. But the number of registered nurses specializing in forensic examination is growing rapidly. For survivors without access to a SANE program, this doesn't mean your doctor's exam will be inadequate. To the contrary, a doctor's exam is a significant advantage as you take control of your health.

Several other considerations may help you achieve the highest possible comfort level during your hospital visit.

Gender

One survivor recalls that she refused to let a male doctor examine her at Atlanta's Grady Memorial Hospital after being raped in her home. She was very satisfied with the woman physician who examined her, and she should be commended for her decision to make her needs known. Not everyone in her situation has such resolve. Hospitals and doctors can be intimidating for anyone, and might seem even more so for someone who has recently been traumatized.

Immediately after an assault, some women feel in complete control of their emotions and thought processes. Others are at the opposite end of the spectrum, physically and mentally disoriented or distressed. That's why it is important to go to the hospital with a supportive friend or a patient advocate who can help you voice your preferences. Even if you feel strong and clear-headed, you might be in shock.

If you have a preference for a clinician, articulating it helps establish your expectations of respect. If you prefer a woman doctor, request one. But don't let the possibility of a male doctor keep you from the hospital. Ordinarily if a male doctor is assigned to you, a female nurse will stay with you during the entire exam to create a nonthreatening atmosphere. Feel free to ask for a female nurse if the physician wants to begin your exam without one.

Race

People from different ethnic backgrounds can have various ways of communicating. Many health care professionals are aware that symptoms can be expressed differently according to your gender, age group, or cultural group. Unfortunately, sensitivity training for health care professionals hasn't necessarily included a racial dimension. Racial biases and condescending attitudes are one way clinicians create a lack of trust with patients, and subsequently a poor-quality exam.

Hutchinson has observed this miscommunication and distrust

particularly with low-income or undereducated patients who felt like their clinician talked down to them and were afraid to ask questions. Meanwhile, the clinicians were oblivious to the problem.

To prevent such added stress, have an advocate accompany you. If you think you might be more comfortable communicating with a Black examiner, ask for one. Just as women practitioners might not be available, African Americans might not be either. But many hospitals will try to accommodate your requests.

Regardless of who ends up performing your exam, expect and demand to be treated in a way that makes you as comfortable as possible. Lean on a family member, friend, or advocate to voice your needs if you don't feel strong enough to do it yourself.

If you encounter insensitive treatment at the hospital, try not to let it distract you from the task at hand, your emotional and physical healing. Address its effect through counseling or the support of friends and family. Consider writing a letter to the offending clinician, his or her supervisor, or anyone with influence over that person, such as the facility's top administrator. Your activism will be another step in self-care, demanding deserved respect as you begin your healing journey. And you just might encourage an attitude adjustment that will prevent the mistreatment of other Black women, men, and children after an assault.

Medical Examination

Hospital procedures vary greatly from place to place, but some similarities can be expected. If you call the police immediately after an assault, it's likely that an officer will escort you to the hospital. Some people elect not to contact the police and instead go directly to the emergency room alone or with a friend. If you want an advocate to accompany you during your hospital visit, call a rape crisis center hotline to request one and she will meet you there. Some hospitals automatically contact an advocate for you.

Before your exam begins, a health care worker will ask you to sign a consent form. Then, in some emergency departments, a physician's assistant will begin the steps of your exam. She may draw blood for various tests and note external injuries in preparation for a doctor. In other emergency facilities, a physician is the only medical professional to treat sexual violence survivors. And in others, a doctor does an initial screening for injuries, and a sexual assault nurse examiner completes your treatment and forensic examination.

The attending medical professional will take your medical history and ask questions about the assault. If a police officer is present, or even a representative of the local district attorney's office, do not be alarmed. It's their way of reducing the number of times you'll have to repeat your story.

Next, you'll be screened and treated for external and internal injuries. The nurse or doctor should explain each step while looking for injuries and collecting evidence. In some jurisdictions, the advocate is permitted to help explain procedures. At the very least, they can be present to hold your hand and comfort you.

Depending on the type of assault, the genitals or anus may be examined at this point. Understandably, this can be the most challenging part of the exam. Whether or not this is physically painful will depend in part on the degree of trauma to the genitals. If genital soreness and injury is minimal, the exam may not be much more uncomfortable than a standard gynecological exam. For men, genital exams are generally not painful. For both women and men, a rectal exam after an anal rape is more likely to be painful.

Having the most private parts of your body probed by a stranger after being assaulted can be unpleasant. Try to focus on the fact that you are now safe and in control of your body. No doctor or nurse will do anything you do not permit him or her to do. This is a brave first step in the healing process. You've made a conscious decision to protect your health and actively participate in the pursuit of the justice you deserve.

The medical professional who treats you should provide information on mental health support, including specific referrals to therapists or rape crisis counseling, sometimes in the same facility. Please see Chapter 3 for detailed information on emotional healing. Also, screenings and preventative treatment for sexually transmitted diseases (STDs) and pregnancy is recommended by the Centers for Disease Control and Prevention and the American College of Obstetricians and Gynecologists.[15]

Preventative Treatment

After being raped, you might be worried about pregnancy and STDs, both rational responses. When it comes to testing for them, protocol varies greatly. Because chances of becoming pregnant or contracting a disease through sexual assault are low, some emergency facilities do not provide preventative treatment. In others, preventative steps are taken routinely.

The risk of pregnancy in survivors not protected by contraception has been estimated at less than 5 percent, but pregnancy prevention treatment is readily accessible, safe, and offers peace of mind.[16] There are two types of emergency contraception pills, also known as "morning-after" pills, both of which contain hormones. One type consists of estrogen and progestin in the same dosage as some birth control pills. The other type contains only progestin and is less likely to cause side effects such as vomiting and nausea.[17]

Emergency contraception pills should be taken starting within seventy-two hours of your assault. In most cases, you will be prescribed pills to be taken twelve hours apart. Even if you aren't able to use birth control pills as your regular contraception, it is likely that emergency contraception pills will be effective.

The *Annals of Emergency Medicine* study found that 20 percent of survivors are given emergency contraception.[18] If it's not offered, request a prescription for emergency contraception during your forensic exam or from your own doctor. You can also access emergency contraception by calling Planned Parenthood or the Emergency Contraception Hotline. [19]

Estimates on the likelihood of contracting STDs as a result of sexual assault range from 3.6 percent to 30 percent.[20] The *Annals of Emergency Medicine* report shows that 58 percent of rape survivors who went to an emergency room were either tested for STDs or given preventative medication.[21] You might also receive preventative treatment for hepatitis B and tetanus, not usually referred to as STDs, during a post-assault exam since they can be transmitted through sexual contact.

Tests done just hours after an assault show only pre-existing conditions. Follow-up testing is necessary to determine if you contracted a disease as a result of the assault. If you have any questions about STDs, including HIV/AIDS, you can call the toll-free Centers for Disease Control and Prevention National STD/HIV Hotline.

There is no proven preventative medication for herpes, but antibiotics can prevent chlamydia, gonorrhea, syphilis, bacterial vaginosis, and trichomoniasis. Although these are not all the conditions that can be transmitted by genital contact or the exchange of body fluids, they are among the most common.

Here is basic information about their signs:

Most people have few or no symptoms when infected with herpes. Those who do may develop blisters near or on the anus or genitals, usually within two weeks of contracting the virus. Signs can also include fever and other flu-like symptoms.[22]

Chlamydia also usually produces mild symptoms if any. For both women and men who show symptoms, they usually appear within one to three weeks and can include an abnormal discharge or burning while urinating.[23]

Most women who contract gonorrhea have mild to no symptoms. They might develop a yellow or bloody discharge or a burning sensation when urinating. Most men with the disease do get symptoms, which can include swollen or painful testicles, a yellowish discharge, and burning upon urinating. For both women and men, signs can take from two to ten days after infection to appear.[24]

Many signs of syphilis look similar to symptoms of other diseases. They begin to appear on average twenty-one days after exposure and can take anywhere from ten to ninety days to appear. In the disease's primary stage, single or multiple chancre sores, usually in the genital area, last three to six weeks. Second-stage symptoms can include non-itchy rashes, often on the soles of the feet and palms of the hands.[25]

Women who contract trichomoniasis often have symptoms, such as a yellow-green discharge accompanied by an odor or genital itching. They normally appear between five and twenty-eight days after infection. Most men do not develop symptoms, but those who do may experience a discharge, burning after ejaculation or urination, or an irritation inside the penis.[26]

Human papilloma virus (HPV) causes genital warts, which can take as long as six months after infection to develop. Small cauliflower-like bumps or flat, flesh-colored bumps in the rectal or genital area, they can be treated with medicine applied directly to the skin. Large warts may require laser removal. Do not treat genital warts with over-the-counter medications intended for the removal of warts on the hand.[27]

If you are concerned about these health risks and testing isn't offered during your exam, get tested by your own doctor. You can also go to Planned Parenthood for low-cost STD screening and treatment. Call toll-free to be connected to the Planned Parenthood health center nearest you. If you are concerned about cost, be open with the staff about your financial situation when you make an appointment. Many centers have sliding-scale fees in order to accommodate everyone in need of medical services.[28]

Perhaps most frightening is the prospect of contracting HIV, the virus that causes AIDS, for which there are treatments but no cure. The risk of contracting HIV after a single sexual contact varies from study to study, but it is lower than for needle sharing, blood transfusion, and other methods of transmission. In cases of rape, the anecdotal evidence of the risk seems low.[29]

If your assailant is charged with a crime, you might have the right to find out his HIV status. HIV testing of sexual assault defendants is either allowed or required before conviction in some states, after conviction in others, and both before and after conviction in still others.[30] The staff at local rape crisis centers should be able to tell you if such laws exist where you live.

It takes an infected person on average three to four weeks, in rare cases as long as six months, to develop antibodies that would indicate if she were HIV-positive.[31] Many HIV-positive people have no symptoms for years. The only way to know for sure if you have been infected with HIV is to get a blood test.[32]

Although the following warning signs can indicate HIV infection, they can all be symptoms of other conditions as well: quick weight loss, dry cough, recurring fever, severe night sweats, extreme fatigue, swollen lymph glands in the neck, armpits, or groin, diarrhea that continues longer than a week, unusual blemishes in the throat or mouth or on the tongue, pneumonia, blotches in the nose, mouth, or eyelids or under or on the skin, or memory loss. Again, none of these are conclusive signs of HIV.[33]

A complicated, costly drug therapy exists that can reduce the risk of HIV infection after exposure to the virus, but it has only been proven to produce positive results in workplace settings, such as when a health care worker is accidentally pricked by a needle. In sexual assault cases, the Public Health Service recommends using preventative treatment, which has numerous side effects, only when the likelihood of transmission is high and treatment can be started no later than twenty-four to thirty-six hours after the assault.[34] If you know that your assailant is HIV-positive, consult with an infectious disease specialist immediately, preferably within a few hours after the assault, about whether preventative treatment could work for you.

As with other STDs, you can get information on HIV testing during your emergency exam or from your doctor, a rape crisis center, Planned Parenthood, or the toll-free Centers for Disease Control and Prevention National STD/HIV Hotline.

Follow-Up

Among medical professionals' responsibilities in treating sexual violence survivors is emphasizing the importance of a follow-up visit. If possible, one should be arranged before you leave the medical facility, but protocol for this varies greatly. It is generally recommended that a follow-up visit happen two weeks after the initial exam.

Some sexual assault nurse examiners want survivors to come back to them in order to document and treat healing wounds. Some clinicians send survivors to other medical professionals in the same hospital, to a state health department for repeat testing for STDs, or even to their own physician for treatment.

Physical Evidence

Some of the best evidence in any rape survivor's case may come off of her or his body. If you don't remember anything else from this chapter, please remember that survivors should not tamper with that evidence.

That means *do not*: shower, bathe, douche, wash your mouth out, gargle, brush your teeth, clean your nails, eat, drink, change or throw away clothes you were wearing when the assault occurred, comb your hair, put on makeup or alter the crime scene in any way.

Health care professionals will use what is commonly known as a rape kit to conduct your forensic exam. Provided by law enforcement authorities, it is a box containing everything needed to collect forensic samples. The kit includes sterile combs for the collection of scalp and pubic hairs, and swabs for vaginal, rectal, and oral smears to detect deposits of semen or other body fluids from the assailant. If a patient scratched the attacker, fingernail scrapings might be taken. Visible bruises and other wounds are documented.

Emergency departments might also test for date-rape drugs, substances misused to facilitate sexual assault by sedating potential victims. For centuries, assailants have used alcohol to diminish their targets' judgment and resistance. In decades past, violators have slipped chemicals such as chloral hydrate, or Mickeys, into drinks to sedate people involuntarily for the same purpose. In recent years, numerous new threats have been added to this list.

More than twenty substances have been identified for their use as date-rape drugs. Among them are Rohypnol, the brand name for flunitrazepam, which is a powerful sedative, and GHB or gamma hydroxybutyrate, a central nervous system depressant. Both illegal in the United States, even for medical purposes, they can cause unconsciousness and memory loss from the time they are ingested. When used to sedate a potential victim, these substances are secretly added to drinks. You may not be able to see, taste, or smell them.[35]

If you seemed disproportionately intoxicated after drinking little or no alcohol, it is a possible indication that you've unknowingly been drugged. Sudden loss of motor coordination, dizziness, confusion, and loss of inhibition are other signs.

A simple urine test is used to identify date rape drugs. If you suspect you've been drugged, get tested as soon as possible after being assaulted. Only tests taken within seventy-two hours would contain enough of a substance to determine if it had been in your system.

Depending on the emergency room's equipment, the forensic exam may not end there. Many facilities use a Wood's lamp, a type of ultraviolet light, shined to highlight traces of body fluids. "It's like a fluorescent stain," says Hutchinson. "If we see that, then we collect swabs of DNA matter, be it saliva or semen or blood, from body parts and the clothes that the client wears." Some ultraviolet light sources used with the correct filters can detect bruising or bite marks not visible on the skin's surface.

The colposcope is another documentation tool. This magnifying camera photographs internal and external injuries. Because it magnifies images as large as twenty-five times their actual size, it is possible to document injuries not visible to the naked eye. One study shows the use of magnifying photography nearly triples the likelihood of finding evidence of sexual assault.[36]

The clothes worn during an assault might be collected at the hospital, if the police haven't already taken them; carrying a change of clothes to the hospital, if possible, is a good idea. Some nurses and physicians only take undergarments to search for DNA-containing matter; others take everything worn. Along with the rest of the rape kit, they are sent to a crime laboratory. Some emergency departments maintain clothes banks so survivors don't have to worry about what to wear home.

When a Child Should Be Examined

Barring mental disability, adults are capable of deciding whether or not to get treatment after being assaulted. Children, on the other hand, may not know that what's happened to them is a crime, or they may be too young to communicate it.

Child sexual abuse is as pervasive in African-American communities as in others. In most cases the perpetrator is someone the child knows. According to one study, in only 7 percent of juvenile sexual assaults reported to police was the assailant a stranger to the victim. About a third were family members and more than 58 percent were acquaintances.[37]

Many abused children who do understand that something wrong has happened, especially when the assailant is a relative or caretaker, believe they shouldn't tell anyone. For sexually abused children old enough to talk, they may have been coerced into silence with threats of beatings, death, or losing the love of a parent. Shame, embarrassment, and fear of being blamed are all common emotions that prevent a child from telling. Kids are even sometimes told that they are being prepared for adulthood and are experiencing a healthy, loving relationship.

Teenagers are more likely to intentionally disclose sexual abuse than young children. Adolescents and teens who don't report being violated often give clues about their abuse and pain through negative behaviors such as compulsive bathing, misplaced anger, fear of being left alone, inappropriate sexual behavior, withdrawing, and lying.

Children are more likely to intentionally disclose being violated by a stranger than a family member. When kids do report sexual abuse by a relative or family friend, it's sometimes done accidentally. One Maryland social worker recalls how a boy revealed being fondled by a teenage baby sitter. When his mother suggested that a joke between she and her son be a secret, he replied, "You mean like my secret with Johnny?" In that case, a silly joke triggered disclosure.

Depending on a child's age, verbal disclosure can be impossible. At about age five, kids can talk about what has happened in a way that others understand.[38] Children can be sexually abused at any age. Even infants have been victimized. In such cases, medical observation and forensic evidence play key roles in determining if sexual assault occurred.

If you suspect that a child has been sexually abused, even if you do not have conclusive proof, you can report your suspicion to police, the child protection agency in your state, or a school counselor for assistance accessing the appropriate medical resources that can help determine if your hunch is correct. (See Chapter 9 for more information about signs of child sexual abuse.) Another option is to take the child to a medical facility yourself.

Some hospitals have departments that specialize in examining and treating child sexual abuse victims, such as the Child and Adolescent Protection Center, part of Children's National Medical Center in Washington, D.C. Some cities have medical facilities for children that are not attached to a hospital, such as the Child Advocacy Center in Mobile, Alabama, which handles nothing but confirmed or suspected cases of sexually violated children. Check with your local rape crisis center to find out what facilities for children are available in your area.

A Child's Medical Examination

Child and adult exams are quite similar. Both begin with collecting a history of assault, abuse, or suspected abuse. At Boston's Children's Hospital, for instance, a social worker interviews the parent or relative present with the child. The doctor follows by questioning the child if she or he is old enough to communicate effectively. To prevent discrepancies that could be used against a survivor in a legal proceeding, interviewers try to limit the number of times a history is taken.

"Thinking about sexual assault makes you want to focus on doing a thorough genitalia exam, but it's equally important, if not more important, to do a thorough physical examination so that you don't miss any other injuries such as fractures or injuries to internal abdominal organs from some type of trauma," says Michael W. Shannon, interim chief of Emergency Services at Children's Hospital in Boston. "The good thing about that approach is that you begin with a physical examination which isn't threatening. It's an opportunity to begin to establish rapport with your patient."

In some hospitals, pediatric emergency physicians conduct exams on children. Some pediatricians specialize in treating sexually violated patients. In other hospitals, gynecologists conduct girls' exams, regardless of age, and general emergency doctors handle boys' exams. Sexual assault nurse examiners are trained to examine children, but are restricted from doing so in some hospitals.

The same rape kit is used to collect forensic evidence from adults and children, although parts may not be applicable for kids. A young child's pubic area cannot be combed for hair samples, for example. The same tests and preventative treatments used for adults can be used with children, including the prevention of sexually transmitted diseases, and in menstruating girls, pregnancy prevention.

Lastly, a genital exam is performed. The attending medical professional should conduct the exam according to what the child will allow. For instance, if a child won't open her legs and permit a thorough genital exam, the doctor or nurse should not force her legs open. "We are not in the practice of traumatizing or abusing kids a second time," says Shannon.

If there is reason to believe that a significant injury needs to be treated, a doctor may decide to sedate the child in order to complete the exam. Barring such a concern, arrange for another appointment as soon as possible so that the examination can be completed.

Physical Evidence from a Child

Children's clinicians encounter the same challenges as health professionals who treat adults. Frequently, parents who suspect that a child has been abused make the mistake of bathing them and changing their clothes before their exam.

The same guideline applies to both adults and children—do not tamper with potential evidence on a suspected victim in any way. That means *do not* allow your child to: shower, bathe, douche, wash out her mouth, gargle, brush her teeth, eat, drink, change or throw away any clothes worn when the assault occurred, comb her hair, put on makeup, or alter the crime scene in any way.

Sometimes evidence can be documented on children even if an assault occurred more than seventy-two hours before an exam. A child's genitals could show abnormalities indicating sexual abuse, for instance. Pregnancy and genital scars are convincing evidence of a child's sexual abuse. Also conclusive is the presence of a sexually transmitted disease, the most common of which in child survivors are gonorrhea and chlamydia. Less confirmatory, but still considered possible indications of violation in child cases, are irregularities in the anal area or hymen. As with examinations of adults, photographs of injuries may be taken with magnifying cameras. Any assaulted child should have a follow-up visit to a health professional within a few weeks for medical oversight of the healing of any physical wounds.

Assistance with emotional healing is as crucial, if not more so, for children as it is for adults. According to Lavdena Orr, a pediatrician in Washington, D.C., "Mental health intervention in the African-American community has not routinely been sought. So we may have a family come in for the crisis and then it's difficult to get them back in for mental health [treatment]."

If your child has been abused, the special care he needs doesn't end with a medical exam. In fact, it's just beginning. If you don't access the appropriate healing professionals for your child, you will decrease his chances of growing into an emotionally healthy adult. Be sure to read Chapter 3 for more information on emotional health.

Once you've taken care of physical health concerns, your or your child's healing journey is off to a good start. Now it's time to think about another time-sensitive issue, the pursuit of justice.

NOTES

[1] Ledray, Linda E. *Sexual Assault Nurse Examiner Development and Operation Guide* (Washington, D.C.: U.S. Department of Justice, Office for Victims of Crime, 1999), 69-70.

[2] *Ibid.*, 63.

[3] National Center for Victims of Crime and Crime Victims Research and Treatment Center. *Rape in America: A Report to the Nation* (Arlington, Va.: National Center for Victims of Crime, 1992), 5.

[4] Sorenson, Susan B., and Judith M. Siegel. "Gender, Ethnicity and Sexual Assault: Findings from a Los Angeles Study," in *Confronting Rape and Sexual Assault* (Wilmington, Del.: Scholarly Resources, 1998), 211.

[5] Bishai, David, and Annette L. Amey. "Measuring the Quality of Medical Care for Women Who Experience Sexual Assault with Data from the National Hospital Ambulatory Medical Care Survey," *Annals of Emergency Medicine* 39 (June 2002), 636.

[6] Littel, Kristin. "Sexual Assault Nurse Examiner Programs: Improving the Community Response to Sexual Assault Victims," *OVC Bulletin* (Washington, D.C.: U.S. Department of Justice, Office for Victims of Crime, April 2001), 4.

[7] *Ibid.*

[8] Koss, Mary P., et al. *No Safe Haven: Male Violence Against Women at Home, at Work, and in the Community* (Washington, D.C.: American Psychological Association, 1994), 222-223.

[9] "RAINN Welcome," *RAINNews: A Monthly Publication for Member Rape Crisis Centers and Friends of RAINN*, April/May 2002, 1.

[10] Bishai, 635.

[11] Littel, 1-4; Voelker, Rebecca. "Experts Hope Team Approach Will Improve the Quality of Rape Exams," *The Journal of the American Medical Association* 275, no. 13 (3 April 1996), 973-974.

[12] Littel, 3.

13 Elliot, Laura. "The Rape Stops Here," *The Washingtonian* (August 1996), 70.

14 See note 12 above.

15 Bishai, 633; American College of Obstetricians and Gynecologists. "Sexual Assault," *ACOG Educational Bulletin* 242 (November 1997), 2-3.

16 American College of Obstetricians and Gynecologists, 4.

17 "Emergency Contraceptive Pills" in NOT-2-LATE.com: The Emergency Contraception Website [cited 10 July 2002]; available at ec.princeton.edu/info/ecp.html. "Emergency Contraception" in Planned Parenthood Federation of America, Inc. website [cited 10 July 2002]; available at www.plannedparent hood.org/ec.

18 See note 10 above.

19 See note 17 above.

20 Koss, M. P., and L. Heslet. "Somatic Consequences of Violence Against Women," *Archives of Family Medicine*, vol. 1 (September 1992), 53-59; Resnick, H. S., R. Acierno, and D. G. Kilpatrick. "Health Impact of Interpersonal Violence, Section II: Medical and Mental Health Outcomes," *Behavioral Medicine* 23(2) (Summer 1997), 65-78.

21 See note 10 above.

22 "Sexually Transmitted Diseases Facts & Info" in Centers for Disease Control and Prevention website [cited 10 July 2002]; available at www.cdc.gov/nchstp/dstd/disease_info.htm.

23 *Ibid.*

24 "Gonorrhea" in Obiakor Obstetrics and Gynecology website [cited 10 July 2002]; available at www.obiakorobgyn.com/medical/crs/gonrha.htm.

25 "Health A to Z" in Intelihealth website [cited 10 July 2002]; available at www.intelihealth.com/IH/ihtIH/WSBOT001/9339/9339.html.

26 See note 13 above.

27 See note 16 above.

28 See note 9 above.

29 Ledray, 73–74.

30 "Issue Brief: Testing of Violent Sex Offenders" in the National Conference of State Legislatures' Health Policy Tracking Service website; available at www.stateserv.hpts.org.

31 "Frequently Asked Questions: How long after a possible exposure should I wait to get tested for HIV?" in Centers for Disease Control and Prevention website [cited 10 July 2002]; available at www.cdc.gov/hiv/pubs/faq/faq9.htm.

32 "Frequently Asked Questions: How can I tell if I'm infected with HIV? What are the symptoms?" in Centers for Disease Control and Prevention website [cited 10 July 2002]; available at www.cdc.gov/hiv/pubs/faq/faq5.htm.

33 *Ibid.*

34 "PHS Report Summarizes Current Scientific Knowledge on the Use of Post-Exposure Antiretroviral Therapy for Non-Occupational Exposures" in Centers for Disease Control and Prevention website; available at www.cdc.gov/nchstp/od/phs_report.htm.

[35] "Rape Drugs" in Rape Treatment Center, Santa Monica-UCLA Medical Center website; available at www.911rape.org/drugs/rohypnol.html.

[36] Voelker, 974.

[37] Snyder, Howard N. *Sexual Assault of Young Children as Reported to Law Enforcement: Victim, Incident, and Offender Characteristics* (Washington, D.C.: Bureau of Justice Statistics, July 2000), 10.

[38] Orr, Lavdena. Interview by author. Tape recording. Bowie, Md., 2 December 1998.

CHAPTER 2
THE PURSUIT OF JUSTICE

My assailants were strangers who were never caught. For some of you, like me, the criminal justice system will have little to do with your healing process. But for those of you whose perpetrator is apprehended, or is someone you know, seeking justice could have a deeper impact on you than anything else you do.

Be forewarned that nothing in this chapter is intended to discourage you from the pursuit of justice. What you are about to read may seem that way, but to the contrary it is intended to provide accurate, realistic information about legal options and their potential challenges. While pursuing criminal penalty or civil redress through the courts can be satisfying, the truth is that it can also be quite unpleasant. As you read on, feel encouraged that you are preparing to make an informed decision that best suits you.

For some of you, deciding to cooperate with a criminal prosecution or to sue an assailant is easy. For others, it's among the most difficult decisions you will ever make. In either case, do not make it lightly.

Seek help from someone with experience. The best place to start is your local rape crisis center. Many have legal advocates who can explain procedures and accompany you on visits to the police, your attorney, even court proceedings. Should your case make it into the court system, you might encounter other support professionals within the system, employees of the court often called victim witness coordinators or victim witness specialists, available to assist you. Take advantage of the resources available in your jurisdiction.

You will consider many factors in deciding what legal steps, if any, you want to take. Once you've made an informed choice, be proud of yourself, whatever it is. This is another step forward, another proactive decision through which you are taking control of your life and treating yourself with the care you deserve.

Progress in the Criminal Justice System

Before the 1970s the criminal justice system so favored men accused of sexual assault over their accusers that, with the exception of White victims in sensationalized interracial cases, no women had reason to hope their assailants would be prosecuted. New rape reform laws and procedural changes since then have finally begun to shift the lopsided scales of justice in the direction of fairness.[1]

The degree of effectiveness of these changes is debatable, but even the most skeptical critic would have to agree that the justice-seeking process has improved. It couldn't have gotten much worse.

Black women have had the most to gain. Throughout the centuries of slavery, raping Black women was perfectly legal, no matter who the perpetrator was.[2] In an 1859 case of a Black man accused of sexually assaulting a Black girl younger than ten, the Mississippi Supreme Court declared: "There is no act (of our legislature on this subject) which embraces either the attempted or actual commission of a rape by a slave on a female slave."[3] In other words, even the rape of an enslaved child was not a crime.

The rape of enslaved women by White men was an accepted, ordinary occurrence. For decades after emancipation, White men continued with impunity their commonplace sexual assault of Black women as a tool of domination over the entire African-American community.

For White women rape was at least acknowledged as a crime in some instances, but the pursuit of justice was no joyride even for them. Particularly if a White rape victim was poor and her assailant was a White man of a higher socioeconomic class, or even in some isolated cases if her assailant was a Black worker whose labor was of value to a powerful White man, White male privilege meant the rapist would not be punished.[4] Historically, a White woman's rape was considered an insult to family honor. It meant White men's property was damaged, its value decreased. Common law rules generally protected White male rapists of White women from being prosecuted. For being accused of the same crime, Black men were frequently tortured, castrated, and lynched by vigilante mobs.[5]

After slavery ended, many accusations of Black men raping White women were fabrications created to justify violence against Black men who refused to be subservient to Whites. It was considered an infringement on White men's power over their women. The belief that Black women were naturally immoral and promiscuous, hence unrapeable, and that Black men were hypersexual beasts who wanted to rape White women were the status quo. The president of the American Medical Association in 1893, Hunter McGuire, wrote that perverted Black men raped White women because of the loss of slavery's discipline—an opinion that was considered solid science.[6] So deeply entrenched were these stereotypes that in trials of White victims' cases, jurors could consider a defendant's race as evidence of his intent.[7]

The legacy of the racist roots of the criminal justice system still impact Black women and men today. Studies show that Black men who are accused of sexually victimizing White women are more likely than other men to be arrested, convicted, and imprisoned. While it is common knowledge that Black men are disproportionately incarcerated overall, there is little focus on how the criminal justice system still discriminates against Black women victims. It has also been shown that men who rape Black women get shorter sentences than men who rape White women.[8]

Until the 1970s, all sexual assault survivors were basically denied access to the criminal justice system.[9] Unlike victims of attempted murder, armed robbery, or other crimes, rape survivors had to prove their stories by presenting evidence of the assailant's identity, the sexual nature of the crime, and the use of force.[10] The basis for this requirement was derived from an English judge's 1671 legal opinion, which stated that rape charges are easy to make and difficult to defend against.[11] Until recent reforms, juries nationwide received special instructions from the courts to be cautious of survivors' testimony. Never mind that sexual assault usually happens in private with no witnesses, and that often no visible wounds result when women submit to a perpetrator in order to avoid further violence or death.

Introduced in the 1970s, new state laws also eliminated proof-of-resistance requirements, and made inadmissible the sexual history of survivors, except for consensual past relations between the assailant and the accuser.[12]

The federal government has been contributing to an improved legal climate for survivors too. In 1984, Congress passed the Victims of Crime Act, creating the Office for Victims of Crime within the Department of Justice to oversee and fund programs for victims of crime, including rape survivors.[13] First passed in 1994, the Violence Against Women Act was reauthorized and strengthened in 2000. It has set harsher penalties for stalking, domestic violence, and sexual assault, and provides funds for legal assistance, among other programs.[14]

Sexual violence, arguably the ultimate personal violation possible, deserves unique handling within the criminal justice system. Because of the factors that make it a unique crime and because of enduring sexism, classism, and racism, sexual violations are singularly challenging court cases to try.

There are now many special units in police departments and prosecutor's offices that handle only sexual violence crimes. Specialized training and increased sensitivity have led to advances like creating separate waiting and interview spaces which allow survivors more privacy, and limiting the number of times survivors have to recount their assault. Not all police or attorneys are sufficiently enlightened, but as a Black survivor, your chances of being treated with dignity and respect are far better than they have ever been.

Overview of Options

The two primary avenues open to you through the criminal justice system are criminal prosecution and civil litigation.

Every state has its own legal definitions for the various types of sexual assault. In most jurisdictions, any unwanted physical contact with any sexual organ is classified as a crime, and in some places, unwanted sexually aggressive comments are also illegal.[15] Force or an articulated threat of harm is not necessary to indicate that a crime was committed.[16]

When one of the participants in sexual activity is younger than the age of consent, even if the minor engaged in the activity willingly, it is a crime called statutory rape. The age at which a youngster can by law consent to sexual activity also varies by state. Most often in statutory rape court cases, parents of the minor pursue criminal charges, but district attorneys do sometimes pursue criminal prosecutions against the wishes of victims.[17]

In a prosecution, the government brings charges against a defendant to determine his guilt or innocence beyond a reasonable doubt. The survivor is officially a witness in the case, sometimes called the complaining witness. If found guilty, the convict's punishment can include incarceration, a monetary fine, mandatory HIV/AIDS testing, sex offender registration, rehabilitation, parole, probation, and the loss of the right to vote, among others.[18]

Civil litigation is an action brought directly by one individual or party against another to determine if it is likely that the defendant caused the harm he's accused of—a lower standard of proof than in a criminal case. The survivor is the plaintiff. Punishment primarily takes the form of financial restitution, and can among other requirements also include court-mandated changes in policy or procedure at an institution.

Justice, the quality of being just, impartial, or fair, can mean much more than punishing a perpetrator. You deserve the support you need, from whatever source available, to help you recover. Explore alternative remedies in addition to reviewing legal options. A good advocate will help you determine what feels right for you.

Yvonne LaMar, a psychology professor and former advocate at Ithaca Rape Crisis, says of survivors: "Sometimes they just want to be moved out of that hallway in a dorm or they want to make some kind of other living arrangements. Sometimes people just want to write a letter and let the person know that that was not what they wanted on that date. And sometimes they don't want to ever confront the person but in fact just want to help themselves feel better. People are very creative and very different on how they deal. We try to honor all that."

For college students, some universities have their own campus justice system. Student jurors or judicial administrators consider evidence and issue binding punishments, such as stay-away orders or expulsions.

Survivors are sometimes eligible for crime victims compensation. The needs provided for by these government funds vary from state to state. Among them are medical expenses, rehabilitation, salary lost as a result of assault, counseling, funds for relocation, emergency services for family, and the repair or replacement of damage to property. Many jurisdictions place restrictions on eligibility, such as reporting the assault within forty-eight hours, cooperating with law enforcement and prosecutors, and submitting the application for compensation within a year of the assault.

If compensation would be helpful for you, inquire about eligibility and application procedures as soon as possible. Compensation is distributed through crime victims services agencies. You can locate them and other victim assistance organizations in your state by calling the National Organization for Victim Assistance or the federal government's Office for Victims of Crime Resource Center.

If you need safe emergency housing, check with local women's shelters or the Red Cross. One survivor who urgently needed to leave town was able to get emergency transportation funds from the Red Cross. As with most sexual violence-related issues, rape crisis center staff should be able to guide you to the appropriate resources.

Police, Black Men, and Your Decision

Even if you're not yet sure if you want to pursue legal action, there are two steps you should take just in case: going to the hospital for a forensic exam and calling the police.

The latter is a simple, logical step for some. For many African Americans, however, it's anything but. Not all Black survivors were violated by a Black perpetrator, but that is the case for the vast majority of us. It's estimated that about 80 percent of rape victims are assaulted by someone of the same race.[19]

Our aversion to the police is no secret, often justifiably based on negative past experiences. Many African Americans mistrust the police because of well-known violent abuses like the Rodney King and Abner Louima cases, because of personal experiences of harassment or simply because they are aware of the disproportionate incarceration of Black men. It is not uncommon for a survivor to decide not to report a Black assailant because she knows he might end up yet another brother mistreated by the system. She might also be worried about disbelief and backlash from Black men and women.

Unfortunately, these very real possibilities present a genuine dilemma for many women, particularly those assaulted by boyfriends, husbands, relatives, or respected community figures like ministers. Such concern for our victimizers stems from Black women's long tradition of selflessness and compassion, and our historic need for absolute racial unity in order to survive this country's most brutal racial oppression.

As you consider the responsibility you feel to protect African Americans, remember to weigh the potential mistreatment of women as heavily as that of men. Sex offenders are known to be the most recidivist criminals.[20] In other words, they are more likely to repeat their crimes, and to do so more frequently, than other types of criminals.

There's no doubt that Black men who rape are rare, tragic exceptions to the norm. There's also no question that Black women deserve to be free from victimization as much as Black men deserve to be free from abuses by the criminal justice system. Black women's right to fair treatment is no more and no less important than that of Black men.

Reporting the Crime

It is the protocol of some rape crisis centers to try to sway you into reporting your assault to the police. Others take a more hands-off approach, simply informing you about what's likely to happen if you do report, and letting you decide with no pressure one way or another. Ultimately, it's your decision. Each survivor and each case are different. Only you know what's best for you.

If you are not up to calling the police or going to the hospital, the most important legal step you can take is to tell someone what's happened. At least contact a friend or relative right away. If you don't feel up to calling the police, have your supporter call.

That first person notified, called an outcry witness in some jurisdictions, is critical. People have numerous reasons for not telling anyone. As rational or justifiable as they might be, keeping quiet makes a case harder to prosecute. Defense attorneys routinely suggest to jurors that if an assault happened, a "real" victim would call the police or at least tell a friend.

If you've waited days, weeks, or months to tell someone, your case isn't necessarily hopeless. Late reporting is better than none at all. Find out what the statute of limitations—the length of time the law allows to pass before a case is filed—is in your state for the specific crime committed against you by calling the district attorney's office or police department.

When the police are notified immediately after an assault, a uniformed officer will come to take an initial report, getting some of the basic facts, and may escort you to a hospital or another safe place. In some areas, police are automatically called to hospitals when survivors go to the emergency room first.

In the midst of crisis, it can be extremely difficult to remember the details that will be of great help to you later. From this point on, keep track of your case by writing down the names and contact information of all police officers and detectives, social service agency workers, advocates, and criminal justice system personnel you deal with. Also, be sure to keep a record of the date, place, and time of your interactions with them, and the number assigned to your case, as well as of the crime itself. If you don't feel up to it, ask a conscientious loved one, friend, or advocate to do it for you.[21]

After reporting the incident, you will be asked to make an official statement, a more detailed account of what happened. This step can be quite challenging. Take a supportive friend or loved one with you when it's time to give your statement. A rape crisis advocate can provide even more than emotional support. With their experience and, hopefully, rapport with police, they can explain questions and interrupt if something is too upsetting and you need a break.

"Often women who have these kinds of complaints are not really comfortable with police, especially with male police, in the interview situation," says Doris Bey, who served with Philadelphia's police department for eighteen years. "There appears to be a hesitancy in revealing these kinds of very intimate details, and a lot of trust has to be established between the person who's interviewing and the victim. And that's not always properly done [because of] time constraints, work overloads."

Some police officers may be a little callous due to work conditions. Others are that way without an excuse. When one survivor entered an Atlanta police station after being assaulted, a Black detective complained that she came in ten minutes before he got off work. One advocate has voiced her frustration with a consistently hostile Black woman officer in her city. And of course, there still are White officers, as well as those of other races, who are sexist and racist.

Consider bringing a man with you when you give your statement, because some insensitive male officers may take you more seriously. Pay attention to what officers do, as well as what they say. One prosecutor has observed policemen who were anything but compassionate in their interaction with survivors, but did a great job of catching perpetrators.

Make it known that you are willing to cooperate fully until your assailant is apprehended. If you are treated disrespectfully or insensitively, complain in writing to the officer's supervisor. Get community leaders or clergy to complain too. Community involvement may also motivate officers who aren't working as hard on your behalf as they should.

If your attacker was a stranger, there are several ways to help identify him. You might be asked to look at a series of identification photographs—now computerized in many police departments, describe him to a composite artist who will sketch his picture, or view a line-up. Bring a friend or advocate with you to these events also.

Despite legal advances that have improved the criminal justice system for survivors, police and prosecutors still have significant discretion in sexual assault cases. Traditionally, if an officer didn't believe someone's story, the case went no further than his opinion. Now many police departments educate officers about the nature of sexual assault and require them to investigate each report, no matter how unlikely it might seem to them.

Not all police officers are so enlightened. One rape crisis advocate recalls officers in a West Central Illinois town stating their belief that between 50 percent and 90 percent of rape reports are false. (Experts say that false rape reports are on par with other crimes at about 2 percent.) Officers in that jurisdiction have even arrested and pressed charges against several women they accused of lying about being assaulted. A local rape crisis advocate can let you know what kind of attitudes or challenges to expect in your area.

If you want to press criminal charges and cannot get police to forward your case to prosecutors, in some places you may have the option to independently swear out an affidavit, a declaration under oath or subject to the penalty of perjury that one's statement of the facts are true. Based on your word, the case is automatically forwarded to the district attorney's office.

Considering Litigation

If you are interested in exploring legal action, there are many factors you should consider. First, be clear about what you hope to gain from the process. Pursuing legal action, even if you win a conviction, is not an emotional cure-all. Some survivors think that if their assailant gets the punishment he deserves, they will automatically feel better. They may end up greatly disappointed to find that their pain lingers on despite a just verdict. The criminal justice system is no substitute for emotional and spiritual healing work done individually, with support groups or in counseling.

Generally speaking, winning a conviction in a sexual violence case is a major challenge. "This system is so imperfect that you can't rest all of your hopes on the system vindicating you, or somehow proving that you are a victim," says Howard Arnette Jr., a former Brooklyn assistant district attorney who was sexually abused by a Boy Scout leader as a child. "You have to know that, because the system may let us down."

Still, he recognizes that whatever the outcome of a trial, there are factors that can make pressing criminal charges worthwhile. "This is me as a prosecutor and as a survivor speaking. Because I didn't come forward, I think it's a real mistake not to prosecute," he says. "Regardless of the ultimate outcome, what you have is the government saying that person is the criminal here, that person is the person who has hurt our society. Not you, them."

While convictions can be part of the healing process, they can also prolong it. "Whatever your natural healing curve, it's now interfaced with the litigation curve," explains Oakland civil attorney Leslie F. Levy. The legal process can bring your assault to the forefront of your mind just when you might have reached a point when you are thinking less about the incident. Litigation can take several months or several years depending on the circumstances of each case. For some people the extended focus on the assault isn't worth the pain. For others, it's a small price to pay.

Depending on the nature of your case, the identity of your assailant, and the attitudes of your loved ones, this could strain your relationships or make them stronger. Enlist family members and friends as a support system. Sometimes the person who winds up helping the most is not who you thought it would be. Accept support from anyone who can genuinely give it.

Criminal Prosecution

Once your case has made it from the police station to the district attorney's office, also called the state attorney's office in some jurisdictions, a prosecuting attorney will interview you to help determine if your case is strong enough to pursue further. This will likely entail recounting another very detailed description of your assault. In most large metropolitan areas, specific attorneys handle sexual assault cases exclusively, and most have been trained to deal with the special needs of survivors.

If this interview is difficult for you, the district attorney's office may provide you with in-house counseling on the spot if necessary, or refer you to an outside therapist. Some jurisdictions permit you to have an advocate with you, although they might prefer you be interviewed alone for fear you'll edit your story with a third party present. At this stage, the prosecutor's office may provide a victim witness specialist who will help explain procedures to you and will become your point person.

Just as the police must decide if there is enough evidence to forward a case to a district attorney's office, prosecutors must decide if there is enough evidence to go forward with litigation. And that decision isn't based solely on whether or not a crime was committed. Every prosecutor wants a winning record. Attorneys are discouraged from taking on cases that are hard to win, and are pressured to reduce charges to make a case easier to win. Survivors are considered bad witnesses when they have qualities believed to reduce their credibility with jurors, such as criminal records or a drug addiction.

Certain kinds of crimes, those involving acquaintance or marital rapes, assaults of prostitutes, or assaults with little or no physical evidence, are labeled bad cases. LaMar says, "I think what happens is, when it comes down to he-said, she-said, that they don't want to take the chance."

Even seemingly angelic survivors are put on the defensive during sexual assault trials, unlike victims of other crimes. Imagine a man in an expensive suit walking down a dark street getting robbed. Would anyone blame him for the crime: "What were you doing there in that outfit at that time of night? That's what you get, you obviously wanted to give your money away."

Laws may have emerged from the dark ages, but not everyone's understanding of sexual assault has kept pace. Prosecutors might focus on the possibility of jurors blaming survivors for their own victimization, instead of the abhorrent criminal conduct of the men who assault them.

"We try to put ourselves in positions as jurors. Based on evidence that's submitted to us, how would we vote if we were in the jury box? And we look at potential defenses," says Johnny O. Scott, criminal investigator in a Mississippi district attorney's office. "We've determined some cases are poor cases. Not that it did not happen, but if we were jurors, we would have to vote not guilty."

From the advocate's perspective, the criminal justice system frequently lacks fairness. "We have people who do all the right things as far as having the evidence collected, and making their statements," says LaMar. "A lot of times when there's been drugs or alcohol involved, our district attorney doesn't want to pursue it."

And racial discrimination in the criminal justice system is not reserved solely for the accused. "Our cases are more likely to be prosecuted less vigorously, because we are not seen as being as valuable as others," says Arnette of African Americans. "We're not seen as being as good a witness as others. If we don't speak a kind of Harvard dialect, we are seen very often as not as smart. All of those stereotypes about promiscuity in the African-American community work against us too."

None of the scenarios mentioned mean a case is impossible to win. But they can mean that your first battle as a survivor might be convincing a district attorney to take your case. If the decision is made to take on your case, a prosecutor will be assigned to you. It is not possible to hire a private prosecuting attorney.

There are a few things you can do to facilitate the prosecution process. First and foremost, cooperate. "Demonstrate in words and action that you are willing and desire to pursue this case. One of the things that turns what someone may consider a bad witness into a good witness is that desire to prosecute," says Arnette.

Arrive on time for your appointments. Show interest in your case by keeping abreast of its progress with periodic phone calls. Try not to take frustrations about the process out on your attorney. You have a right to have your questions answered and to know the status of your case, but asking with a combative attitude or trying to tell an attorney how to do his job won't help anything.

Also, when interviewed, don't omit any relevant information about the incident, your assailant, or yourself. It's not unusual for survivors to hold back important details because they want to hide something about their own behavior from loved ones. For instance, a teenager might want to avoid telling her parents she knew a boy's parents weren't home when she went to his house. Or a woman might want to hide her drug use from her husband. You do yourself a disservice if you do not tell everything, because if the defense surprises your attorney in court with such details, it could irreparably harm your case.

Some jurisdictions automatically do a criminal record check on survivors. Whether or not yours does, it's a good idea to let your attorney know if you have a record. It's another potential disaster if the defense should come across that information and your attorney hasn't. But if the prosecutor knows in advance, he can explain it to the jury in a way that won't harm your case.

Pre-Trial Proceedings

The first court proceeding is a bond hearing at which a judge sets bail. If the defendant can pay it, he will not be jailed before the trial. He might also be released on parole, without paying anything, if the judge believes he won't attempt to flee prosecution. When a judge believes the defendant dangerous, he can be incarcerated without bail. If you are afraid of being harassed or attacked again, your attorney can request a stay-away order as a condition of bail.

At the second court date, the arraignment, the defendant is told whether he faces felony or misdemeanor charges. Generally, a felony penalty is a year or more in prison, and a misdemeanor penalty is less than a year in jail. Both charges can also carry a fine. The accused will then plead guilty or not guilty. If he pleads guilty, the judge sets a sentencing date. A judge can also dismiss the charges if he thinks the evidence is insufficient.

In some jurisdictions, the arraignment and bond hearing occur in a single court proceeding. At any time after the accused enters a not guilty plea, he can change that plea. The defense and prosecution can also reach a plea bargain agreement after the arraignment, meaning the prosecution and defense agree on a lesser charge to which the defendant pleads guilty. Any plea bargaining attempts by your attorney should meet with your approval.

In some areas, the next court proceeding is a preliminary hearing or preliminary exam. Your prosecutor's goal here is proving reasonable cause for trial. Your attorney tries to convince the judge there is sufficient evidence that the crime happened and that the defendant is responsible.

You will likely testify at the preliminary hearing and be asked to identify your assailant. The defense attorney will have the opportunity to cross-examine you. The judge determines if the charges are appropriate, and forwards the case to its next stage. If you are required to testify, the district attorney should prepare you for the questions you'll have to answer. Fortunately, rape reform of the 1970s and '80s eliminated this step in many courts.

In some jurisdictions, a grand jury takes the place of a preliminary exam. Instead of a judge deciding if a case merits a trial, based on evidence and your testimony jurors can vote to indict—officially charge the accused with the crime as a felony, reduce the charges to a misdemeanor, or dismiss the charges. Generally less stressful than a preliminary exam, this hearing is closed to the public and the defendant is not present.

The next proceedings, pre-trial hearings, can happen in every jurisdiction. They are court proceedings at which details of the trial are determined. The prosecution and the defense may make motions, which are requests for a judge to decide about specific things. For instance, the defense can make a suppression motion asking that a particular piece of evidence be barred from trial. Pre-trial hearings also involve discovery, the ongoing process of each side sharing its evidence with the other. Pre-trial conferences are meetings between the prosecution and defense to reach a plea bargain.

Only under rare circumstances would you be required to testify at a pre-trial hearing. Otherwise your attendance is not necessary. But there is still a way to take a proactive role in your case. "If you feel that you're not getting the right type of treatment, then one way to add pressure is pack the courtroom," says Arnette, emphasizing that your supporters sit on the prosecution's side of the courtroom. "It says to the judge and it says to the prosecutor, 'We expect something to be done.'"

The pre-trial period can be frustrating. Attorneys with a heavy workload probably won't take time to keep you informed of each phase. If a victim witness specialist within the prosecutor's office is working with you, it may be easier to get information about your case through her. If there's no victim witness specialist and your attorney is not keeping you up-to-date, call periodically for an update. If you don't want to be kept abreast of each detail, that's fine too.

If you are approached by a private investigator, a member of the defense team, or an unidentified person asking about your case, tell the police and your prosecutor immediately. If the defendant or anyone else harasses you, report that right away too.

At the pre-trial stage, ask community members to show interest. Says Arnette, "The reality is that in sex crime cases and in other cases, if I got a phone call from the mayor's office, that case got a lot more attention. If I got a phone call from a very prominent pastor or clergyman, that case got a lot of attention, because I knew that I was being watched." Even if your contacts are not well known in your community, ask your minister, your local city council representative, even concerned friends, to inquire about your case's status and demonstrate their support.

If you are concerned that your prosecutor is performing inadequately on your case, talk to a victim witness specialist within the court system or at a rape crisis center to find out if your expectations are realistic and your worries merit action. If after that step you are convinced that your case should be getting better quality treatment, try talking to your prosecutor in a nonthreatening manner to try to find a mutually agreeable way to remedy the situation. If you are still dissatisfied, let your prosecutor know that you would like to speak with his or her supervisor. Again, if possible, try to frame your conversations in a way that will not earn you the label of being unreasonable or difficult to work with. Instead of accusing your prosecutor of being incompetent, for example, convey that you are simply convinced that a natural clash of your philosophies or personalities may be preventing you from working together effectively. Another tactic is to write a letter to the head of the prosecutor's office, an elected official called a state attorney or district attorney, and have prominent community members do so as well.

The Trial

The prosecutor's goal in a trial is to prove beyond a reasonable doubt that the suspect did in fact commit the crime of which he is accused. Numerous people may testify at a trial, including the defendant, witnesses, character witnesses for the defendant, and experts, such as the police or sexual assault nurse examiners. You will also most likely testify.

Your physical appearance may be the last thing on your mind as you prepare for trial, but even the clothes you or the defendant wear can leave an impression on a jury that might affect the verdict. "If he's dressed in a suit and a tie and you're not dressed comparable to him, what is it going to look like? I tell [survivors] to be conservative and be the best you can be," says Zephree Brinson, a victim witness specialist for the Cook County State's Attorney's office in Chicago.

She explains that if survivors don't own suitable clothes or have enough money to buy some, she'll help them find appropriate clothing through a church or other source. When substance addiction is an issue, she will work with them to find suitable services and make sure they understand that coming to trial under the influence of drugs or alcohol would be disastrous for their case.

Your district attorney will help you prepare for testifying. Make sure she reviews everything she'll be asking you on the witness stand and rehearses questions that the defense is likely to ask. You can also visit your local rape crisis center and request to go through a mock trial.

Part of your preparation should be learning some stress relief techniques. Ask a therapist, advocate, or counselor at your rape crisis center to teach you some deep breathing, meditation, or stretching exercises. These quick tools can help you get through your most tense moments, from testifying to awaiting a verdict.

The importance of preparing for your testimony cannot be over-estimated. "It's going to be an extremely hostile experience," warns Arnette. "It's the job of the defense attorney to exploit every possible weakness in the survivor's story."

If your assailant was a stranger, his defense will most likely be mistaken identity. His attorneys will likely say that you are not sure if their client is indeed the assailant because you were under great stress. They may suggest, for example, that you focused on the rapist's weapon, not his face. However, because of the increased use of DNA testing, which defense attorneys have difficulty refuting, this defense is becoming less common.[22]

If your assailant was someone you knew, the defense's strategy will probably be to suggest that you consented. A common tactic is to avoid attacking the survivor while trying to gently discredit her story. The defense will try to refute all the evidence presented by the prosecutor, including any scientific proof.

Also be prepared for a possible attitude adjustment in your attorney. "Prosecutors are under a tremendous amount of stress," says Arnette. "They may have been up a day and a half. Suddenly, sometimes, they're not as nice and understanding as they were. Because now we're in that adversarial system and they're trying to win this case." Some district attorneys may become less patient and more irritable in the heat of battle. Try not to take this personally. It may signify how deeply invested in your case she feels.

Some courts don't allow you to be present in court during the trial except when you must testify. Others permit you to sit in after you've testified. Rape crisis advocates will accompany you to court proceedings. Have as many supporters attend as possible. Not only does it help you to have friendly, reassuring faces to look at during your testimony, it might help influence the jury, or judge in a bench trial. Make sure all your supporters sit on the prosecutor's side of the courtroom to send the judge and the jurors the message that many people care about you and are concerned that you receive a just trial.

Your prosecutor will tell you if at any time your family members should leave the courtroom. "There are times when you don't want the fathers and brothers in the courtroom. They're saying things like, 'I'm going to kill you, bastard,' and that kind of stuff. And that doesn't help," says Arnette. "There are other times if they're being supportive and they're giving the impression that this is a caring family, you want them there."

If you are permitted to remain in court after your testimony, consult with your district attorney or advocate about whether this is a wise decision for you. For some people, it's too stressful to hear their case, even their character, being maligned by the defense. Others feel it's important to be aware of the details of the trial.

Verdict

In bench trials, which are less common than jury trials, a judge alone decides a verdict. In a jury trial, jurors must vote unanimously to reach a verdict of guilty or not guilty. Whatever the verdict is, you should be proud of yourself. You've endured a grueling, flawed process in an effort to seek justice and protection for yourself and your community. Not everyone has the strength or will to make it through a trial.

Survivors have a variety of reactions to guilty verdicts. Some are elated or relieved. Some feel a step further in their healing process, while others are just glad to get this episode over with.

The acquittal of an assailant can be traumatic, but not for everyone. Felicia McGruder of Los Angeles's Rosa Parks Sexual Assault Crisis Center says, "In my experience, a lot of survivors feel relief in just trying. It's a vindication that empowers them."

Arnette agrees. When he's seen district attorneys on the verge of tears, survivors have provided them comfort. "I've seen survivors go to prosecutors and say it's okay. It's all right. I know that you did everything you could and I know you believe me," he recalls. "It seemed like it's therapeutic sometimes despite all that trauma."

This is a time to surround yourself with support. If you've been fortunate enough to work with a victim witness specialist or advocate, continue to reach out for the resources and support they provide. Brinson says that if clients don't have successful prosecutions, she calls to check on them and continues to be accessible if they need to talk. She again gives counseling referrals if they are not already in therapy. Rape crisis centers, of course, provide counseling and support services you may find helpful after a trial. At this point, consider whether or not bringing a civil suit against your assailant is an appropriate option. For more information on this decision, see the section on civil litigation later in this chapter.

A conviction may provide you with additional rights, depending on the laws in your area. Some jurisdictions will inform you if your assailant dies in prison or escapes. Some parole boards accept letters from survivors expressing opinions about whether to release a prisoner. You might be notified when your assailant is released from prison or jail, and eligible to receive by mail a picture of him upon his release. Check with your prosecutor's office or rape crisis advocate to find out what post-conviction rights apply to you.

Sentencing

The judge will schedule a convicted defendant's sentencing date, usually at least several weeks up to a few months from the trial's conclusion. The convict will be imprisoned immediately following the trial.

You still have the opportunity to play an active role in the criminal justice process at this stage. You can write a victim impact statement, explaining in detail how the assailant has affected your life. Don't leave anything out. Every personal, professional, material, financial, physical, emotional, and spiritual difficulty that has resulted from your trauma is fair game. A rape crisis advocate, victim witness specialist, or crime victim coordinator will help you craft your statement.

A written victim impact statement, in some jurisdictions, is included in an assailant's permanent record. The judge will read it at the hearing before pronouncing the sentence. If you prefer to give your statement orally instead, you can attend the hearing and do so. If you don't attend the sentencing hearing, your attorney should call you with the results. If not, feel free to call her.

The sentences an assailant can receive run the gamut depending on the statutes in your state, the type and number of offenses he committed, his criminal history, and his age. He could get anything from life in prison to no jail time. There are even some states in which certain sexual assault crimes are punishable by death.

Your assailant has the right to appeal his verdict. You will have no responsibilities in an appeal, although you still have a right to know its results. A felony appeal can take years. A convicted felon or misdemeanant will remain imprisoned through an appeal.

Civil Litigation

The second of the two primary court processes is the civil lawsuit. A civil trial is very similar to a criminal trial, but the steps preceding it and its end goal are quite different. A fundamental difference between criminal and civil proceedings is who brings legal action against whom. In civil cases, a plaintiff sues a defendant. Unlike criminal cases in which the government is always the plaintiff and victims are witnesses, civil plaintiffs can be any individual or legal entity such as a corporation.

Plaintiffs can sue individuals who've caused them harm directly, for instance the assailant in sexual assault cases. They can also sue third parties such as institutions or individuals whose negligence somehow enabled the damage to happen. For instance, a company that left unchecked complaints about a manager's violent behavior, or a church that provided inadequate security for employees expected to work late hours, could be responsible. A civil suit can be filed whether or not a criminal case is tried. It can be filed before, during, or after a criminal trial. However, simultaneous criminal and civil trials will likely work against you.

A civil suit against a convicted criminal is easier to win than one against someone who has not been convicted of a crime. If you bring a civil suit during the criminal proceedings, your assailant's defense may suggest that you want his client declared guilty in criminal court in order to facilitate you winning money from him in your civil suit.[23]

While criminal trials determine *beyond a reasonable doubt* if a defendant committed a crime, a civil action determines *by a preponderance of the evidence* that the defendant did what he was accused of. In other words, in order to win a civil suit, it must seem at least slightly more likely than not that the accused caused the alleged damages, even if he was previously acquitted in a criminal trial.

In a successful civil trial, the judge or jury then dictates how much and what kind of damages the defendant will give the plaintiff. If the accused was convicted in criminal court, the civil case serves only to determine the amount and type of damages the plaintiff should receive.

Damages in a civil case primarily take the form of financial restitution. If you are suing a third party such as a company or school, you can request that the court force changes in its internal policies, called injunctive relief or equitable relief. You can be quite specific, demanding actions that will minimize the chances of future assaults and maximize the organization's response in the event that an assault does take place.

When deciding whether to sue a perpetrator, you should consider the same factors mentioned in the criminal prosecution section of this chapter, as well as some factors unique to civil action. As with criminal proceedings, your emotional healing curve is likely to be delayed. And civil trials can strain relationships, especially if the person you are suing is a relative.

Civil suits are often the most appropriate remedy for adult survivors of child sexual abuse seeking legal remedy. The civil statute of limitations for child sexual abuse is longer in many jurisdictions than the civil statute for adult sexual abuse.[24] These laws vary a lot between states, so be sure to check the laws where you live. Rape crisis centers may have such information on hand.

You have less privacy in civil trials than in criminal court. Medical records and conversations with therapists relevant to damages you are claiming are admissible in court. Even your diary can be subpoenaed. Do not destroy or try to alter any personal documents, including journal entries, if you are considering civil litigation. In some jurisdictions, rape shield laws don't apply to civil cases, meaning your past and present sex life can be used in a trial.[25]

A major consideration unique to civil litigation is the cost. Unlike in criminal trials, you will have to hire and pay a lawyer. Cost varies from place to place. In California, for example, plaintiffs pay thirty-five thousand dollars or more, not including the attorney's labor fees.[26] Most civil cases are taken on a contingency basis, meaning that attorneys agree to be paid by collecting part of the winnings upon settlement or a trial's end. You and your attorney will determine how he will be paid in a retainer agreement, your contract with him, before he begins working on your case. Make sure you understand everything in the contract.

Ask yourself what you hope to get out of a lawsuit. According to Levy, most of her clients have at least one altruistic motivation. "In 90-plus percent of the women who walk into my office," says Levy, "the primary reason they're doing this is because they don't want it to happen to anyone else." Most sex offenders commit multiple crimes, with pedophiles being the most recidivist criminals of all.

Another primary motivation is a desire to recover the costs survivors have incurred as a result of being violated, including medical and mental health expenses for the future as well as the past, the inability to fulfill their potential, and the loss of childhood.[27] Of course, if an assailant is acquitted in a criminal trial or a district attorney refuses to prosecute, some survivors choose to sue as a continuation of their pursuit of justice. Remember, like a criminal trial, a civil suit can be gratifying, but it's unlikely to bring instant healing to your wounds.

Choosing an Attorney

If this process seems appropriate for you, you'll first have to select an attorney. This should not be a rushed decision, but a thoughtful, deliberate process. You'll likely be working closely with your choice for at least a year, possibly as many as five years.

There are two categories of lawyers you should check out. Few fall in the first category, those who specialize in sexual offenses. The second group consists of personal injury lawyers, who handle all kinds of injuries, such as accidents. Call rape crisis centers for attorney recommendations. Local and state bar associations often have lawyer referral services. They can also tell you if an attorney's license has been suspended, or if he has been disciplined.[28] Another resource for finding a civil attorney is the National Crime Victim Bar Association in Washington, D.C. They can be reached toll-free by calling the National Center for Victims of Crime. The One Voice project of Justice for Children maintains a list of civil attorneys, and the National Organization for Women Legal Defense and Education Fund has a directory of attorneys by state in its *Incest and Child Sexual Abuse Legal Resource Kit*.

Schedule initial meetings with several attorneys, making sure to clarify by phone if they'll charge for it. Many provide a first consultation for free. You will be asked specifics about yourself and the abuse. Also, be prepared to ask questions of the attorney. The publication *Long and Mature Considerations: A Legal Guide for Adult Survivors of Child Sexual Abuse* contains a two-page worksheet with questions designed for an initial consultation.

Find out about their experience with the type of suit you plan to file and their knowledge of current laws. Also, get a sense of their awareness of issues unique to sexual assault survivors. Both you and she should understand that it may take longer to develop a healthy, trust-filled rapport than with other types of clients because of the nature of your experiences. Adult survivors of child abuse in particular might have a lasting distrust of authority figures that inhibits a trusting relationship.

Ask if any of their former clients would be willing to speak with you about their litigation experience. The attorney may feel it a breach of attorney-client privilege, but some lawyers are willing to connect you with clients they've served.

As you narrow down your choices, be sure that you feel at ease with the attorney you are considering. "A lot of survivors get a sense about the lawyer just from talking to them," says Levy. "Is the lawyer answering your questions? Are they patient with you? Do they seem to have an understanding about why it's difficult for you to talk about certain parts of [your story]? Have they explained the process to you so that you're comfortable to the extent that one can be with this process?" Good quality lawyers give their potential clients an overall evaluation of the potential case, explaining the likelihood of success, an overview of the process, and how long it could take.

You can also check with law schools in your area to see if they offer free legal guidance, as does the Rape Crisis Advocacy Project at the University of Virginia School of Law. Such an organization can support you throughout your legal process.

How Attorneys Choose Clients

As with prosecutors, civil attorneys have the final say about taking on a client. Your first or second meeting will be a detailed interview about your abuse, which will allow the attorney to evaluate your case. The more specific information you can give the better. The attorney might ask you about the damages you have sustained, including emotional injury, the healing services you've procured, and the amount of money and work time you and your spouse have lost.

The lawyer will likely want to know how much you know about the assailant, including his employer's name, social security number, birth date and assets. And you should be prepared to discuss the abuse, when and where it happened, if there were witnesses or evidence, and details about police involvement and criminal prosecution if they occurred.[29]

Perhaps the primary factor attorneys weigh is whether or not any of the parties being sued have money that can be recouped. Another major consideration is the survivor's emotional health and the strength of her support network.

If the survivor was abused by a relative, the attorney may take into consideration a survivor's realistic expectations of potential effects on her relationships. Says Levy, "There will be people in the family who will turn against her, swear she's lying. It's never my job to judge whether it's worth it to the survivor to deal with it. It's my job to just make sure she understands what litigation can do to a family."

Attorneys may want to know that you are emotionally strong enough to withstand the legal process. Someone who is involved in a positive, ongoing counseling experience may be better suited for a civil suit than someone who has just recently remembered being sexually abused as a child.

To take your case, an attorney will have to find sufficient evidence to back up your case, such as a medical history or school records documenting problems sometimes triggered by child sexual abuse, or proof that you told someone about the crime long before considering filing suit.[30] And your story must be consistent. "She may be telling me the absolute truth, but if I can't find a way to make it understandable to a jury, then it's not going to be a successful case. Doesn't mean it didn't happen," Levy explains.

Like prosecutors, civil lawyers generally take on only cases they think they have a significant chance of winning. So if an attorney turns you down, do not assume that she didn't believe you. Ask why she declined to take you on as a client in case it is something you can change to bring about a favorable decision later on. If you still believe civil litigation is right for your case, continue to look for an attorney.

Pre-Trial Period

After you and your attorney agree to work together, the first step will be to file with the court a complaint or petition, the legal document that describes why you are suing and what you expect to gain. If your jurisdiction permits it, you may want to use your initials or a pseudonym to file if you are concerned about protecting your identity because the document will be accessible to the public, although in some cases you can get a court order to seal your file. If you are worried about your story being publicized in the media, that usually only happens if someone with a high profile is involved, or if you and your legal representation decide it would be advantageous to the case to drum up media attention. Be aware, however, that the long-standing editorial policy of many media outlets to not publish sexual violence survivors' names is becoming less common.[31]

A copy of the complaint and a summons demanding that the defendant reply to the court within a specified amount of time will be delivered to him. Usually given a month or longer to admit or deny the charges, the defendant has the right to make a counter-claim against you as part of his response. He could sue you for libel, for example.

The discovery process happens next, with each side gathering information about the other. An interrogatory is a written response to the opposing side's questions. A deposition is the oral testimonies of witnesses under oath, including you and the defendant, recorded in the opposing lawyer's office. Whether or not you attend your assailant's deposition is up to you and your attorney.

Each attorney can also request physical evidence and documents relevant to the case, such as diaries and medical records. And you will probably be evaluated by a psychiatrist or psychologist hired by your attorney, as well as one hired by the defendant's attorney. That expert witness will produce a report about issues you are claiming in your suit, and may later testify as an expert witness if your case makes it to trial.

As in criminal cases, motions to suppress a particular piece of evidence or dismiss a case entirely can be made. At any time during the pre-trial period, a settlement can be reached. Most civil cases are settled before they reach trial, which means both parties agree on damages before a trial starts. Another alternative being used more frequently in recent years is alternative dispute resolution. Sometimes ordered by a judge, it can be less expensive and less time consuming than a trial.

The two main forms of dispute resolution are arbitration and mediation. In arbitration, a neutral third party negotiates a settlement, which is legally binding. In mediation, a third party negotiates, but resolution is only reached when both the plaintiff and the defendant agree to it. It is not legally binding. If no settlement or dispute resolution is achieved, the next step is the trial.

The Trial

Your attorney will present your case through evidence and the testimony of witnesses, including you. The defendant's attorney will do the same for him. The lawyers can cross-examine each other's witnesses.

Expect a civil trial to be as stressful and challenging as a criminal proceeding. Civil trials tend to last longer than criminal trials, as witnesses who aren't used in the latter must testify, such as expert witnesses who examine your mental health. You should go to trial with supportive friends and family and take advantage of the advocacy resources in your area. Rape crisis center staff work with survivors involved in civil litigation as well as criminal litigation. Pack your side of the courtroom with supporters, just as you should in a criminal trial.

Verdict

A lower standard of proof in civil court improves your odds as a civil plaintiff. In California civil trials for example, instead of reaching a unanimous decision, only nine out of twelve jurors have to vote together to hold a defendant responsible for the charges. Depending on regulations in your area, you might not have a jury trial. In a bench trial, the judge makes a decision.

In civil litigation, both plaintiffs and defendants have the right to appeal a decision with which they disagree, unlike criminal cases in which only defendants can appeal. An appeal will generally add at least another year to your litigation. Although it is extremely rare, the assailant has the right to file a claim against you in some circumstances.

If you win, the judge or jury decides how much the defendant must pay you, or which conditions you've set out that a defendant must fulfill. Unfortunately, winning doesn't necessarily ensure that you will receive the damages you've been awarded. If the assailant doesn't have enough money, his property can be seized. There have been instances of perpetrators having liquidated their assets so that little or nothing remains in their name as a way of getting out of paying damages. Federal employees' pensions can be garnished. Should the assailant acquire assets in the future, they can be used to fulfill your winnings, depending on the jurisdiction, for up to fifteen years or more.[32]

Now that you are prepared to decide whether pursuing a criminal or civil case is appropriate for you, proceed by consulting with the rape crisis and criminal justice system professionals who can help guide you. No matter how much time you spend navigating police stations, district attorneys' offices, and courts, never stop tending to your emotional health. Regardless of where you are in the legal process, even if you have no involvement with it at all, now is the time to embark on an emotional healing journey.

NOTES

1 Bohmer, Carol. "Rape and the Law," in *Confronting Rape and Sexual Assault* (Wilmington, Del.: Scholarly Resources, 1998), 254-256; Berger, Ronald J., Patricia Searles, and W. Lawrence Neuman. "Rape-Law Reform: Its Nature, Origins, and Impact," in *Rape and Society: Readings on the Problem of Sexual Assault*, edited by Patricia Searles and Ronald J. Berger (Boulder: Westview Press, 1995), 223-232.

2 Wriggins, Jennifer. "Rape, Racism, and the Law," in *Rape and Society: Readings on the Problem of Sexual Assault*, edited by Patricia Searles and Ronald J. Berger (Boulder: Westview Press, 1995), 215.

3 Wriggins, 220.

4 For an excellent analysis of the historical intersection of race and class in the criminal justice system, including the case referenced here, see Berry, Mary Frances. *The Pig Farmer's Daughter and Other Tales of American Justice* (New York: Alfred A. Knopf, 1999).

5 Wriggins, 215-216; Berry, 203-212.

6 Berry, 204.

7 See note 2 above.

8 Crenshaw, Kimberle Williams. "The Marginalization of Sexual Violence Against Black Women" (speech given at the National Coalition Against Sexual Assault Conference, Chicago, Illinois, 1993).

9 Fairstein, Linda A. *Sexual Violence: Our War Against Rape* (New York: William Morrow and Company, 1993), 17.

10 Fairstein, 15.

11 *Ibid.*

12 Berger, Searles, and Neuman, 224.

13 Koss, Mary P., et al. *No Safe Haven: Male Violence Against Women at Home, at Work, and in the Community* (Washington, D.C.: American Psychological Association, 1994).

14 "The Violence Against Women Act of 2000 (VAWA 2000)" in Office of Justice Program's Violence Against Women Office website [cited 11 July 2002]; available at www.ojp.usdoj.gov/vawo/laws/vawa_summary2.htm.

15 "What is sexual assault?" in Sex Laws website [cited 11 July 2002]; available at www.sexlaws.org/assault.html.

16 *Ibid.*

17 "What is statutory rape?" in Sex Laws website [cited 11 July 2002]; available at www.sexlaws.org/statrape.html.

18 See note 13 above.

19 Rennison, Callie Marie. *Criminal Victimization in the United States, 1999: Statistical Tables* (Washington, D.C.: U.S. Department of Justice, Office of Justice Programs, January 2001), Table 42.

20 Fairstein, 27.

[21] "Keeping Records" in National Organization for Victim Assistance website [cited 11 July 2002]; available at www.try-nova.org/Victims/keeping_records.html.

[22] "City Attorney Shares Reality of Prosecuting Sexual Assault Cases" in University of Virginia School of Law website [cited 11 July 2002]; available at www.law.virginia.edu/home2002/html/news/2001_02/zug.htm.

[23] Schafran, Lynn, Hecht. Interview by author. Silver Spring, Md., 17 June 2002.

[24] Levy, Leslie F. Interview by author. Email, 24 September 2002.

[25] *Ibid.*

[26] *Ibid.*

[27] *Ibid.*

[28] Brent, Elizabeth A. *Long and Mature Considerations: A Legal Guide for Adult Survivors of Child Sexual Abuse* (Washington, D.C.: One Voice: The National Alliance for Abuse Awareness, 1997), 63.

[29] "Information for Victims" in National Crime Victim Bar Association website [cited 11 July 2002]; available at www.victimbar.org/victim_information.html.

[30] See note 23 above.

[31] See note 23 above.

Unless otherwise specified, the primary sources for information in this chapter are interviews by the author with Howard Arnette, Jr., Doris Bey, Zephree Brinson, Yvonne LaMar, Leslie F. Levy, Felicia McGruder, and Johnny O. Scott.

Chapter 3
Emotional Recovery

How can I go on?

The day after I was raped, I called the D.C. Rape Crisis Center hotline. I remember asking if, after such an assault, women went on to have normal lives, get married, have children, be happy. It sounds silly to me now, but on May 16, 1995, I found it inconceivable that someone could be normal, much less happy, after experiencing what I had. That was my intellectual perspective. At the same time, on some deeper level, I had already decided to struggle to feel better. My emotional pain was too agonizing to accept indefinitely.

I began therapy less than twenty-four hours after I was attacked. That first day, my mother and sister accompanied me. The next day, my boyfriend and I went together. Over the next several months, I attended weekly private counseling sessions that helped me heal emotionally and spiritually.

Mine was a far from average scenario. Most people who are sexually violated in childhood or as adults never seek help. Estimates of the number of victims who get mental health treatment range from 25 percent to 40 percent.[1] And we know that Black folks in particular are more likely to go to family and friends for help than professionals.[2]

It is impossible to know exactly how many survivors never tell anyone, not a parent, sister or brother, or best friend, much less a therapist. But in studies of Black women's sexuality conducted by renowned psychologist Gail Elizabeth Wyatt, half of interviewees who had experienced childhood sexual abuse never told anyone and less than 5 percent ever got counseling.[3]

Healing is not easy; on the contrary, it can be a painful process that takes years. But no matter what kind of violation you've suffered, feeling better is possible. And getting professional help can be an essential part of recovery.

"It's such an easy thing to say and such a hard thing to do. Because we really do want to believe that we can get a good shower, we can pull ourselves together, and we can go on with our routine," says Rosa McDaniel-Ashe, a psychotherapist at Pathway Center for Psychotherapy in Norcross, Georgia.

There are many reasons survivors of sexual violence choose not to get help, or not to tell anyone at all. They might think they won't be believed or supported, or don't want to burden an already overburdened family. They may dread that a loved one will seek violent revenge. Women who are sexually abused at work may be afraid they will become jobless. Some women who are financially dependent on their abusive partners are scared they won't be able to make it on their own.[4] And as African Americans, we don't want to air our dirty laundry in a society that tends to emphasize what's wrong with us.

"It becomes a luxury to heal. That's how we look at therapy," explains Davine Del Valle, a psychotherapist at Sine Qua Non: Allies in Healing in New York. "You can't afford the time. You can't afford the money. It's not a priority. . . . It doesn't matter if you're suffering and depressed and all the grief is trapped in your body."

Survivors sometimes feel so overwhelmed by what happened that they think no amount of counseling can help. Black women often believe if we can't handle our problems alone we are weak, crazy, or just not praying hard enough.

"Black women, I tell you, we think we are superhuman," says Joyce Estes, a psychologist in private practice in Columbus, Ohio.

"We're the worst offenders when it comes to not coming for treatment early enough. We're not supposed to be in pain. And by that time we have brainwashed everybody else around us to believe that we don't have pain. We just take care of their problems, and so [we]'re the last ones dragging in the door."

Some women don't seek help because they don't understand that they've been violated. Maybe you haven't recognized that incident that you didn't want to happen on that date in high school as rape. Perhaps you consider that scary, confusing episode with your cousin when you were seven years old as just child's play. Even if you were violated years or decades ago in a seemingly minor way and experienced no apparent negative consequences at the time, it is quite possible that you will be negatively affected by the incident at some point later in life.

Some survivors will make strides in healing without the help of a professional. For them, tackling the healing process alone should mean much more than just going on with life. It requires self-education, discipline, and the willingness to challenge oneself to grow and to work through pain.

But among those who decide to go without help, there are untold numbers of walking wounded. Whether their dysfunction is obvious or obscured, they live months, years, even their entire lives, depressed and anxious, or unable to sustain relationships, or trying to deaden their pain with alcohol or drugs, or mistreating their children because unresolved anger spills into their family life, or with any number of other symptoms.[5]

Many people think that someday they will suddenly and miraculously feel better. With any goal you set for yourself, you must take steps to achieve it. Authentic healing is no different.

Whether you were assaulted as a child, teenager, or adult, whether you tried to physically fight off your assailant or went along with abuse because you felt scared and powerless, what happened to you was not your fault. It is unfair that you may need to put some hard work into being emotionally balanced, peaceful, and healthy. You could not control the violation, but what happens next is primarily up to you. Bluntly put, you now must choose whether or not you will strive to heal.

You can choose to let your pain serve as a catalyst for emotional and spiritual growth. Many survivors who report triumphant recoveries say they've become stronger, wiser, more deeply spiritual and loving, even more appreciative of life through their healing process. Healing is worth the struggle.

"At some point a total healing can take place. But it is taken in steps," says Atiba Vidato-Haupt, an ordained minister and psychotherapist in Washington, D.C. "The degree to which the individual is willing to work on the healing process will determine how complete their recovery is."

Depending on where you are in your healing process, that might be hard for you to believe. Are you still asking: Is healing really possible? If by that you mean, will you go back to being the same person you were before you were assaulted, the answer is probably not. But if you mean, can you be free of emotional pain and other negative effects of your trauma, the answer is a resounding yes.

In this chapter, you will become aware of how sexual violence affects people mentally and emotionally. And you will learn about some of the healing options available. Not every approach will appeal to you. Because healing is a unique process for every survivor, a broad variety of healing modalities are gathered here in order to help you make informed choices about your recovery. You will also learn some proactive steps you can take on your own in your healing journey, either in addition to professional help or independently.

How Sexual Violation Can Affect You

Experts may have different opinions about how to heal, but they are in agreement about this: Anything you are feeling, thinking, or doing in reaction to sexual trauma is normal.[6] Everyone has their own coping mechanisms for dealing with grief, a major issue that results from such violations. You are surviving as best you can.

Perhaps you're experiencing physical pain for which there is no medical explanation. Maybe you never go outside after dark anymore. If you were sexually abused as a child, it could have taken years to remember what happened because your mind repressed those memories. These are all coping mechanisms.

Self-injury responses to sexual violation, while clearly not healthy behaviors, do not mean you are strange or crazy. In response to trauma, survivors sometimes develop challenges such as eating disorders, substance abuse, self-cutting, or burning.[7]

Incompleted incest or rape attempts, even voyeurism, can cause long-term consequences. For example, if a teenager found out that a brother had been watching her undress through a hole in her bedroom wall, she could experience the same kind of survivor's reactions as someone who was physically assaulted.

There are infinite responses to sexual violence. No two people will react alike. All kinds of factors influence responses, including the severity of physical injury, the number of perpetrators, the state of your emotional health at the time of the attack, your beliefs about sexual assault, and other people's reactions.[8]

"I'm surprised at the number of [Black] women who say, 'It doesn't really bother me. It's really not a problem,'" declares Estes about sexual violence survivors. People underestimate the gravity of sexual violence every day. The most private, sensitive parts of your body were attacked. For many of us, we were literally attacked inside our bodies. We have experienced the most intimate violation possible.

The truth is that sexual assault is one of the most traumatic crimes there is. Psychologist Hawthorne Smith, who counsels foreign torture survivors in New York, explains that torture and rape are interrelated. In fact, sexual violence is a common tool of torture.

"Torture is something that is used to try to denigrate, to break down someone's spirit, to have them question their own humanity, to have them feel that they are dirty or that somehow they brought this upon themselves," he explains. Rape can have identical repercussions.

Convincing yourself that it was not harmful or significant or that it didn't really happen might be a way to keep from feeling overwhelmed. But those mindsets hinder your ability to recover, to get to the point where you really are no longer overwhelmed by the violation.

So serious is sexual violation that it commonly leads to a condition normally associated with war combat veterans, post-traumatic stress disorder (PTSD), a debilitating reaction to serious trauma experienced by about 80 percent of rape survivors at some point after their assault.[9] Believed to be the largest group of PTSD sufferers, sexual violence survivors are more likely to develop it than victims of car accidents and natural disasters.[10] Its symptoms can include recurring nightmares or flashbacks, withdrawal, and hypersensitive behavior such as startling easily.

If you have high blood pressure, a heart attack could cause more damage and require a longer recovery time than for someone who is healthy. The same can be said of your emotional health. If you have experienced incidents of classism, racism, sexism, or violence that have drained your mental energy and strength or diminished your self-image, you may be even more vulnerable to negative consequences of sexual assault, and you might find that you have an even harder time healing than someone who is unaccustomed to being harmed, devalued, or discriminated against. Black women are particularly likely to have sustained numerous assaults on their overall well-being, leaving us vulnerable to PTSD when we are assaulted.[11]

If friends, family, police, counselors, or hospital workers treat you negatively, their secondary victimization, also called a second assault, can further damage your emotional state and cause your healing to take even longer.[12]

It is possible that you will recognize many coping mechanisms and reactions to sexual violence that will be described here, or only a few. You might have reactions other than those mentioned here as well. They may come and go over periods of weeks, months or years. Being able to recognize the mental, emotional, and behavioral repercussions common to survivors may save time and energy as you delve into your healing. Hopefully, it will help direct you to the healing approaches appropriate for you. Rest assured that untold numbers of people have not only survived, but victoriously transcended these very challenges.

Survivors' Feelings and Behaviors

In the first days after a sexual violation, survivors commonly experience shock. You may be disoriented, restless, or numb. Your emotions may feel like they are racing out of control: anger, fear, humiliation, grief, relief at being alive. At the other end of the spectrum, some people become emotionally distant or cold, handling their personal business like robots.

In the short or long term, you might find your eating and sleeping patterns drastically changed. You might cry a lot or not at all. Some people cry and laugh simultaneously, or experience nervous laughter. Chronic sadness, depression, and anxiety are common expressions of a survivor's period of mourning.[13]

A lot of women blame themselves after an assault.[14] People think they could have prevented the incident if they had tried harder, said the right thing, screamed louder, run faster, or stayed home that night, for example. Others think that they deserve to be mistreated, that the abuse must mean they are a bad person. Sometimes religious or cultural influences make us feel dirty, ashamed, embarrassed, and even ruined.

Some survivors speak of feeling isolated—that they've become different from everyone they know, and no one will understand what they're going through.[15] You might feel irritable or sensitive to things people say or do, or into violence on television or in movies.

Many people lose their ability to focus at home, school, or work. Decisions large and small can seem overwhelming. Choosing a sandwich for lunch, for instance, can seem like a monumental task. You might find yourself without interest in hobbies or social activities.[16]

People try various ways of escaping the emotional challenges left by sexual assault. Television watching or shopping, for instance, might increase dramatically. These and many other activities may take your mind off unpleasant thoughts or feelings, but if you do them so much that they become disruptive or prevent you from working through your pain, they have become addictions or harmful avoidance mechanisms.

According to the report *Rape in America*, rape seems to catalyze substance abuse. Compared to people who have never been victimized by crime, rape victims were about five times more likely to have used prescription drugs in a non-medical way, 3.4 times more likely to have used marijuana, six times more likely to have used cocaine, and ten times more likely to have used other hard drugs.[17] Alcoholism and drug abuse are methods of self-medicating to avoid emotional pain.

"I've found that a lot of our patients who are drug users were abused very early in life," says Deborah Dyson, a physician assistant at a high risk prenatal clinic in New York. "[The survivor] begins to feel that she's not worth anything. And if she's not worth anything, why not try the drugs? It makes you feel better, you don't have to deal with things. They are ways to avoid the pain."

You might have nightmares rehashing the attack.[18] Some survivors dream about injuring or killing an assailant or someone else, or even fantasize about it while awake. Such dreams or thoughts are satisfying to some women, but other women are disturbed by them.

To other people, it might seem like a survivor is going to extremes to feel safe. The owner of an Internet company that sells chastity belts made of metal and plastic with a high-security lock says many customers are female survivors of child sexual abuse who wear the belts for that reason.[19] Repetitively checking locks on windows and doors or looking under beds and in closets are common ways survivors reassure themselves. If you begin to repeat a habit so much that it interrupts your daily activity, or if anxiety develops when it's not done, you could be developing obsessive-compulsive disorder, a mental health condition characterized by ritual behaviors and intrusive, distressing thoughts.[20] Becoming overly frugal can be a way of establishing control and safety, of proving you don't need anyone else.

Sexual assault can shatter your belief system, including what you think of yourself and your body, your sense of security, power, and control over your life, how you view and relate to other people, men in general, strangers or relatives, depending on who assaulted you, your ability to trust your own judgment, other people, and even your faith in God. You may feel as if everything has been turned on its head.[21]

Phobias, common after assault, are intense fears that cause serious distress. Ordinary fears are not disruptive, but phobias cause people to go to great lengths to avoid the situation they fear. If someone has developed a phobia of answering the door at night, for instance, a late doorbell could cause panic-like reactions. She might experience an accelerated heart rate, and decide to hide in a closet and pretend no one is home.

You might experience panic attacks, sudden, fierce blasts of anxiety and fear with physiological manifestations: sweaty palms, shortness of breath, flashbacks, or any other fear-based reactions. They can be triggered by something that reminds you of the assault, or by your own thoughts, and can last seconds, minutes, or even hours.

When a trauma is too overwhelming, particularly in children, it can be mentally suppressed so effectively that the victim has no memory of it. Years or decades may pass before the repressed memories are recalled, or it may never happen.

Similarly, an overload of emotional or physical pain can result in the formation of split personalities, called dissociative identity disorder, formerly known as multiple personality disorder. In this condition, a person forms two or more distinct personalities in order to disconnect from a current reality or a memory. When one personality is dominant, the other is dormant, and each has its own memories and memory gaps.

Some survivors experience physical pain despite having no muscular, tissue, or structural damage. Unexplained headaches or stomachaches, for example, often result from stress and trauma.[22] One woman forced to perform fellatio during an assault later experienced severe throat pain, though no detectable physical damage existed.

"All pain is real," notes Estes, who recalls a client who had vaginal pain that was disrupting her sex life with her husband. Medical doctors found nothing wrong with her, but Estes was able to trace the pain to a sexual abuse incident that had occurred years ago. The woman had never dealt with it or even told her husband about it.

Some survivors' self-worth diminishes after abuse or assault, which can leave them vulnerable to dating unsupportive or abusive men, or to patterns of sexually irresponsible behavior.[23] A woman who was raped by her cousin as a teenager says that for years afterward her sexual activity was more frequent and riskier than it would have been had she not been assaulted. The rape made her feel like she didn't own her body, like she didn't have the right to say no to a man who wanted a sexual relationship with her. Another woman, who was repeatedly molested by her brother as a child, says she became promiscuous as a result. By the time she was a teenager, she had mistakenly learned to look for love through sex. Casual, risky sex or promiscuity is something some survivors do to feel like they are in control of their own body.[24]

Loss of appetite sometimes develops into eating disorders. In one study of a group of bulimics, 23 percent had been raped, and 29 percent sexually abused in childhood.[25] It is generally thought that few women of color have eating disorders. But Estes sees it frequently among African Americans in her practice. "They're bingeing, they're dieting, they're purging, and turning all of that pain into focusing on their bodies," she says. We might overeat, taking comfort in food or subconsciously trying to thwart further victimization by making ourselves less physically appealing.

There are also Black victims of trauma who mutilate themselves. "Some people cut themselves because they can't feel anything. That's a way of feeling. Some people cut because that's a way of releasing the pain that they feel. They're overwhelmed by pain," says Davine Del Valle. She's treated women of color who have cut themselves, burned themselves, hit themselves with objects, or banged their head. Any unhealthy physical behavior, even smoking or poor diet, in response to the stress of victimization, can create worse health conditions in the survivor, making it more challenging to concentrate on efforts to heal emotionally.[26]

No matter what your trauma was, no matter what your coping mechanisms and reactions are, and no matter how mild or severe they are, it is possible for you to become healthier, stronger, happier, and more balanced. Look at this period in your life as a crossroads at which you commit to a path of growth and wellness. There's no one right way to get there. No matter what your circumstances and challenges may be, there are many options available to help you on your healing journey.

The Therapy Option

Psychology. Therapy. Mental health. Counseling. These words make some people very uncomfortable. Do they make you think of a monotone doctor making a powerless patient quack like a duck by hypnotizing her with a pocket watch? Or worse, do they conjure up images of hysterical people tied in straitjackets and locked in rooms with padded walls? If so, rest easy that these stereotypes have nothing to do with the mental health services millions of Americans benefit from every day.

When a physical trauma happens, no one thinks twice about going to a doctor for guidance, physical therapy, and pain relief. Since the mind is essential for the healthy functioning of your entire being, why not seek professional help to restore your mental and emotional health? Even if you don't have health insurance or money for therapy, there are community-based healing resources available. We've explored how seriously sexual violation damages emotional and mental health. Now let's delve into ways to heal.

Mental health practitioners are trained to help people reduce pain, heal their self-image, eliminate disruptive or dangerous behaviors, and restore themselves to wellness. Simply put, psychology is the study of mind and behavior, and psychological therapy or counseling is the treatment of mental and emotional difficulties.

After sexual assault or abuse, you are in unfamiliar emotional and mental territory. Expecting to be able to navigate it alone is asking a lot of yourself. Being strong and brave is getting help, not suffering in silence.

"Therapy is like problem solving, normalizing, understanding what's going on, thinking about why the usual stress strategies or techniques are not working anymore. It's developing some new or embellishing [old strategies]," says Estes. Counseling more often than not is a series of conversations between the person seeking healing and the healer. Some professionals may include complementary tools in the pursuit of recovery, such as relaxation exercises, meditation, aromatherapy, or yoga, to name a few.

By necessity, African Americans have historically made use of support systems other than mental health services. We are accustomed to calling on sister-friends during difficult times, which is particularly helpful when they are trustworthy and caring. There's no question that a worship service can have huge therapeutic benefits, and the ear of a compassionate pastor can work wonders. If any such opportunities to advance your recovery exist for you, don't hesitate to make use of them.

According to Brenda Ingram, clinical coordinator at the YWCA of Greater Los Angeles Sexual Assault Crisis Program, "I don't think that everybody has to go to therapy. It's not the answer for everybody. But I do think that you need to talk to people. So if you have friends that you can talk to, if you have a minister you can talk to, if you have family you can talk to, and it works for you, you don't necessarily have to go to a therapist."

It's important to be able to discern when these support systems work and when they don't. There are still many ministers who are not knowledgeable about the nature of sexual violence and have never been trained to handle such traumas. And it is possible that some friends or relatives have been socialized to blame victims, or don't want to deal with the reality of your assault because they feel overwhelmed and scared. Often people want to believe an assault happened because of something the survivor did or didn't do, in order to maintain their own sense of security.

Not everyone is aware of some other benefits of a nonjudgmental, stable therapy experience. In counseling with a trained professional, your conversations won't be tainted by personal considerations like whether or not you baby-sat for her child last month. It is a space for you to focus solely on you, and not have to worry about the other person's problems being included in the mix. You need and deserve to be believed, encouraged, and informed. If family, friends, or your church or mosque don't meet that need, then seek out professionals trained to help people overcome exactly the challenges you are facing.

If challenges other than sexual violence bring you into counseling, you are not alone. "People come in with other issues: depression, inability to have a healthy relationship, low self-esteem," says Del Valle. "It's only in doing the work with somebody that it's revealed that some kind of sexual trauma is the basis for those experiences."

One psychiatric nurse has observed that women hospitalized for depression, an anxiety disorder, post-traumatic stress disorder, a sleep disturbance, or substance abuse frequently have experienced some kind of sexual assault or abuse in the past, although it wasn't the primary issue that brought them in. If you do have a substance abuse problem, the first step should be getting help to begin to overcome the addiction before delving into healing from the abuse or assault. Once you are stable, you will have less risk of a relapse when you start to engage in emotional healing work.[27]

Individual therapy or counseling consists of confidential, one-on-one sessions during which a therapist helps her client to resolve negative thoughts and behaviors, relieve stress, develop coping strategies, and, ultimately, move beyond the pain of trauma.[28]

Counseling isn't necessarily limited to conversation. Some therapists incorporate tools such as dream analysis, visualization, or journaling, as well as various non-Western traditional healing methods. Called complementary, alternative, or holistic, such approaches assume the interconnectedness of mind, body, and soul, and seek to restore balance to the whole person. Considering that sexual violation impacts people mentally, physically, and spiritually, it's logical that integrative therapy incorporating holistic treatments may help facilitate total healing.

Group therapy or a support group, another type of psychological counseling, can be particularly helpful for some survivors. Comprised of a small group of people at differing points in their recoveries, groups are facilitated by a counselor.[29] "It allows the person to see that they're not alone. This has happened to other folks. 'My reactions are normal because everybody who's sexually assaulted goes through this.' It helps reduce the stigma attached to being sexually assaulted," explains Ingram.

By encouraging each other, offering advice to someone facing a challenge you've already dealt with successfully, being a safe, dependable source of comfort, you raise your own esteem. Instead of feeling defined by your victimization, helping others in group therapy can help you feel empowered.

Group therapy is not advisable for someone who is extremely sensitive, however. It could be overwhelming for them to listen to other people's stories of abuse. But for those who will not feel retraumatized by others' stories, it can be a great relief to talk with peer survivors. One survivor reports benefiting from group therapy in quite an unexpected way. College age at the time, she began attending a group at her local rape crisis center which included survivors in their fifties or sixties who hadn't progressed much since assaults that happened decades earlier. Their situations motivated her to pursue healing with greater vigor because she realized she didn't want to spend year after year in pain as they had.

Choosing a Therapist

Immediately following an assault, some people may find they don't have much energy or focus for finding a counselor. Meeting with someone at your local rape crisis center is the simplest way to start counseling. You can rest assured that therapists there are trained to handle your challenges.

Rape crisis workers provide crisis intervention, whether it's during a hospital visit or an in-house counseling session, by providing information, active listening, and giving emotional support. "Our counseling starts from the time a person calls us," says Ingram.

Rape crisis centers usually offer individual and group therapy. "They're recognizing that most of the people who come in, having been victimized by sexual assault, may have other histories of victimization that complicate the current sexual assault, so they need to have more in-depth psychotherapy as opposed to just crisis therapy," Ingram reports. "They're offering a wider range of therapeutic intervention."

If you are fortunate enough to know someone who's had a positive counseling experience, check out her therapist. You can also contact a variety of organizations for referrals. The Rape, Abuse, and Incest National Network, commonly known as RAINN, offers crisis intervention through its National Sexual Assault Hotline, as well as referrals to rape crisis centers. Check with your local YWCA to see if crisis counseling is one of the services they offer.

The National Center for Victims of Crime, the National Organization for Victim Assistance, the National Mental Health Association Resource Center and the federal government's Office for Victims of Crime Resource Center all have toll-free phone numbers you can call for referrals to therapists or community-based mental health resources nationwide. Among them are services offered on a sliding fee scale, which means lower income survivors pay less for counseling.

You can also call the Association of Black Psychologists in Washington, D.C., and the American Association of Pastoral Counselors in Fairfax, Virginia, for a recommendation. The National Organization on Male Sexual Victimization has a toll-free number that refers male survivors to support groups, and they list counselors who specialize in working with men on their website.

If you have health insurance and want to see a private therapist, check to see if the professional you select participates with your health plan so that you don't have to pay the full fee out-of-pocket. You may also be eligible for financial support for counseling from your state compensation board. Get information on compensation from the National Center for Victims of Crime, the National Organization for Victim Assistance, or your local rape crisis center.

Contrary to popular belief, not all mental health practitioners are psychologists or psychiatrists. As a matter of fact, you are less likely to receive treatment from a psychiatrist than other types of counselors. At the YWCA of Greater Los Angeles Sexual Assault Crisis Program, for example, only if it seems that medication such as an antidepressant is needed to best treat a survivor will she be referred to a psychiatrist. Psychologists and other mental health professionals cannot prescribe medicine because they are not medical doctors.

Therapists come in many disciplines, with a variety of credentials. Psychologists might have a doctoral or master's degree in psychology or education. Many counselors earn degrees in social work and might be licensed clinical social workers, certified social workers, or marriage and family therapists. A pastoral counselor might have a master's or doctorate in divinity or philosophy. Many psychiatric nurses are therapists. If you've developed a specific chronic problem like debilitating phobias, you should seek someone with expertise in that area.

When searching for a therapist, if you are up to it, request a free phone or in-person consultation to determine if she is adequately prepared to handle your challenges. It will also give you a sense of your personal comfort level with her. Even if the person is a pastor you already know, there are some questions about training and experience you should ask. If you are not up to a consultation, have a friend or family member do it for you. If a therapist refuses to answer your questions before beginning counseling, unless they come highly recommended by someone you trust, you might want to keep looking.

During the consultation, find out if the therapist you are considering is skilled in working with sexual assault or abuse survivors. Having an appropriately trained therapist is crucial because negative therapy experiences can also amount to a secondary victimization and compound your trauma.[30]

"If you go to a therapist who has never done any work with someone who's been victimized or traumatized, they could do more damage," says Ingram. "They don't know how to work with someone who's been a victim of sexual assault if they're somehow blaming you: 'Why were you drinking and why did you go off with that guy? Let's talk about what that might have meant from your childhood.' That ain't got nothing to do with it!"

Some survivors ask personal questions in a pre-therapy consultation. They might want to know about a therapist's religious background or family life, for instance. Since you are about to reveal extremely private, painful information, it may feel comforting for you to know if you share some common life experiences with a therapist, or it may make no difference to you. Take their responses into consideration as you decide who will help you heal.

Discuss with the therapist her philosophy about healing and her strategies for achieving it. For instance, "Helping the person find balance in mind, body, and spirit is the ultimate goal for me," says McDaniel-Ashe. "Anyone who comes to me, particularly through referral, they understand that they're likely to be hypnotized, they're likely to be chanting, they're likely to be doing relaxation exercises. They're certainly going to be reading. They're certainly going to be reconnecting to their physical body. It's a very, very interactive healing process for me." You should feel comfortable with the philosophy of the counselor you choose.

Following are some questions to ask during your consultation. There are no absolute right or wrong answers, although for the first question it is best to go with someone with more than a workshop or two under her belt. Add any questions that will help you decide if you will be comfortable with a particular counselor.

- How much training and experience do you have handling sexual assault in particular and trauma in general?
- What is your professional category: social worker, psychologist, etc.?
- What academic degrees and professional certifications or licenses have you earned?
- What is your philosophy about healing?
- How long have you been practicing?
- Do you suggest any complementary healing techniques such as yoga or reiki?
- (For counselors in private practice) Do you accept my medical insurance company? If so, what is my co-pay? If not, how much do you charge?
- Do you have any current or former clients willing to speak with me about their experience in therapy with you?

After your consultation, ask yourself some questions. Are you comfortable talking with the person? Did you sense that she was really listening to you and interested in what you were saying? Was she patient? Were you comfortable in her office space? Did you feel physically and emotionally safe?

When meeting someone new in a social situation, you can feel immediately comfortable, have an instant dislike, or be without a strong feeling one way or another. Pay close attention to your intuition in this situation, too. Even if someone comes highly recommended, if she rubs you the wrong way, continue looking for a person you feel comfortable with.

Unfortunately for some survivors, their ability to trust their instincts may be damaged because of abuses they've experienced. If you are unsure about whether a therapist will be a good fit for you, there is no need to feel worried or anxious about your decision. Remember, you can leave therapy or find a new counselor at any time.

When considering your comfort level during therapy, race can be a major factor. Some African-American therapists say they have clients who have turned to them after negative experiences with White counselors. Reports Del Valle, "They don't want to be scrutinized, sidestepped. People come in and say, 'Well, I tried to work with somebody else I wasn't comfortable with. They stared at me or they took notes or they just look so horrified by anything I said that I just felt like I couldn't talk.' I hear that over and over and over again."

Therapists of color may be more likely to understand your special needs, but there are always exceptions. Of course, not all Black therapists are good, and not all therapists of other races are unable to work successfully with Black clients. Whatever the race or ethnicity of your counselor, your comfort level is the key to successful therapy because you will have to be honest about your experiences and feelings in order to progress. Therapy should be a respite for you, a place where you can say anything on your mind, even things you aren't comfortable sharing with family or friends. If you can't maintain a high level of comfort with a practitioner, don't feel bad about finding someone else. Remember, the therapist works for you.

Your comfort with the gender of your therapist is also important. One male survivor says he selected a female counselor because it's easier for him to share private thoughts and feel vulnerable with a woman than a man. According to McDaniel-Ashe, "I'm not sure that for women entering therapy initially, going to a male is the thing to do. Perhaps later on, as they're beginning to restructure and rebuild trust, connecting with a male therapist would be a healthy thing to do."

Evaluating Your Therapist

There are some common denominators of effective therapy for sexual assault and abuse survivors: The survivor is never blamed, the violation is dealt with as a crime without stigma, the client is informed about possible reactions to trauma, and perhaps most importantly, the therapist sets the expectation of improvement and healing.

If your therapist ever says or implies that being violated was in any way your fault, you are not receiving the help you deserve. Look elsewhere for therapy.

If at any time your therapist suggests any kind of sexual contact between the two of you, get out of there as fast as you can and don't look back. Anything beyond a handshake, pat on the back, or a friendly, comforting hug is inappropriate and unethical on the part of the therapist. Even these touches are okay only if they are not crossing personal boundaries that make you uncomfortable.

Also, be wary of therapists who push you to forgive, as frequently happens in a religious context, or to confront the offender. Neither is necessarily a requirement for your healing. Such emphasis demonstrates a counselor's lack of understanding of sexual violence. If she spends what feels like too much time talking about her own issues, even if they are sexual violence-related, or if she seems too emotionally disturbed by something you've said or done, she probably needs to work through some things on her own before helping you.[31]

In therapy, you should be learning about trauma's effects and what you can expect during recovery. You should also be learning some self-help techniques to use between sessions. And you should feel like you are working toward your own goals.

When you start therapy, clarify together the concerns and symptoms you need to address. From that point on, you should feel that you are working as a team. Says McDaniel-Ashe of her clients, "I come on board to help them achieve what they want. I don't set the agenda." Make sure your therapy stays focused on your needs, not her goals for you. Counselors should not tell you how you feel or what you think. They should not make decisions for you.

"I tell [my clients] to challenge me, to question me," Del Valle agrees. "I cannot be the ultimate authority about somebody else's life." She suggests that you voice your disagreements instead of just leaving angry when something upsets you. If you don't tell the therapist on the spot, call back later, giving them a chance to correct the problem. If they don't, it's probably time to move on.

If there are distractions or things you find unpleasant in the physical environment where your sessions take place, clearly explain the problem to your therapist as well. For instance, a cat or a dog roaming around would be inappropriate. If your complaint is not handled in a timely and respectful way, consider finding someone else.

Over time, take note of whether your challenges are becoming less difficult. "The person may be having nightmares. They may be having heart palpitations, sweaty palms, fears. As those things start to decrease, they start to feel less depressed," says Ingram. "So they want to look at a reduction of the symptoms that they first came in with."

Your emotional recovery probably won't happen in a linear process. There is no standard sequence for a healing process, and no standard recovery time. You can feel like you have made great progress one week, then feel like you've backtracked the next, and still be moving toward healing.

Evaluate yourself, too. Are you being honest and open in therapy? Do you believe that you will feel better? Both you and your therapist should be optimistic that you can heal; however, your expectations are more important than anyone else's. You've got to have hope.

Holistic Healing Practices

Consider enhancing your recovery process with one of the following techniques. If you are visiting a therapist and decide to use complementary healing techniques on your own, let her know so you can be in agreement on strategies in your healing process. Many of these healing practices can be used independent of counseling as well.

Following are brief descriptions of some alternative healing practices, none of which require the removal of clothing, with the possible exception of acupuncture depending on where needles need to be placed. Organizations that can make referrals for each are listed. If necessary, ask if low-cost services or sliding-scale fees for violence survivors are available. These are just a few of the holistic healing methods that exist. You can always research others at a public library or online to become aware of the full range of options.

Acupuncture

Thousands of years old, this Chinese treatment is based on the belief of life force or natural energy in all living beings, called chi or qi (pronounced chee). If the flow of chi is blocked from traveling along fourteen internal, invisible paths or meridians, a person's emotional, mental, spiritual, or physical functions become imbalanced. This upset can be caused by stress, injury and other challenges.

To restore energy flow, an acupuncturist inserts hair-thin, sterilized, stainless steel needles into the skin's surface at some of the hundreds of acupuncture points. The usually painless procedure is believed to cause the brain to release serotonin, a chemical that has a calming effect. Treatments usually last between fifteen minutes and an hour. Acupuncture has successfully helped treat depression, alcoholism, drug abuse, and other disorders.[32]

Medicaid and some private insurance companies help cover the cost of acupuncture in some cases. The National Certification Commission for Acupuncture and Oriental Medicine and the American Association of Oriental Medicine can refer you to a licensed acupuncturist. For a medical doctor who is also an acupuncturist, call the American Academy of Medical Acupuncture.

Aromatherapy

Aromatherapy, believed to be some six thousand years old, has been used in various forms by civilizations all over the world. Liquid extracts distilled from various flowers, herbs, and other plants, called essential oils, are sprayed or steamed into the air so their aromas can be inhaled, or in some cases applied topically, to produce a particular effect. They should never be ingested.

Essential oils' scents can stimulate the release of brain chemicals called neurotransmitters, which can have a variety of effects. Among the essential oils used to relieve stress are basil, vanilla, orange, frankincense, and geranium. Lavender and chamomile are sleep aides, as well as stress relievers. Palmarosa is said to ease grief and anger.[33]

Although some aromatherapy schools license their graduates, there is no single accrediting body for practitioners. The National Association for Holistic Aromatherapy can help you find practitioners. And since aromatherapy is not dangerous, you can practice it by yourself. Get an aromatherapy book from the library or bookstore. You can buy essential oils at some health food stores or even at some skin care product stores like The Body Shop.

Biofeedback

Biofeedback, one of the techniques referred to as a mind-body therapy, is used to teach people to relax. Electrodes wired to a biofeedback machine are placed on the skin to gather information on body functions such as blood pressure, brain wave activity, skin temperature, and heart rate. A practitioner guides you through meditations, deep breathing patterns, visualization, relaxation, or other techniques, and monitors your physical responses. By assessing the machine's feedback she can teach you which techniques have most effectively relaxed these bodily functions. Soon you learn to relax yourself without the machine. You become more conscious of and able to control your body functions.[34]

Biofeedback is commonly used for stress-related disorders like PTSD and symptoms of anxiety and depression. It's also been known to help with treating alcoholism, drug abuse, and sexual dysfunction as a complement to talk therapy. Many biofeedback therapists are psychologists. Call the Biofeedback Certification Institute of America for referrals or search for one on the organization's website.

Creative Arts Therapies

Creative arts therapy is an umbrella term for therapy that integrates the arts and psychological counseling. By using artistic forms of expression such as music or drama, people can express things they may not be able to express verbally.[35] Following are descriptions of two types:

Art: In art therapy, conducted in individual or group settings, clients create visual art such as paintings, sketches, or sculptures. It is a way for people to express things they are uncomfortable talking about, and can draw out subconscious emotions and memories. The process helps develop self-awareness and helps engage clients as active participants in the treatment process. Moreover, creating art can simply be uplifting.[36]

Dance: Dance or movement therapy is based on the premise that the mind and body are interconnected and that movement is the most basic form of expression. Often after sexual violation, survivors feel physically uncomfortable and need to improve their relationship with the body. Dance therapy takes into account that muscular memories of trauma remain in the body just as mental memories stay in the mind. Movement is used to release anxiety and tension, enhance self-awareness, and draw out emotions to be processed. A natural advantage to dance therapy is that it's a way to get exercise into your day. Exercise causes the release of serotonin, helping alleviate stress and depression.[37]

There are several expressive therapy professional organizations that make referrals: American Dance Therapy Association, American Music Therapy Association, National Association for Drama

Therapy, National Association for Poetry Therapy, and American Art Therapy Association.

EMDR

Only a few decades old, Eye Movement Desensitization and Reprocessing (EMDR) is a psychotherapy said to rid survivors of negative trauma-related feelings, thoughts, and behaviors in relatively short periods of time. EMDR combines many elements of mainstream psychology with eye movements or other rhythmic stimulations such as hand taps. The movements seem to stimulate the brain in processing information unusually rapidly. People who have been treated with EMDR have experienced improved self-esteem and the elimination of feelings such as anger, fear, shame, and guilt.[38]

EMDR is not appropriate for everyone. The client needs to be emotionally stable and strong enough to deal with painful, difficult memories and feelings that may surface unexpectedly during sessions. The therapist should be certified EMDR-trained, and should have sexual trauma training. Not yet widely available, due in part to the expense of training, its popularity is growing. For referrals of certified practitioners, contact the EMDR Institute.

Hypnotherapy

Hypnotherapy is a procedure of deep relaxation that leads to a state of intense concentration, sometimes called altered consciousness. It can be used to help recall memories suppressed as a result of trauma and to address addictions, phobias, PTSD, anxiety, and depression.[39]

Contrary to common misperceptions, people cannot be forced into a hypnotic state unwillingly or forced to do anything against their will while in that state. A hypnotized person is always in control of herself and aware of what is being said and done in her presence. It can be used to treat food and drug addictions and relieve anxiety and stress. It can also facilitate positive attitude and behavior changes and the recall of repressed memories.[40]

If you are considering legal action against your assailant, do not use this healing modality. Some judges may dismiss your claims of abuse because they think that hypnotherapy can plant false memories in one's mind.[41]

Many healers, including social workers, pastoral counselors, and psychologists integrate hypnotherapy in their practice. Some therapists become certified in the technique through the American Board of Hypnotherapy, preferable but not a must. People can even learn self-hypnosis to help relax and overcome anxiety. The American Society of Clinical Hypnosis gives out a list of practitioners.

Reiki

Reiki, a type of bodywork, is based on a principle of internal energy pathways similar to acupuncture. Created in Tibet some twenty-five hundred years ago, it relaxes, and releases anxiety and negative emotions. By placing her hands near the body or lightly touching a client along energy centers, called chakras, a reiki healer helps restore the healthy flow of energy in the body. In so doing, she helps revive spiritual, physical, and emotional balance. It is believed that reiki, which means universal life force, works particularly well when done as soon as possible after a trauma has taken place.[42]

Clients often report feelings of warmth during sessions. Some feel emotional disturbances as negative emotions are released. There is no central accrediting body, but you can contact the International Association of Reiki Professionals or Reiki Alliance for referrals. Reiki is another completely safe treatment you can learn to do on yourself with the aide of a good book or in a local class taught by a reiki master.

Yoga

Thousands of years old, yoga is a traditional practice from India designed to create physical and spiritual balance. You can do yoga, of which there are various types, at any age, and in any physical condition. People who practice yoga relax and strengthen themselves physically and mentally through breathing, meditation, and various postures. Whether as a complement to therapy or independently, it can be used to reduce stress and anxiety, and develop self-discipline. It has also been integrated into drug addiction treatment. [43]

A few therapists include yoga during counseling sessions. You will find yoga instruction in local classes offered at the YMCA or YWCA, health clubs, or community centers and recreation centers. You can also learn on your own through books, videos, magazines and online resources. Every December issue (and year-round online) of *Yoga Journal* lists a directory of about a thousand yoga teachers nationwide. There is no single accrediting body for teachers.

What You Can Do on Your Own

Whether or not you decide to get counseling, there are many things you can do to spur your recovery. "Even if it looks weird to everybody else, [survivors] need to make sure that they feel safe, short of doing something that's going to be dangerous," says Ingram. Double-check locks on doors and windows if that will help you sleep. Stay with family or friends for a while, or have them stay with you. Make your home safer by installing security devices like alarms and window bars. Move to a place where you feel safer if necessary.

Ingram does not recommend carrying a weapon but acknowledges that some women do feel more secure packing a gun or a knife. If that is the case for you, it is absolutely crucial to get trained to use the weapon you are interested in and continue to practice using it. If you are not knowledgeable about how to use a weapon to protect yourself, or even if you got some training and then let your skills get rusty, it may be easy for an attacker to use your weapon against you.

Taking self-defense classes may help you to feel safe. Many martial arts schools, women's safety organizations, and rape crisis centers offer classes. You might start a neighborhood watch program to help keep your area safe from crime. For more information about weapons, self-defense, and safety, see the chapters on risk reduction.

For women who are assaulted at home by family members, feeling safe can become an even greater challenge. "Home takes on a different meaning. There's no place of refuge. The home or the bedroom represents a place of stress and fear," says Estes. If you are living with an abuser, try to remove yourself from the situation.

Writes Evelyn C. White in *Chain Chain Change: For Black Women in Abusive Relationships*: "Keep in mind that the longer you stay in an abusive relationship, the clearer the message is to your partner that there is nothing wrong with his behavior and that you are 'strong' enough to take it."[44]

Leaving an abusive relationship is never an easy proposition for people who are financially or otherwise dependent, or are afraid of their partner's reaction. There are many resources to help women escape domestic abuse. Call a domestic violence hotline or a women's shelter in your area.

Not only is it important to be physically safe, it is important to be physically healthy. Emotional healing takes physical energy. Drink lots of water, at least eight glasses a day, and eat plenty of fruits and vegetables. Regular exercise is proven to help relieve tension, stress, and depression. Go walking, swimming, or running. Work out at a gym—some health insurance companies provide discounts on gym memberships. An even more economical option is to buy or rent exercise videos, or borrow them from your public library. You can also exercise to fitness shows on television. Check early morning public television, or sports channels on cable if you have it, for exercise programs. Sign up for salsa, African dance, belly-dancing or hand dancing lessons at a local community center or dance school.

You can even schedule time in your day to dance around your home to your favorite music.

Immediately after an assault, many people find it necessary to take some time off from work or school to begin to recover from shock and any physical injuries, while others prefer to maintain their daily routine. Don't push yourself too hard, and don't stay home just because other people think you should if that's not what you want to do. If you have children, get someone to help you care for them for a few days. Contact your state compensation board if you need to apply for funds to supplement your income if you've had to miss work.

If you are having trouble getting back into the swing of everyday life, you probably need to do things to ground yourself in the present. Take note of whether or not you are eating and sleeping enough. Are you grooming yourself adequately? And are you able to engage in activities at work, at school, or at home? You will be able to tell when these aspects of your life stabilize.

Del Valle suggests writing weekly or monthly goals on a wall calendar, as opposed to weekly planners, so you have a sense of how much time is passing. She also recommends nurturing something like a plant or a pet as a way to keep you engaged in life, particularly if you are not feeling motivated to take good care of yourself.

As soon as possible, begin creating a healing, comforting environment. If you were assaulted at home and you have no other place to go, try rearranging the furniture to change the atmosphere. Listen to soothing music. Rent light-hearted movies. Think of ways you've comforted yourself before and use those techniques again now.

Your environment includes the people in your physical space. Experts agree that survivors need an emotional support system.[45] Choose nonjudgmental, trustworthy, compassionate people to talk to about your feelings, and don't keep grief trapped inside. Part of your communication with loved ones should include being clear about your comfort level with physical touch, from hugs to returning to intimacy with your partner.

If the person you've selected to talk to turns out not to be supportive, if they blame you for what happened for instance, don't spend too much energy trying to convince them to have a different attitude. If you feel strong enough, instruct them to get educated by a rape crisis center counselor before talking to you again about your assault. One survivor who directed her mother to a counselor reports that her attitudes about assault have changed drastically and resulted in a greatly improved relationship between the two. But don't feel that it is your responsibility to educate people brainwashed by myths about rape.

"You might say, 'It's very unfortunate you believe what you believe, and I choose not to respond to that.' And just leave them with that," says Estes. "We have to be really clear in our minds that 'It was not my fault. There's nothing I did to deserve this.' If that person is not there, it's not your job or your goal to educate them." Move on to someone else who can offer the support you need.

Let people help you. This is a foreign concept for many Black women. If ever there is a time in your life when you should rely on others and not feel guilty about it, it is now. This doesn't mean letting other people make decisions for you or tell you what's best for you. If friends can pick up some groceries, baby-sit your kids, or escort you somewhere you are afraid to go alone, accept the support.

If and when you feel ready, talk to your loved ones about their feelings regarding your trauma. They might be hesitant to bring up their feelings as they focus their energy on you. Honest communication about your emotions, and your transforming roles and expectations of yourselves and each other, can help avoid misunderstandings and unnecessary tension. When things are too difficult to say, try writing what you need to communicate in letter form.

Positive self-talk will be key in your recovery process. Recruit a dependable friend you can call anytime to help you concentrate on healthy thinking. Generally be mindful to use compassionate, gentle words with yourself. Do you spend time criticizing or blaming yourself for what happened? Or do you tell yourself: I know I will feel better, I am determined to heal, I refuse to let this tragedy ruin my life? Affirmations like these are an excellent way to keep your mind and your spirit from getting stuck in pain. They can be as short or elaborate as you like. You can repeat the same affirmations every day. You can also make books like Iyanla Vanzant's *Acts of Faith: Daily Meditations for People of Color* part of your everyday routine.

When confronted with moments of panic or flashbacks, explains Estes, "One of the things I find helpful for individuals is to come up with what we call a focal point. It could be something that they make, something that's really meaningful that helps them feel better." She suggests something small like a paperweight or rosary. Once you've selected or created your focal point, keep it with you, on your desk at work and your nightstand at home, or in any convenient place that will allow you quick access to it. "So at the time when you really feel like you're losing it, not focusing or coming apart at the seams," she says, focus in on the object. Look at it and touch it to remind yourself that you are now safe and well. Know that it might not work for you in every instance, sometimes you might still feel overwhelmed, but other times it will be exactly what you need to get through that moment.

Learn relaxation techniques. You will no doubt need to relieve stress and anxiety. Get some books on deep breathing, meditation, or other relaxation strategies or search for such techniques on the Internet.

Journaling is highly recommended by many healers.[46] Writing out feelings is one way to purge negative emotions, help you organize your thoughts, and better understand your behavior. There may be times when you really want to express something, but no one is available to talk to or you just don't feel comfortable saying whatever it is. You can journal any time of day or night. And with that record of emotions and experiences, you will be able to look back and see your progress over time. You can also write about your negative experiences and then burn what you've written. Use that ritual as a method of releasing anger and pain, visualizing your hurt disintegrating.

There are a plethora of self-help books to help readers work through challenges. You can choose from African-American oriented books that deal with general emotional and spiritual growth or books specific to healing from sexual abuse or assault, including some interactive workbooks. See the Resources section for a book list.

Go out of your way to lift your mood. If you can, take a trip to somewhere new or to a place that is comforting to you. Go on picnics in a nearby park. Spend time with friends doing things you enjoy like going to museums, sporting, or music events, or free outdoor festivals. Get pampered with a manicure, pedicure, or trip to the hairdresser. Or get together with friends and create a spa at home. Make sure you include your favorite hobbies, such as making crafts or cooking, into your schedule. Now is a great time to take that class you've been thinking about, be it yoga, photography, Swahili, or whatever interests you.

A simple healing tool available to everyone is laughter. Not simply a matter of lightening up your mood, laughing can stimulate the release of antibodies and endorphins, natural chemicals in the body that fight anxiety. It has also been documented to reduce stress hormones. Stock up on humorous books and movies. Get the tapes or CDs of your favorite stand-up comedians and watch comedies on television. Again, don't forget your public library as a source for materials that will fit in any budget.[47]

African Americans' spirituality has helped us as a people survive some of the worst atrocities committed on this planet. Whatever your religious background, incorporating your tradition of faith into your recovery will be an advantage. McDaniel-Ashe has observed that her more spiritually attuned clients have less difficulty with some aspects of the healing process, such as developing the ability to trust again.

And if you've never seriously engaged in any spiritual practice, it doesn't mean you can't heal deeply or begin to develop a spiritual consciousness, even in the midst of crisis. If you can open yourself to the possibility of connecting with a higher power, seek out spiritual guidance in friends and family, in religious services, and in reading material. A great way to start exploring spirituality is to subscribe to inspirational booklets such as *The Daily Word* or *Daily Thoughts from the Hill*. Find some gospel music that suits your taste—and it comes in every form, from rap to jazz to traditional down-home classics—and play it often. In some areas, gospel radio stations provide nothing but uplifting music programming all day long.

Spiritual healing may not be easy for everyone. Even the most devout believer, after the devastation of sexual violation, might experience doubts, fears, or other challenges in their relationship with God. If you find yourself facing such feelings, seek counsel from a compassionate spiritual teacher, or friend whose spiritual practice you respect, to help you adjust and rebuild your spiritual life.

If a pastor or another person at your church or mosque abused you, or if you experienced the secondary victimization of a negative reaction from someone you confided in there, the thought of religion might be a source of pain instead of solace. Do not go to church or mosque if it is a traumatic experience for you. Know that you can heal without participating in organized religion.

If it is not a painful idea for you, maintain your personal connection with the Creator, even if that simply means taking nature walks or spending quiet time at the beach. Or when you catch yourself sinking into negative thinking, change mental gears with affirmations or scriptures.

Spiritual practices can play a vital role in healing for many people. Certainly other survivors have healed deeply without it by nourishing themselves physically, emotionally, and mentally. The best kind of healing strategy, with or without deliberate spirituality, is comprehensive and holistic.

Stages of Recovery

Although people heal in different ways, some experts break the process down into several major stages. The initial *shock* stage can manifest itself in many forms including denial, numbness, confusion, and feeling slow or weak, out of control or in extreme control.

In the *adjustment* phase you are beginning to move on with day-to-day living. It may become apparent that denial won't work, and you intensely feel emotions in reaction to the assault. They could be fear, anger, depression, anxiety, or negative attitudes about sex, to name a few. Often during this period you may believe you've improved and then feel yourself slip into negative emotions you thought you had gotten past. You are learning to cope with what happened.

In the final *integration* phase, you've accepted that the assault happened and that you've been changed by it, and you've dealt with the range of emotions you felt in response. You understand that it was not your fault, but that the attacker was looking for a victim and selected you. Even if you still feel emotions such as anger, you express them constructively. You spend less and less time thinking about how horrible the assault was. Instead it has become a negative experience that you've been able to overcome, that you haven't allowed to keep you from enjoying life.

Jumping back and forth between stages of the healing process doesn't mean you aren't making progress. "Often times you'll come into therapy and you'll feel really badly because you're remembering a lot of things, you're getting in touch with pain. It really doesn't feel good. You think, 'You know, I was feeling a little bit better before I came,'" says McDaniel-Ashe. "So you really can expect to feel more sad, more depressed, but you have to. That's a part of the work. You have to go back and do a grieving process."

And McDaniel-Ashe points out these markers of a survivor who has triumphed in her healing process: "There's a healthy sense of self again. There's a freedom in her sexuality. There's no interruption in her ability to trust and look forward. She is really restored to prior functioning or even a more heightened functioning."

Ingram agrees that sexual violence survivors have the potential to transform their pain into profound emotional wellness and happiness. "Your life has been forever changed as a result of that experience, just like every experience you have changes your life," she explains. "It's not that you are always going to be controlled by this experience. You can grow from that and become a stronger person. That's where the hope lies, in that you can use that experience to better yourself."

Now you are well prepared to embark on a deep healing journey that will leave you healthy and whole in every aspect of your being.

NOTES

1 Campbell, Rebecca. "Mental Health Services for Rape Survivors: Current Issues in Therapeutic Practice" in Violence Against Women Online Resources website [cited 16 July 2002]; available at www.vaw.umn.edu/FinalDocuments/Commissioned Docs/campbellfinal.asp.

2 Wyatt, Gail Elizabeth. "The Sociocultural Context of African American and White American Women's Rape," *Journal of Social Issues* 48 (1992), 77-91.

3 Wyatt, Gail Elizabeth. *Stolen Women: Reclaiming Our Sexuality, Taking Back Our Lives* (New York: John Wiley and Sons, 1997), 59-60.

4 Odem, Mary E., and Jody Clay-Warner, eds. Introduction to *Confronting Rape and Sexual Assault* (Wilmington, Del.: Scholarly Resources, 1998), xvii.

5 See note 1 above; Koss, Mary P., et al. *No Safe Haven: Male Violence Against Women at Home, at Work, and in the Community* (Washington, D.C.: American Psychological Association, 1994), 165-166.

6 Lindquist, Scott. *The Date Rape Prevention Book* (Naperville, Ill.: Sourcebooks, 2000), 115.

7 "Rape Fact Sheet" in National Center for Injury Prevention and Control website [cited 16 July 2002]; available at www.cdc.gov/ncipc/factsheets/rape.htm. Frawley-O'Dea, Mary Gail. "The Long-Term Impact of Early Sexual Trauma" (paper presented at the National Conference of Catholic Bishops, Dallas, Texas, 13 June 2002).

8 Koss, 203-207.

9 Stovall, Carole. Interview by author. Silver Spring, Md., 27 September 2001.

10 Koss, 192.

11 See note 1 above.

12 See note 1 above.

13 Lindquist, 115-121.

14 Koss, 185.

15 See note 1.

16 Koss, 191.

17 National Center for Victims of Crime and Crime Victims Research and Treatment Center. *Rape in America: A Report to the Nation* (Arlington, Va.: National Center for Victims of Crime, 1992), 7.

18 See note 1 above.

19 Edut, Ophira. "What?" Ms. (October/November 1999), 9.

20 See note 1 above.

21 Koss, 186.

22 "Rape Fact Sheet" in National Center for Injury Prevention and Control website [cited 16 July 2002]; available at www.cdc.gov/ncipc/factsheets/rape.htm.

23 Wyatt, *Stolen Women*, 136-137.

24 Stovall, Carole. Interview by author. Silver Spring, Md., 27 September 2001.

25 Koss, 180.

26 *Ibid.*, 183.

27 Wallace, Barbara. Interview by author. Bowie, Md.

28 Bruce, Debra Fulghum, with Harris H. McIlwain. *The Unofficial Guide to Alternative Medicine* (New York: Macmillan, 1998), 156.

29 Lindquist, 123.

30 See note 1 above.

31 Singer, Ken. "A Consumer's Guide to Therapist Shopping" in National Organization on Male Sexual Victimization website [cited 20 July 2002]; available at www.nomsv.org/articles/singer1.html.

32 Bruce, 55-57; Rosenfeld, Isadore. *Dr. Rosenfeld's Guide to Alternative Medicine: What Works, What Doesn't and What's Right for You* (New York: Random House, 1996).

33 Bruce, 104-109; Trivieri, Jr., Larry. *The American Holistic Medical Association Guide to Holistic Health: Healing Therapies for Optimal Wellness* (New York: John Wiley and Sons, 2001).

34 Bruce, 158-160; Trivieri, 109-110.

35 Home page of The National Coalition of Creative Arts Therapies Association website [cited 17 July 2002]; available at www.ncata.com.

36 "Art Therapy: Definition of the Profession" in American Art Therapy Association website [cited 17 July 2002]; available at www.arttherapy.org;.

37 Bruce, 156-157; American Dance Therapy Association, "Dance/Movement Therapy Fact Sheet."

38 Trivieri, 127-128; see note 22 above.

39 Rosenfeld, 229-241.

40 Trivieri, 114-115.

41 "Civil Remedies for Victims of Sexual Abuse" in Smith Law Firm website [cited 11 July 2002]; available at www.smith-lawfirm.com/remedies.html.

42 Bruce, 81-82; Young, Jacqueline. *The Healing Path: The Practical Guide to the Holistic Traditions of China, India, Tibet, and Japan* (New York: Thorsons, 2001).

[43] Bruce, 51-52; Trivieri, 40-42.

[44] White, Evelyn C. *Chain Chain Change: For Black Women in Abusive Relationships* (Seattle: Seal Press, 1994), 29.

[45] Koss, 207.

[46] Trivieri, 31-32.

[47] Clarke, Sherrill. "The Best Medicine" *Essence* (March 2002), 76.

CHAPTER 4
TO FAMILY AND FRIENDS

If you are reading this, it is probably because your worst nightmare has happened to someone you care about. You may be in shock, exploding with anger or paralyzed with sadness. You have a right to be.

You are a victim too. Some experts call you the secondary victim. After all, you are experiencing many of the same emotions sexual assault victims feel. Whatever your reactions, in order to do your best to serve your loved one, concentrate on her needs first.

You have already taken a giant step forward. By reading this book, you've demonstrated a level of support that many survivors never get. Thank you for the strength, courage, and commitment it takes to educate yourself in order to help your loved one as best you can.

What to Do First

Immediately after an assault, encourage your loved one to get medical attention. A forensic examination must be conducted within seventy-two hours after an assault in order to collect evidence from her body. An exam is of primary importance because she may have internal injuries and not know it. Take her to a local emergency room if she is willing to go, and afterwards, make sure she goes to her follow-up appointment. After suffering a trauma, some people feel too emotionally and physically drained to take basic self-care steps. See Chapter 1 for more information on physical health issues.

Your reactions will influence how well your loved one heals. If you are anything other than supportive, you will contribute to her problems. She may actually have to spend time working through the pain of your response in addition to the trauma of the abuse itself. On the other hand, if she receives good emotional support immediately following the assault, it can reduce the amount of time she needs to heal.[1]

The single most important thing you can do is believe what she tells you. No matter if the victimization happened a day or a decade ago, no matter how minor or horrific it seems, acknowledge that it happened and that it was traumatic. Affirm that she is safe now and that you are sorry she has been hurt in this way. Tell her it was not her fault.

What happened was a crime. The only person responsible for it was the criminal who decided to commit it. By questioning what she did or said, you are being sympathetic to the assailant instead of to her.

"Don't ask her questions in any way that can seem to her to be judgmental or that somehow it was her fault because of something she did or didn't do," says Rosa McDaniel-Ashe. "You have to be very careful to work out of an attitude that says, 'It doesn't matter where you were, what you wore, who you were with. You did not deserve to have this happen to you.'"

Staci Kitchen, a survivor and executive director of the Ohio Coalition on Sexual Assault, agrees: "It is not appropriate to ask a person why they didn't do such-and-so. We know that's a knee-jerk reaction, and many times [the person asking is] not trying to hurt or further traumatize." But that's the effect.

Even if your loved one did make what you consider to be an unsafe decision, one that left her more vulnerable to violence, now is not the time to deal with it. Wait until she understands that the assault was not her fault and is emotionally stronger. For more information on risk reduction, read Chapter 8 and Chapter 9.

Some folks might think it's best to go on with life as if nothing happened or encourage the survivor to get over this tragedy as she would a cold. But minimizing what is likely the most devastating event of someone's life is a harmful response. If the people she depends on most decline to acknowledge the devastation she feels, it will only add feelings of isolation to her pain.

Flying into a rage or running out to seek revenge will probably further frighten her or make her feel neglected. For her sake, you've got to put aside your anxieties, anger, and fear. Even though you are not blaming the victim with these responses, you are removing your focus from where it should be—providing comfort and support to your loved one in whatever way she wants it.

You can be honest about your feelings and still be supportive. It's okay to say, "I feel very angry. I know you feel badly right now, but I want you to know things will be all right. I will support you however I can for as long as you need me." Such statements create a solid foundation for a healing environment. With that kind of support, she'll be less likely to feel ashamed or guilty, which, unfortunately, survivors commonly do. And you will maintain a balance between acknowledging her trauma and being optimistic about her healing.

Open communication can help you avoid misunderstandings in what is already a period of confusion and shock. When you see that someone has a physical wound, it's easy to determine how to avoid causing more pain with your touch. In the case of survivors, the only way you can know is to ask. Your instinct may be to hold her or touch her in ways you think will be comforting. That's important because she does need to know you don't think of her as damaged. But you need to be sure what she's comfortable with.

For days, months, or even longer, she may want a lot of attention or very little. If she does not want attention or affection from you, do not take it personally. It's how she is coping, and is in no way an indication of her feelings about you. Your loved one might want to talk about the details of her assault or might not ever tell you. Make clear to her that you are ready to listen, but don't force her to talk when she's not ready.

You are already doing one of the most important things you can: educating yourself. Learning what to expect during the grieving and healing processes alleviates a lot of anxiety for survivors' supporters. Read some of the books written specifically for survivors' families and friends. (See Resources section for book listing.) Rape crisis center counselors and other assault and abuse experts can offer advice on how to handle the survivor's ups and downs as well as your own. Some centers host support groups for loved ones.

It is not uncommon for significant others, in particular, to feel overwhelmed by sexual violence. One study showed that men who were partners of female survivors experienced similar emotions as women partners of male war veterans, including powerlessness, isolation, and frustration because of their partner's changing emotions.[2] If you need emotional support, particularly if you are feeling unable to provide optimum help for your loved one, call your local rape crisis center and see if you can get counseling for yourself. If you were ever sexually abused, it may be even more difficult for you to try to help someone else. Now is the time to work on your own healing.

For family and friends who don't live with the survivor, if you are emotionally and logistically able, offer to be "on call." Let her know that you are available if she needs to talk in the middle of the night or spend the night at your home, or wants you to accompany her somewhere she is afraid to go alone. If you cannot help in this way, encourage her to identify someone who can. Perhaps you can work cooperatively with other family members and friends to create a network of support. Be sure that she knows whom she can call on for help. Be honest about the level of support you can give.

There may come a time when you think your loved one needs more help than she is getting. If weeks or months pass and she is still unable to function in daily activities, she could likely benefit from professional counseling. Gently encourage her to go.

If she is in therapy, find out if her counselor recommends that you participate in any sessions with her. Even if you think you are adequately prepared to help with your loved one's recovery, going with her to counseling at least once, if the therapist recommends it, will reassure the survivor about your commitment to her healing. The three of you can agree on how to work cooperatively to further the survivor's recovery process.

Watch out for any signs that your loved one might do physical harm to herself, or to others. In such an emergency, get professional help immediately. Call her therapist if she has one, or a rape crisis hotline for help.

Your Job's Not Over

During the months, if not years, following an assault or the recall of earlier abuse, there are a variety of ways you can continue supporting your loved one. Safety is a major issue for many survivors. Talk with her about ways to make sure she feels safe. She may want to consider getting a dog, moving to a more secure location, or taking self-defense classes.

She needs energy to heal. Make sure she is eating nutritious meals. Cook for her when you can. Invite her to exercise with you and choose an activity you both will enjoy. Regular exercise can reduce depression and stress.[3]

Help make her environment as comforting as possible with touches like fresh flowers, her favorite music, or aromatherapy candles. Make sure she is doing things that she enjoys. Buy her that book she has wanted to read, or take her fishing, to a sports event, or to a craft workshop—whatever lifts her spirit. Laughter is very healing and lessens anxiety.[4] Try to work some amusement into her environment through books, films, jokes off the Internet, or any other creative ways you can think of. This may be difficult, but try as best you can to maintain your sense of humor.

While doing all this encouraging, you don't want to make her feel that she has no control over her life. Whether it's about what to eat for dinner or whether to cooperate with the police, ask her what she wants. Even though you're naturally trying to be protective, do not make decisions for her, assume what her needs are, or treat her as if she's helpless. If the people surrounding the survivor continuously see her as a victim, it can be difficult for her to see herself as a person who is gaining strength and healing. It could also cause her to pull away from you.

Whatever your connection to the survivor, do not be surprised to find your relationship strained.[5] Her world has been turned upside down. Maybe you don't understand how she's been acting since the assault, or she may be expecting you to behave differently than before. Some survivors take out their anger on the nearest person. Others withdraw. Be patient with these new currents in your relationship. Things may or may not go back to being just like they were between you, but they are sure to settle down if she is working toward healing. You may have to release your frustrations to a confidant, perhaps a rape crisis counselor or group for the loved ones of survivors.

Not surprisingly, past or recent sexual trauma can present unique challenges for the survivor's partner. In cases of recent assaults, men often feel that they should have been able to protect their beloved. It's not your fault any more than it is hers. Blaming yourself will not help either of you.

For men, partner or not, it can be particularly difficult to understand what your loved one is going through. Women often have concerns about their physical safety that never even occur to most men. Now your loved one must try to readjust to life having experienced a level of terror unfamiliar to most people, the loss of control over her body, the invasion of her very being. Keep that in mind when frustrations and challenges arise for you after learning of her victimization. Use that thought as motivation to focus on doing what's best for her. And of course, do not encourage her to revive your sex life together before she is ready. If you rush her, you will without doubt complicate her devastation and prolong her return to healthy sexual functioning.

Deciding what to say to a survivor's young children can be tricky. Changes in her behavior will likely be apparent to them, but explaining specifics of the trauma will do more harm than good. When thinking about what to say, ask yourself: Will this information help or harm the children? Will it be helpful for the survivor for her children to know, or will it cause more complications for the family?

If they are too young to understand sexual functioning, crime, and violence, simply tell them she has been hurt and the injury is not visible. Tell kids they can help their mother feel better by being as responsible as possible, by doing their homework and chores and by getting along.

When the Victim is a Child

If you think your child has been sexually abused, the worst thing you can do is deny the problem for any reason. No matter how hard it is to accept or how many doubts you have, believe it. According to experts, it is very rare that children lie about sexual abuse. It is better to act as if the accusation is true and risk being embarrassed than to deny your child the help she desperately needs. If you suspect abuse, consult a rape crisis center expert about the signs you have observed. They can help you determine if you should have your child examined to prove or disprove your concern.

If your child tells you about his abuse, it is imperative for you to stay calm. Your anger and fear will further frighten him. If you do express strong emotions, be sure to tell your child that you are not upset with him. Make sure he understands that it was not his fault, that he is now safe, and that you are glad he told you what happened. He needs to be reassured that his status and value in your eyes have not at all changed.

Aside from not believing your child's disclosure of abuse, the worst response is to do nothing. By not taking action to ensure your child's healing, she may get the message that she is still not safe, or that what was done to her wasn't so serious. No sexually abused child goes unaffected, even if you can't currently see any signs of emotional problems.

Arrange for professional counseling with someone trained specifically to work with child survivors of sexual abuse as soon as possible to help prevent the range of problems that could develop when she grows up. [6] You and your family should get counseling as well to prepare you to best help your child and to enable you to get past your pain. For age-appropriate therapy for the survivor as well as the entire family, contact your state's Child Protective Services agency or a rape crisis center. You can also call the National Child Abuse Hotline or the National Sexual Assault Hotline toll free for more information on counseling and other related issues. Mothers Against Sexual Abuse provides referrals, too.

It is essential for you to maintain privacy for your child to the greatest degree possible. Do not tell family members or friends what has happened unless they will play a key role in helping the child heal or supporting you. You want to minimize the possibility of your child feeling embarrassed or ashamed around anyone.

A family member is the victimizer in a significant portion of child sex abuse cases. In cases of incest, it's especially important that you believe your child. Learning that someone you love could abuse your child is, of course, agonizing. It can mean the destruction of an entire family. You have to muster up the courage and strength to do what is best for the victim. Most importantly, that includes ensuring that the abuser does not have access to your child.

Your child must get the message, through your words and actions, that you will support her above all else. That means making sure she is safe from the abuser and placing the blame solely on the perpetrator. As devastated as you feel, know that your child can grow up to be emotionally healthy if she gets the help she needs.

NOTES

1 Campbell, Rebecca. "Mental Health Services for Rape Survivors: Current Issues in Therapeutic Practice" in Violence Against Women Online Resources website [cited 16 July 2002]; available at www.vaw.umn.edu/FinalDocuments/Commis sionedDocs/campbellfinal.asp. Koss, Mary P., et al. *No Safe Haven: Male Violence Against Women at Home, at Work, and in the Community* (Washington, D.C.: American Psychological Association, 1994), 207.

2 *Ibid.*

3 Trivieri, Jr., Larry. *The American Holistic Medical Association Guide to Holistic Health: Healing Therapies for Optimal Wellness* (New York: John Wiley and Sons, 2001), 23.

4 Trivieri, 10, 33-34.

5 See note 1 above.

6 American Academy of Child and Adolescent Psychiatry. "Child Sexual Abuse" in National Organization on Male Sexual Victimization website [cited 20 July 2002]; available at www.nomsv.org/articles/csa.html.

CHAPTER 5
SEXUAL HEALING

When Marvin Gaye sang "Sexual Healing," he made it seem so simple. But for people who have been sexually violated, this natural, normal part of life can be one of the most challenging dimensions to heal and appreciate, much less celebrate. Dr. Carole Stovall, a psychologist with a private practice in Washington, D.C., specializes in trauma. She answers questions about achieving healthy sexuality in the aftermath of sexual assault and abuse.

Q: What are the main characteristics of a sexually healthy person?

STOVALL: From a psychological perspective one of the main characteristics of sexually healthy people is that they are comfortable with themselves and with another person. Healthy sexuality means lacking inappropriate guilt, shame, and sadness, and being able to experience happiness and joy through sexual expression. Sexually healthy people are honest—both with themselves and with another person—about their emotional and physical reactions as well as about their feelings.

Q: How much emphasis should a survivor place on healing his or her sexual life? I ask that question because some people rush back into sex after an assault because they want everything to "just be normal" again.

STOVALL: It is normal to want to reclaim our life after any traumatic event. However, sexual healing is a process, and how quickly each person moves through this process is highly individual. After a sexual assault, it is difficult for survivors to hold on to the reality that they are safe and that the assault is over. But, just like it is important to acknowledge and work toward healing a broken leg or any other physical part of us that is injured, it is important to acknowledge and work toward healing ourselves emotionally and sexually after trauma. It is not uncommon for trauma survivors to act as though their sexuality does not exist, or to go to the other extreme and push themselves to respond sexually, even if they don't want to. The healing process is about reconnecting to our sexual feelings and making middle-of-the-road choices based on what is best for us. Finding this important place is what allows people to move from being a victim to becoming a survivor. Our sexuality and its expression is an important part of who we are. The process of healing helps survivors to trust themselves to know when they are ready for sexuality and to understand and accept that human beings deserve to feel whole, healed, and joyful.

Q: Should sexual health and intimacy be addressed after a successful emotional healing process, or should it be done as a complementary, simultaneous part of emotional healing work?

STOVALL: Sexual abuse survivors often try to function by containing, separating, or shutting out any thoughts, feelings or physical sensations that remind them of the abuse. The overall therapy process helps survivors reconnect with themselves, and know that healing can take place. Survivors need to work through many tangled feelings and assumptions about themselves and their sexuality that result from an assault. For example, after an assault, survivors can feel terribly guilty, wrong, dirty, sinful—even responsible—for what happened to them. They can be confused and forget that an assault is about violence and not about sex. This sorting through of feelings and responsibility needs to be done as survivors progress through therapy. Good therapy facilitates survivors' integrating sexuality back into their life and helps them to normalize their reactions as they work through and heal the trauma.

Q: Are there ever any kinds of behaviors that have to be dealt with first before addressing sexuality and general healing? For example, a survivor may have a chronic problem such as alcoholism or a harmful compulsion.

STOVALL: Absolutely. When people put themselves in danger of any kind, this needs immediate attention. This would include the threat of suicide, suicidal behavior, or suicidal thinking. Additionally, people need to have knowledge and coping skills in place if alcoholism, drug abuse, severe depression, anxiety, eating disorders, or other self-abusive behaviors are present. Healing from trauma can be very stressful and can possibly trigger underlying issues.

Q: What are some of the common ways that sexual abuse suffered as a child affects sexual functioning and intimacy for adult women?

STOVALL: The clearest effect is that sexual abuse is damaging to a child because it is a violation of a child's boundaries. Our boundaries define our physical and psychological sense of who we are and how we relate to the rest of the world. Boundaries form the cornerstone of rules and assumptions about how the world works, and our personality develops around this lexicon. Therefore, the younger the child when abuse occurs, the greater the damage because the boundaries are more vulnerable to the violation. As a result, a child who is sexually abused at two years of age can suffer more severe wounds than one who is sexually abused at an older age.

It is typical that people who suffer sexual abuse as a child develop post-traumatic stress as well as other types of anxiety disorders, depression, self-abusive behaviors, and perhaps dissociative identity disorder. The severity of each of these disorders depends on when the sexual abuse occurred developmentally, the length of time the child was abused, and the severity of the abuse. There are also some individual differences in how a child reacts to abuse, and the severity of its effects depends on the child's life circumstances, how much neglect is present in general, and a whole host of other factors. Of course, all of these things mean that, in terms of sexuality, there is a broad continuum of sexual disruption. At one end, there are very severe disruptions in sexuality in which the person's identity is totally distorted and he or she may engage in activities such as prostitution. At the other end, there can be a general distrust, even a total disinterest in sex.

Q: Are men affected differently than women?

STOVALL: In the sense that the damage is the same, no. But men are taught to suppress their emotions, and the resulting buildup of emotional pain makes them much more likely to "act out"—to have behavioral problems. Research suggests that a significant number of male teenagers who are constantly in trouble have been emotionally abused, sexually abused, or both, as children. Statistics indicate that many incarcerated males were sexually abused early in their lives. Rather than crying or perhaps exhibiting depression outwardly, men will often turn to violence, alcohol, or drugs as a reaction to abuse.

Q: Could you talk more about the issue of men in prison being sexually abused?

STOVALL: Some of the most horrendous sexual, emotional, and physical abuse I've seen has occurred to children who later became criminals or prostitutes, who are often in and out of jail. Criminal and self-degrading behavior often comes from people who are running away from traumatic life experiences. Very early childhood experiences of abuse made them feel so badly about themselves that they engaged in certain negative behavior to try to combat the painful feelings. That's why they become prostitutes so early—twelve, thirteen, fourteen—to quickly try to regain feelings of control.

Q: It seems that such counterproductive responses to abuse would have the opposite of the intended effect. Instead of making a person feel better about themselves, they would make them feel worse.

STOVALL: When children are treated abusively, they lose the perspective that many of us take for granted—that we are decent human beings who have a basic inalienable right to control our bodies and our personal and psychological boundaries. Abused children grow up feeling out of control, powerless, and defective. Since bad things happened to them, it is not uncommon for them to take responsibility for the abuse: "The abuse happened to me so I must be a bad person." Simply put, getting into trouble and being self-destructive is a way of desperately trying to be in control, expressing rage over being violated while at the same time acting out the hopeless resignation of being "a bad person." The goal of therapy is to help them integrate the experience, to help them accept and work through it, so that they can heal and move on. Good therapy helps abuse victims separate who they are—victims of someone else's crazy behavior—from what happened to them.

Q: I understand that men are raped at a far lower rate than women, that much of male rape happens in prison, but that adult men are also raped in society.

STOVALL: There is very little data about male rapes. I suspect that men are not likely to report a rape because it goes against the male stereotypes of what it means to be a "man." Although rape probably does not happen as much to men as it does to women, it does happen. The consequences of the rape are the same: depression, post-traumatic stress, anxiety disorders, lower self-esteem, increased rates of alcohol and drug abuse, and other abusive behaviors.

Q: Can male rape survivors have the same hypersexual response to rape as women, or the opposite response of completely avoiding sex?

STOVALL: Absolutely.

Q: How can sexual violation affect sexual orientation?

STOVALL: The data is not completely clear on this issue. At this point there is no evidence of causal factors that make a person become gay solely because of sexual abuse.

Q: What are some of the common ways that a recent incident of rape affects sexual functioning and intimacy for adult women?

STOVALL: Rape represents a massive violation of physical, personal, and psychological boundaries. In that act, the most creative and intimate of human experiences—sexuality—is pounded by violence and subjugation. It is no wonder that research shows that 80 percent of women who are raped experience post-traumatic stress disorder (PTSD)—a disorder we usually associate with combat war veterans.

Women who are raped often feel shattered and blown apart after the initial shock and disbelief wear off. They are usually plagued with PTSD symptoms, such as reliving the details of the rape attack and experiencing difficulty sleeping, eating, and even thinking. Many victims of rape are also plagued with depression, as well as an extreme sense of loss, grief, and anxiety. Frequently they blame themselves for the attack and they feel dirty, damaged, betrayed, and distrustful of life and—in many victims—of men as a whole. As such, rape survivors can engage in extreme behavior such as becoming hypersexual or totally celibate in order to try and feel in control.

Q: In what ways do sexuality and intimacy problems resulting from sexual violation manifest themselves differently for African Americans than for other racial and ethnic groups?

STOVALL: I don't think there's a way in which those things manifest differently. I do think there can be differences in what happens afterwards that are culturally related and culturally bound. For example, people of color are less likely to seek out help from mental health professionals. The longer it takes to get help, the longer a person suffers. Also, the symptoms worsen and they become more resistant to treatment. So, getting help early is very important.

Black people are more likely to believe that what happens to them is their fault—that if they feel badly about something, then they're not pulling themselves up by their bootstraps. Unfortunately, they also feel that they are not being prayerful, religious people. I've had more than one person tell me that God helps those who help themselves. Fortunately, things are changing. The African-American community is more accepting of the idea that a good mental health professional can be a prayer answered.

Q: What are some of the main messages survivors need to understand during the sexual healing process?

STOVALL: After a sexual trauma, people are normally trying to avoid the feelings, the physical sensations, and the emotional manifestations that are part of the sexual assault itself. It's a type of phobic response that is part of PTSD. We, as therapists, know that in terms of actual phobias the best thing we can do is to teach people that they may have sensations and feelings that remind them of the assault, but those things in and of themselves do not present a current danger.

The work has to proceed in a way that clients are reminded that whatever happened to them is in the past. The trauma is over. It's done. What they are now dealing with are merely feelings, thoughts and physical sensations controlled by one region of the brain. So the work is actually reteaching them not only to tolerate, but to know what to do with those physical sensations in order to regain their life.

Q: If a survivor does not access professional help for problems with sexual functioning and intimacy, will their problems improve naturally over time?

STOVALL: If the abuse has been long-term, then it's very unlikely that these symptoms would go away on their own. The more we know about the brain and how people respond to trauma, the more we know that it is far better for victims to get treatment with somebody who understands the trauma response. It can help them change their physiological responses to an overwhelming, negative event. If it is a more recent trauma, such as a rape, or single-event trauma, sometimes the symptoms will go away over time.

The symptoms may go away, but the person is then still more vulnerable to post-traumatic stress in the future if another trauma happens. Even in a single-event trauma situation, survivors are still better off if they see a mental health professional. It should be someone who is a trauma specialist and thus understands the healing process and how to help patients ameliorate the symptoms—not just to learn to live with them, but to actually reduce the symptoms.

Before EMDR (Eye Movement Desensitization and Reprocessing) and some of the really good specific techniques designed to help people with trauma, therapists would tell clients, "You're going to have to learn to live with this for the rest of your life." This is no longer necessarily true. Treatments like EMDR can actually help some trauma survivors completely regain their life.

Q: How are survivors' problems with sexuality registered and played out biologically?

STOVALL: When sexual assault happens—whether it be a rape or ongoing sexual abuse to children—the victims' brain tells them that they are in danger because something is happening to them that is overwhelming their boundaries, something that they don't want to happen. After the trauma has occurred, their bodies stay on alert, and it's very easy for a part of the brain called the amygdala to "flip on a switch" and say "danger." All of the sensations, feelings, and connected sensory material are stored here. It's the part of the brain that is the earliest and the most primitive.

While experiencing normal events, victims are using the cerebral cortex, the rational part of the brain that's operating quite well. But when an event happens that reminds the victims of the abuse, they go right into feeling heart palpitations or any number of physical or emotional sensations they experienced at the time of the abuse. The amygdala kicks in with its "danger" warnings when stored memories of the abuse are accessed. There is only a one-cell difference between the cerebral cortex, which is the logical, external, highly developed part of the brain, and the amygdala. So when victims experience symptoms that remind them of the trauma, I call that an "amygdala hijacking." And if the victim understands what happens in an amygdala hijacking, then they're prepared for it.

Q: Such triggers can happen when a survivor is participating in a consensual, joyful sexual activity, right?

STOVALL: Absolutely. They can experience it with a partner who's acting very appropriately. The sexual experience can trigger earlier traumatic memories, sensations, feelings, and beliefs. The person then feels as if she is back in time, back when she was sexually abused or raped.

Q: So it's an automatic response, which you're not consciously controlling?

STOVALL: In short, yes. People who have been sexually abused can be with a partner who is appropriate and toward whom they feel love, but when the partner touches them in a certain way or says something to them that reminds them of the sexually abusive event, then the "amygdala hijacking" will occur and survivors can feel like they are being abused all over again.

Q: How can survivors know if they need professional help with sexuality or intimacy?

STOVALL: There's a problem if they're experiencing anything other than joy during the sexual act, and this includes feeling depressed after sexual interaction. If they feel anxiety, sadness, or anything other than the relaxation and peace that are associated with joy, then survivors need to take a look at their emotional responses to sex and address them immediately. Appropriate sexuality shouldn't feel bad.

Q: Do survivors complain of an inability to achieve orgasm during sex?

STOVALL: It would not be unusual for sexual abuse survivors to have difficulty achieving an orgasm. Survivors often report feeling pain with intercourse, feeling very little physical sensation when touched, or generally feeling "deadened" sexually. It is important to have a medical exam to be certain that nothing is occurring physiologically that would interfere with normal sexual responses.

Q: When you've sent people out for physiological testing for sexual problems, do the results usually come back one way or the other?

STOVALL: Usually the problem is not physiological; usually it's psychological. But it's always best to make sure. All psychological work needs to come after there's been a thorough physical exam, because depression and anxiety can be caused by thyroid problems, viruses, multiple sclerosis, or a number of other biological problems. Usually there's nothing physically wrong with the patient, but having a thorough physical is a good idea regardless. When sexual abuse survivors come to me for help with sexuality issues, this is one of the first things I have them do.

Q: If you were to guide a survivor through the process of selecting an appropriate therapist for sexuality and intimacy issues, how would you go about it?

STOVALL: I would normally tell them to start by investigating the background of the therapist. What is his or her experience in treating and understanding trauma? After that, survivors need to trust their own instincts. They need to like the therapist they are working with, and they need to feel that they can trust that person. They need to follow their gut feelings about who that potential therapist is. Most important, therapy is about empowerment—about connecting to our strengths as we go through a process of healing, learning and making the choices and decisions that are right for us.

Different types of specialists have different means of treatment, so it's important to find one that meets your particular needs. Simply talking to clinicians about their specific experiences working with traumatized people is key. For example, have they worked with rape survivors? Have they worked with sexual abuse survivors? Also, do they frequently use some of the new treatment techniques? For example, a treatment called EMDR can significantly help trauma survivors. In fact, it is one of the most powerful techniques that exist. Asking these questions is important. A victim needs to establish a trusting relationship with the clinician. There should always exist openness and the ability to put things on the table without the patient feeling bad about what they've said.

Another thing about a good therapist: being helpful doesn't mean that the clinician is always really nice or that the patient always feels really good after every session. A therapist who is helping a victim work through those very tender issues of sexuality is going to make the patient uncomfortable at some point. It's analogous to getting close to a physical wound, because the trauma has caused the victim so much intimate, private pain over such a long period of time. The trust that exists between therapist and patient is of paramount importance because good, effective therapy is about getting closer to those things that victims want to run away from. Without that trust, patients won't want to let their therapist help them as they work through issues on a very deep emotional level.

Q: Should survivors who want to improve their sexual functioning necessarily seek a sex expert?

STOVALL: I think the answer depends on the individual clinician and the needs of the person. There are some sex therapists who are primarily researchers and they do work with a wide variety of sexuality issues, but that doesn't mean they understand trauma. Other clinicians who are trauma specialists don't necessarily have experience treating sexuality issues. Again, I think patients need to feel free to ask therapists about their individual style of therapy, their areas of expertise, and how much experience they have had related to sex and trauma issues. Another possibility might be having two separate therapists at the same time. The therapeutic picture might include a trauma specialist as well as a sex expert. There are not hard and fast rules. People need to do what is the most helpful for them.

Q: When survivors come to you with sexuality and intimacy issues among their other potential problems, what are your primary goals for them?

STOVALL: I work with survivors to look at where they are in their life and where they want to go. Helping them get there is usually about helping them reduce, or hopefully remove, the symptoms that are causing the suffering. I help patients to stabilize their life, as well as to work through other, non-sexual issues that may be holding them back. There are usually a variety of things that need to happen and a variety of issues that need to be addressed—both physical and psychological.

All of these things are done through a process in which the therapist is working *with* the patient. If the therapist is the one who takes the power, if the therapist is the one who decides the primary goals for that individual, then he or she may essentially be doing the same thing to the survivor that was done by the sexual abuser. So therapy should be an empowering process in which survivors get more in touch with and more aware of their own ability to be in control, to make decisions and to act in a powerful way that positively affects their life. A therapist giving them anything less than that is disrespectful.

Q: What expectations should survivors working to achieve positive, enjoyable sexual experiences have of therapy and its impact on their relationship with their significant other?

STOVALL: If the patient has an experienced clinician who understands what he or she is doing, the patient should know first of all that it *is* possible to achieve a positive, enjoyable sexual experience. There are always going to be tensions in any relationship, regardless of whether or not one partner is in therapy. This is appropriate and normal. Part of the therapist's work is to help people whose boundaries have been violated understand where their comfortable boundaries begin and end. As patients are going through this learning process, it does create tensions, because they're experimenting with their identity and their power. This can understandably be confusing to the important people in their lives, but it's a necessary part of the healing process. The amount of time needed in therapy to completely recover often depends on where survivors already are in the healing process. Sometimes a single trauma can be resolved in a very short period of time. However, if the abuse is more extensive than that, such as repeated sexual abuse during childhood, successful therapy can take a lot longer.

Q: Is total sexual abstinence necessary for at least some period of time during the healing process?

STOVALL: The need for abstinence varies from person to person. Honoring our feelings and what we feel is best for us is never wrong. However, I do think people need to understand that abstinence can sometimes be avoidance. Only survivors can know what is best for themselves, but they should also understand the factors that influence their decision.

Q: So, depending on the individual and the particular circumstances, you might make a patient aware of the option to abstain from sex, but it's not a necessity.

STOVALL: What I *do* say to patients is that the decision should be based on their honest feelings—that being true to themselves sexually is the only way to recover. They should never have sex unless they want to; they should never feel forced into it. Survivors can be responsive to their partners even when they're not particularly in the mood, because they love them and that, in and of itself, is a nice feeling. But there is never a time when they have to tell themselves that they *must* do it. That works against honoring their boundaries and their sense of self.

Q: What life conditions or personal characteristics help make the healing process most effective?

STOVALL: One of the most important decisions survivors need to make to achieve success is to decide that they *want* to do the work, and they are *ready* to start down the road to healing, which can be a long and emotionally difficult process. This decision must be made primarily for themselves, not to please someone else.

Q: As a complement to therapy, or for those who cannot access therapy, what steps do you suggest survivors take for working toward healing on their own?

STOVALL: Reading is one of the best tools for this "independent study," and many good books and workbooks are available. An excellent book is Wendy Maltz's *The Sexual Healing Journey*. She has also edited a lovely poetry book, *Passionate Hearts: The Poetry of Sexual Love*, that helps survivors reconnect with a desire for positive, appropriate sexuality. I also recommend a book called *I Can't Get Over It* by Aphrodite Matsakis, which is about trauma in general. She deals with some of the specifics related to sexual trauma and includes a large variety of resources. She does an excellent job of helping victims understand and put into perspective the physiology of what's happening in their brains during trauma flashbacks.

Other useful resources include basic emotional support from friends and family, as well as from themselves. Most communities have support groups available for survivors, and many hospitals now provide support groups too. Rape crisis centers offer support for single-event trauma victims, but they also can direct victims of long-term sexual abuse to other support groups. Finally, victims can access such groups through college campus counseling centers, community mental health centers and most women's hospitals.

Journaling is another great tool for self-healing. It gives victims a place to "store" a lot of the feelings, both positive and negative, that they understandably experience. Lastly, there are specific sexual exercises, like the ones in Wendy Maltz's book. She discusses the most common exercises, which people can try on their own. They work by helping victims learn to desensitize their negative responses.

Q: Does a survivor need to be in a sexually intimate relationship to address the healing of sexual wounds?

STOVALL: No. Sexual healing begins with the relationship victims have with themselves. To love and respect oneself is a good place to be in *before* starting a sexually intimate relationship anyway.

Q: Studies suggest that many African Americans have negative views of masturbation. What role does this belief play in the sexual healing process?

STOVALL: It has to do with the relationship people have with themselves. If people are comfortable touching their hands, then there is no reason to be uncomfortable touching their sexual parts. It's about owning all of who they are. Part of having a healthy sexual relationship with themselves and with another person is understanding this myth of dirtiness—that their bodies are not dirty.

Q: Ideally, what are a partner's roles and responsibilities in the sexual healing process?

STOVALL: Whether the sexual trauma was a single-event rape or long-term sexual abuse, the victim's partner has the same roles and responsibilities—to communicate, to support, to accept, and to respect. It is particularly important for survivors of long-term sexual abuse to understand that they deserve and are worthy of these intangible gifts from their partner. Survivors should expect the very best from their partner and work toward being open and honest in order to help their partner understand their needs.

Quite frequently, adult victims of childhood sexual abuse can find themselves in emotionally or physically abusive relationships as well, not necessarily *sexually* abusive ones. The common thread here with adult survivors is the abuse; the *type* of abuse doesn't always repeat itself.

Q: Are there ever times when it would be helpful for the partner to come in for therapy with the survivor?

STOVALL: When the communication is not working or there is a lack of any of those other ingredients I talked about—support, acceptance, and respect—joint counseling is very helpful, if not essential, for successful therapy. It is frequently the case that a male partner in a relationship with a sexually abused woman doesn't know what to do, doesn't know how to act. The man may deeply love and care about the woman, but if she cries when he approaches her sexually, he doesn't want to hurt her, and the result is that he backs away and is often very upset and silent. This is not helpful or therapeutic for either partner.

Q: What is the greatest challenge to sexual healing for African Americans?

STOVALL: The biggest barrier that exists for African Americans is the notion that they're not supposed to ask for help. This is the single, largest issue that gets in the way.

Q: What do you say to African Americans who believe that asking for help is a sign of weakness?

STOVALL: Fortunately, I think that belief, on the whole, is changing. There are a lot of ministers who are now putting mental health services in the church. They are performing a great service for the community and are speaking out. So, people have more options to get help, and the message is clear that perhaps one of our greatest gifts from God is the ability to learn, to think, and to make different choices. Through free will, we are being taught that suffering is not required to have a good and blessed life.

CHAPTER 6

REFLECTIONS ON THE SPIRIT:
A Discussion with Two Womanist Preachers

African Americans are a spiritual people. As descendants of Africans in the Western Hemisphere, we have relied on our relationship with God to survive and transcend some of the most horrendous experiences known to humankind. The Most High has indeed brought us a mighty long way.

The colonization process cut enslaved Africans off from their spiritual traditions, including Islam and various African religions, and many of our ancestors integrated Western religion into their lives, even if by force. Despite White efforts to use Christianity as a justification for oppression, African Americans connected with its universal truths. It has been central to individual and collective Black struggles for freedom, justice, equality, and human rights ever since. Today it is believed that 85 to 90 percent of African Americans self-identify as Christian.[1]

Although the Black church has been a premier social service and political organizing institution since slavery, it is often among the least progressive institutions in the Black community when it comes to sexual violence. While most Black church leaders are men, an estimated 60 to 70 percent of members of historically Black church denominations are women.[2] Statistically, it would be impossible not to have sexual violence survivors among any majority-women congregation. According to some Black women clergy, the leadership of far too many Black religious institutions is ill prepared to handle the crises of rape, childhood sexual abuse, and domestic violence.

In the aftermath of assault, it is quite common to seek comfort, healing, and explanations for the seemingly inexplicable from God and from the leader of your spiritual home. Be careful in your quest for answers, because the wrong information can cause more harm than good.

In this chapter, two womanist preachers answer questions commonly asked by survivors of sexual violence. These sisters share spiritual insight and encouragement learned not only in seminary. Both women's ministries specifically addresses violence against women, and both are survivors.

Rev. Dr. Linda H. Hollies is a United Methodist clergywoman who lives in Grand Rapids, Michigan. A self-defined transformational agent, she is the owner and spiritual director of WomanSpace, a retreat center for bodacious, professional women. Hollies is also the author of many inspirational books for women, including *Jesus and Those Bodacious Women: Life Lessons from One Sister to Another.* She is an incest survivor.

Rev. Aubra Love is the founder and executive director of the Black Church and Domestic Violence Institute in Atlanta. She founded this educational ministry to train pastoral leadership and other professionals to serve victims after recognizing that Black women in abusive relationships commonly go first to clergy for help. A retired commercial banking officer, Love is ordained as a United Church of Christ minister. She is a domestic violence survivor.

No matter what religion you practice, these sisters' reflections about God and spirituality will bless your healing process.

Q: Why did this happen? Did God abandon me?

HOLLIES: God did not abandon us. God was there weeping with us and over us and for us. Assaults happen because of the [misuse of] free will that is a gift from God.

LOVE: I don't believe that God ever abandons us. When something happens to us that another person inflicts upon us, it is a decision of that person. This is mostly people continuing to act out their own hurts on others.

Q: Was I being punished for something?

LOVE: God would not choose another person to inflict punishment upon us. When a person does something cruel or harmful to us, intentionally, this is not an act of God. Sexual violence is so traumatic that survivors will often ask, "Why me? What did I do?" . . . and actually come up with very elaborate reasons why it happened. It is an indication of our sanity to go in and do some self-reflection when horrific things occur. We want to believe that we have some control over what happens to us. But rape happens randomly.

HOLLIES: It has nothing to do with a punishment from God because it did not come from God.

Q: The Bible says, "An eye for an eye, a tooth for a tooth." Should I get revenge?

LOVE: The scriptures remind us that vengeance belongs to God and that we might put all of our focus and energy on praising God for our own recovery.

HOLLIES: What that is saying, my sister, is that we want to go out and rape somebody else. And that is not God's way either. That is not God's way. And an eye for an eye, and a tooth for a tooth, is something that happened under the old covenant. That is a

123

Hebrew scripture that you're quoting. We no longer live under that covenant. We live under the new covenant, which is called grace and truth.

"Vengeance is mine," said the Lord (Romans 12:19). I'll take care of it. We are told to pray for our enemies. We are told to love those who despitefully use us (Matthew 5:44). It is a hard thing to do. And yet we cannot go around looking for revenge. It is the first thing that comes to our mind. But if you went and did what the person did to you, you would become the evil that you deplore.

Q: I can't stand the fact that the perpetrator is walking around free and I am still suffering. Will there be justice?

HOLLIES: That's a very human concern, that we want God to get them. And yet what we have to understand is that your statement is not true. You said the people who raped me got away. They did not get away. Because God was right there watching all the time. It is written in God's book. It will never be forgotten. And God promises us justice. God promises us restoration. We might not see them get it, but we have to believe that God will not lie.

Even though we cannot tangibly see the justice, we cannot tangibly see the retribution, we cannot tangibly see the punishment that God metes out, know that God does not play. Jesus says it this way: Whatever you do to one of these, the least, you did it unto me (Matthew 25:40). When they rape you, they rape God.

LOVE: Given the frequency of the assault on the person and spirit of African-American women, many times we find ourselves just thankful that we got out of a harmful situation with our lives. However, we have begun to explore what avenues are available to us in our justice seeking. The criminal justice system is charged with providing recourse in cases of sexual assault. Only the tiniest fraction of sexual assaults is tried through the system for a number of reasons: trauma, the victim cannot identify the assailant, the perpetrator is a family member, undue embarrassment of the victim, lack of victim support, etcetera. Vigilante justice is practiced in a handful of insular communities.

Our national network of rape crisis centers and sexual assault response teams within urban hospitals can gather essential, preliminary evidence of the sexual assault if the victim goes immediately and asks that a rape kit be prepared. Time is of the essence here because the victim must make this decision, literally, within hours of the assault.

Our elders might say, "Know that God sees all and you simply leave it in the hands of the Lord." Ultimately, each victimized person must decide, based on their emotional (and often financial) resources, their method of seeking justice.

Q: The experience of being violated has made me feel so vulnerable and afraid. How can I deal with this fear?

HOLLIES: God does not give us the spirit of fear, but of power and love and a sound mind (2 Timothy 1:7). That's scripture. Fear comes out of our humanness.

There is healthy fear. There is energizing fear. There is paralyzing fear too. You surely don't want to have a paralyzing fear. We have to make sure that the fear of what has happened to us keeps us alert. Not to keep you from enjoying life, not to keep you paralyzed so that you never grow up, move on, experience healthy sex, that kind of stuff, but it does keep you apprehensive enough so that you will be motivated to take better care of yourself.

The other thing I wanted to say about the energizing kind of fear is that no social movement in this world has happened without somebody having energizing fear. I don't care what kind of social movement it is, it comes about because [somebody says,]

"I don't want it to happen to anybody else." Whether it's domestic violence, whether it's welfare reform, whether it's older citizens getting together to get more rights for seniors, it's the energizing kind of fear that says, "This has happened to me. Let us use this, let us create community around this fear so that we can prevent this from happening or being repeated like this again."

LOVE: The first step in dealing with fear is just acknowledging that you are afraid and that your sense of vulnerability is increased. Most people who appear courageous are simply managing their fear—some better than others.

Sometimes what we call fear is simply increased caution. And caution can be a very sensible thing. In an environment where a human being will prey upon another sexually, caution makes sense. In Ephesians 6:13-17 ". . .the whole armor of God," the imagery here is of a righteous warrior being spiritually dressed for protection "to quench the fiery darts of the enemy." There is a breastplate of righteousness, a sword of truth, helmet of salvation, safety, a warrior's girdle. I am not referring to how a victimized woman is physically dressed, here, but about good and useful spiritual preparedness. The fear can be used to inspire caution and a deeper experience with spirituality.

Q: I've never prayed much or been very religious. Will God help me?

LOVE: Absolutely. All of us are God's people. Just begin to talk to God openly the way you would talk to a friend in the room. Sometimes when we say we're not religious, we're really thinking about the form. Religion is the "training wheels" on spirituality. What I would liken it to is teaching a person to dance, where footsteps are drawn and numbered on the floor. We don't really need the footsteps are drawn to access the dance in us. We don't have to have a formal religion in order to access God. God belongs to us, we belong to God. God is with us and in us.

HOLLIES: Everybody has the choice as to whether or not they're religious. Nobody has a choice as to whether or not they're spiritual. All of us are spiritual beings. And God is with us regardless of whether or not we acknowledge and follow God. And so a person who wants to begin a spiritual journey, they only have to say, "Hey God, I'm here. I need You. I can't do this by myself." God is there. And the shortest prayer I know to get started is: "Help." That's it. "Help." God is there. God is as close as our breath, as the breath that we expel. Say the word, God is there.

Q: I was abused a long time ago. Why do I feel worse now than at the time I was victimized?

LOVE: If you can notice feeling worse now it's because it's safer to notice. We have internal protections that keep us from noticing the full horror of something until we're safe.

Q: I've been praying for healing for a long time. Will God ever heal me completely?

LOVE: I believe that God heals completely. Once we're victimized by sexual violence we're never the same. Healing doesn't have to look the same. Some people think healing is about being returned to how and who they were in the former days. But we are changing every moment. And in the moment where we are most able to notice our healing, we will likely be stronger, more perceptive, more compassionate, and simply more alive to ourselves and the spiritual realm. Time spent with God shows up on us like that. Healing doesn't have to look the same.

HOLLIES: Healing is a two-way street. Healing is part God's responsibility and part our responsibility. No victim can ever get rid of the scars. But you can move past that debilitating hurt and anger and unforgiveness. You can live because Jesus said, I've come that you might have life, and that you might have it more abundantly (John 10: 10).

Some of us who have been rape victims choose to live lives of desolation. We choose. Because you don't have to stay in the place that you're in, because the potter really does want to put us back together. We were broken to be glued together in a better way. We were not just broken and dumped.

Q: Sometimes I wonder if I'm not praying hard enough or if my faith isn't strong enough. People have even said it's about time I get over this. How long should healing take?

HOLLIES: Healing is a process. Healing is not a right now, it's over, it's done, kind of event. You can get a scab on something and really think that it's okay, but healing is an inner process. It happens from the inside. It doesn't happen from the outside. And so therefore what we have to remember is that in a process we don't heal at the same rate. And so you can't measure how your body or how your emotions or how your spirit heals. This is something you have to walk through. It's something that you have to go through day by day.

If [the perpetrator] was a father, a brother, a cousin, a grandfather, an uncle, a teacher—I think the closer the person was to you, that you have to see them over and over and over again, the longer it takes for you to get through that. Repetition of seeing the person causes us to relive the event.

Q: I used to be very open with family and friends. But now I don't feel comfortable talking to them about what happened and how I am feeling.

HOLLIES: I have to go to the book of Revelation where John says, Who are these and where did they come from? And the angel responds, these are they who have been washed in the blood and have overcome by the word of their testimony (Revelation 12:11). You have to find a safe place to talk about it. You don't ever want to talk about it to any and everybody because you have to pick the people that you trust will hold your confidence. But you cannot hold stuff in like that. It will eat you up. It will cause all kinds of physical manifestations. And so you have to find a safe space.

Now if you don't talk about it, you are asking for all sorts of trouble because then you end up looking at the world through your very narrow lenses. What you do when you talk is to get it out of you, and then to have somebody else say to you, "I absolve you too. It was not your fault." And that starts the healing process, when you can stop holding yourself hostage.

There has to be somebody in your family, somebody in your church circle, somebody in your friend circle, somebody even in your work circle. It can be an EAP rep, employee assistance person. It can be a chaplain at a hospital. It can be a pastor on the phone. It can be the crisis hotline, but there has to be somebody that you can go [to] and cry about this, talk about this, get it out of you.

Q: What about traditional mental health counseling? Some people call therapy the enemy's workshop.

LOVE: There are a number of modalities that can work in our healing process. African-American tradition and culture have historically dictated that worship and a good, cathartic shout on Sunday morning would bring about mental and emotional health. While jubilant praise has many redemptive characteristics and benefits, the healing process is facilitated by trained persons able to assist with the exploration of the victim's feelings, value systems, and early learnings. Counseling provides a companion on the journey to healing.

Q: How can I deal with my feelings of guilt?

HOLLIES: That's why I said we have to talk to folk. The incest for me started when I was thirteen years old. I didn't get absolution until I was forty. Hello! It was in a clinical group at forty years old when I was told you have to tell the story. And I sat there and I told it just like I'm talking to you and telling some story that was written in a book. And the youngest person in that group was sitting curled up in a chair. And she looked at me and she said, "Linda, you need to cry. You told that story like it happened to somebody else. That happened to you. It was horrible. You need to cry. You're not the guilty person." That's when the healing began. For all the other years, I held it against myself. That was thirty-something years of walking in the victim role, [of] "It had to be something I did."

Q: I know you are supposed to go to your church family in times of crisis, but I don't think people at my church will understand and be sympathetic. I've heard about how they've treated other victims.

LOVE: It is important to find someone you can trust, whether or not they are a member of your church. If there is no one in your church who has been properly trained, the Black Church and Domestic Violence Institute recognizes the safety needs of victims and survivors in faith communities. The organization provides training to sensitize clergy, lay leaders, and congregants about the issues of violence against women. It is important that you find someone that you can trust without complicating your relationships to the point that you lose your spiritual refuge, the places where you go to seek support on other issues.

Q: I want faith-based counseling, but I'm not sure I'm comfortable going to my own pastor.

HOLLIES: Can I say something that will be extremely controversial? Pastors and church folk are often the worst folk in the world to go to for confession and absolution. The average pastor does not have a clue about counseling. And what pastors need to do when they find somebody in a situation like ours is to refer them to a counselor, refer them to a spiritual director, refer them to a chaplain, refer them to somebody who knows what they're doing with somebody's emotions.

LOVE: There may be a trained lay leader in your congregation such as someone in the women's fellowship. Other sexual assault survivors may be able to help you find someone. Word of mouth is often a most effective way to identify who can be helpful.

Increasing clergy awareness and response to violence against women is one of the most critical issues of the day. Religious leaders and faithful congregants must advocate for appropriate faith-based response within your church community. In the meantime, a rape crisis center may be a source of referral for a chaplain or clergy person who will understand your particular needs.

Q: One pastor said to me, "Jesus forgave. Why can't you?"

LOVE: The whole push can be toward trying to make the one who is victimized forgive the abuser. If we believe in One greater than ourselves, we have to believe that forgiveness is of the Lord, and that we cannot truly absolve someone of their wrongful act that they put in the universe. The forgiveness that a survivor develops is really for her own recovery and her own path, not for the perpetrator's release.

HOLLIES: When people say we can forgive and forget, that's a lie. Even when you forgive, to forgive means to take it off of your agenda for retribution and put it on God's agenda. That's all it means. I'm going to take you off my hit list. I will not expect you to come back and apologize. I will not expect you to come back and make amends. I will not expect you to feel sorry. I will not expect you to ask for my forgiveness. I turn it loose. You did it. That was yesterday. You will not ruin my today. God knows you will not hold me captive in tomorrow. And so when I think about it, when it comes back, when it's fresh, I have to say, "God, I gave this to you. You keep it." It's never to say I won't think about it.

Q: Why is there this emphasis in churches on survivors to forgive?

LOVE: Placing the emphasis on forgiveness, rather than on giving full acknowledgment to the pain and devastation of sexual violence, serves to inappropriately minimize the experience of the survivor.

The attitude of some churches is like, "Just suck up and deal!" Faith communities can be uncomfortable with the victim's just anger. In the same place where unforgiveness lives, there is some healthy anger. And in that place of anger, there's also some passion to create social reform. And through doing what we believe that God has called us to do, the forgiveness will come; and we will find that we are no longer operating out of anger but out of a love ethic. And this journey of forgiveness comes from our relationship with God, not from pressure by human beings to coerce forgiveness.

Q: What does the Bible say about rape?

HOLLIES: Most folk, when they go to church, go to hear the word of God. You know and I know that the word of God contains many references to women. Anything that has happened to us in life has happened in scripture. One of the scriptures that is most applicable to women who have been raped is found in 2 Samuel. It starts with David raping Bathsheba (2 Samuel 11).

That's a story that most of us never hear anybody preach. And when you look at it in any kind of spiritual journal or biblical journal, you will always see where they had an affair.

He committed adultery. That's a lie. He raped her. Let's get real, real plain. Anytime he is a king, she is a married woman, he sends the guard after her, and he has sex with her, he raped her. So you don't find men telling that story from the pulpit.

David didn't say nothing and most men ain't going to say nothing. It's all in the Bible. It's all in there. God tells the truth on everybody and every family. There are no secrets hidden.

Q: My husband forces sex on me. Doesn't the Bible say that women must submit to their husbands?

LOVE: It's no wonder, based on the culture of regarding a body as a commodity, that the stealing of that body is something that is not even regarded. I am reminded of a colleague who consulted with me concerning a court-mandated class on batterer intervention. He asked where in the Bible permission is given for a husband's ownership of the body of the wife. It seems that the text in I Corinthians 7:4, ". . .for the wife does not rule over her own body but the husband does," had been misquoted and taken out of context. This text was being cited by the convicted batterer as a justification of marital rape. Now, the remaining part of that text is, "likewise, the husband doesn't rule over his own body but the wife does." Here, the text is referring to mutual conjugal considerations of a married couple. Summarily, one partner is not to ignore the desires of the other; however this is not about one forcing sexual contact on another in an intimate relationship. Marital rape is wrong and a violation of trust.

Q: At my church, I am being encouraged to stay with my husband even though he is abusive. What about my wedding vows?

LOVE: Good point! What about your wedding vows? You are under no obligation to honor a broken covenant. When one side has dishonored the covenant, then it allows the other side an opportunity to rethink, renegotiate, forsake, or abandon. That's the point of a covenant, to lay out the nature of an agreement.

Q: As a survivor of incest, I feel betrayed and hurt not only by the perpetrator, but also by the adult who suspected abuse but did nothing. I'm not sure if I should even try to rebuild my relationship with them.

HOLLIES: There is a great difference in trying to have a relationship with people who are unrepentant as opposed to trying to have a relationship with people who are repentant. If your parents, whoever violated you, if you know that the other one was aware, if your parents have not confessed to you their need for forgiveness, you really don't have an obligation of being in that same sort of tight, harmonious, loving relationship that you see on television with folk who have wonderful relationships.

You've been violated by both of them. And there must be a time of repentance. You should not keep going around where the scene is continually brought into your mind with people who are unrepentant and uncaring. Until your family treats you like part of the family, you have to make new family. That's what I had to do.

My dad raped me and it was many years later when I asked my mom [if she knew]. And my mom said, "I thought so, but I really didn't want to know." That was probably harder for me to deal with than the rape, because it makes you feel so alone. It makes you feel so—vulnerable is not even the word—tossed away, cast aside. It made me feel abandoned; it made me feel like I was the sacrifice. And so the truth of the matter is I took a year off from my family.

I had to go into therapy and find out what was wrong with me. Why would my mother sacrifice me? Why would she bring me into the world to sacrifice me? And what I found out was that

God had given me somebody else who cared for me with a mother's love. And it was an aunt who had helped to raise my mom and she helped to raise me. And so when I found out that God did not abandon me, that God had put somebody in my life, when this therapist began to help me go back and to see what parts of other people had been placed into my heart, what parts of other people did I emulate, what parts of other people did I cherish and who did I actually cherish, then I began to get into a place where I could move back into a relationship with my mother. It was never the way that it was. I loved my mother. I miss her greatly. But I have to really say my mother was a bad mother.

Q: What can my church do to support sexual violence survivors?

LOVE: Your church leadership can demonstrate their commitment to caring for sexual violence survivors by devoting the time for adequate, culturally competent training on this and related issues. Many faith communities of various denominations have begun to participate in the BCDVI's national Domestic Violence Sabbath Observance in October. These are worship services designed to acknowledge the current state of violence against women. Similar observances are held in April, the month for sexual assault awareness.

Seminaries must prepare future pastors to take on the responsibility of their congregants by offering reality-based training. Clergy should not come out of seminary having earned a Master of Divinity but never having been trained regarding issues that affect women—because 70 to 80 percent of their parishioners and tithers are female.

HOLLIES: God is not a man.

In the Black church, we are so limited because we only know how to call God "Father." When you have been raped by a man, especially if that man happens to be in your family, well then of course it gives you a double bind to be close to a God that you call "Father." God is bigger than a male image. God is bigger than a female image. We don't have to call God "Mother" or "Father." We can call God "Creator." We can call God "Sovereign." We can call God 1,001 titles. You know, Dream of the Night, Hope of my Heart, Help for the Hopeless. There are so many adjectives. You will never have enough words to describe God. And we cannot limit God to being one or two genders, male nor female.

I don't want a male God because of the relationship to my dad. I don't want a female God because of the relationship to my mom. Both of them were weak people. I don't need that. I need a God that's bigger. My God is a rainbow. My God is a butterfly. My God is the Spirit of lifting, the Spirit that is higher than I am, the Spirit that is more great, that rules the world. That's the kind of God I need. I don't need a little image of a little puny human being.

That's what inclusive language is about. If we continue this pattern of always referencing God by "He," "Him," and "Father," we shut down about one out of three women that sit up in our church service. If we refer to God as "Mother," we shut down [lots of] men that come to church. Many mothers have abused their sons. We don't like to talk about it, but they do. And many men have been abused by uncles and brothers and fathers and grandfathers and neighbors. So we have to find more metaphors to describe God. Because language is powerful. Words create. God created the whole world with words. And so we have to be more expansive with our words.

Q: Can any good come out of all of this pain and suffering?

LOVE: The vulnerability and brokenness to really intimately know God's healing power, to know that God can lead and direct, while we actually just rest in God's love. The elders would say, "The Holy Ghost is a keeper!", able to keep us from perishing.

I want to be really clear that I wish that rape did not ever occur, and I don't think we have to have this experience to know God. I just know that from this experience, we can.

HOLLIES: As we walk through it, we're able to reach back and tell somebody else, "Come on, you can come out of that." You know, the Bible tells us that the comfort that we get from God is the same comfort that we have to measure out to others (2 Corinthians 1:3-4). Praise be to God, the Creator of our Lord Jesus Christ, the Creator of compassion, and the God of all comfort, who comforts us in all of our troubles, so that we can comfort those in any trouble with the comfort we ourselves have received of God. And remember, that comes from the Beatitudes, which says to us, "Blessed are they that mourn for they shall be comforted." (Matthew 5:4)

Thanks be unto God we survived. Because in spite of the trauma, in spite of the victimization, God carried us through. We're on the other side of it. And like Mahalia Jackson said, we can look back and say "My soul looks back in wonder," because it has taken down a lot of people. But thanks be unto God, we walked through it. We didn't get taken down by it. And our job is to help other folk, to let them know if God has done it for me, God will do it for you.

NOTES

[1] Mamiya, Lawrence H. Interview by author. 25 September 2002.
[2] Pinn, Anthony. Interview by author. Email, 18 September 2002.

CHAPTER 7
PRAYERS: Tools for Spiritual Healing

Arguably, sexual violence does more damage to the spirit than to the body or the mind. The disease of the spirit can manifest problems in every aspect of one's being. No matter which religion you practice, or whether you practice one at all, the healing of your spirit is essential for overall wellness.

While most African Americans affiliated with a religion today are Christian, a variety of spiritual systems have attracted Black worshipers. In 2000, 64 percent of converts to Islam were African American.[1] African Americans are Buddhists, Hebrew Israelites, and Baha'i. People of African descent practice traditional African religions, such as the faith of the Yoruba people of Nigeria, and other forms of spirituality.

This chapter is full of spiritual tools for use by survivors and their supporters, congregations, and communities. You will find prayers, affirmations, chants, and a sermon excerpt. Most are written by African-American Christian clergy, but a few come from other cultures and religions.

Use these spiritual tools to address your particular needs. Consider them practical resources for personal healing and community mobilizing. Repeat and memorize selections that comfort and uplift you, that speak to where you are in your healing process and where you want to go. Incorporate them into counseling sessions, meetings, rallies, and religious services. Open your heart to the possibilities of healing, of violence-free families and communities. Accept that God can work miracles in and around you that you cannot even imagine. Be blessed by these gifts.

Self-Talk for Thrivers
by Rev. Dr. Melinda Contreras-Byrd

I began as a victim, but I will move to being a survivor, and
    finally a thriver.
I will survive and thrive by saying the right things to myself.
I acknowledge the power of my mind to heal myself.
I claim the biblical promise that "truth will make us free."
Therefore I will speak to myself only in truth
And pledge from this day on to stop the voices of blame and
    shame that constantly talk inside my head.
I will affirm that: There is no way I could have known—
    unless I suspected every man of harboring wicked motives.
Only psychologically unhealthy people suspect everyone of
    wicked motives.
He was not a monster, able to be everywhere at once, all-
    powerful and omnipresent to keep me inside, in fear, in
    pain and surrendered.
Only God is all-powerful and omnipresent.
We cannot know why God allows such horror to occur,
    but we can affirm what we *do* know with certainty
    about God.
We can affirm that God is with us in our suffering.
No one deserves to be abused; I will never say that I caused
    this in any way.
No one is within his rights to behave this way toward another
    human being.

This did not happen because I was too free, too open, too
    sexy, or too trusting.
This happened because he was lacking in some essential
    human part.
I refuse to let this sick individual change my whole life.
I refuse to become fearful, untrusting, depressed, and
    silenced.
I will develop a plan for my own healing.
I will include a support circle in my healing process.
I will tell my pain, and shout my rage
Until it has no more power to silence or disable me.
In the future I will sleep peacefully again.
In the future I will trust again.
In the future I will not dread the night, or being alone, or the
    footsteps of men.
In the future I will not need medication or ongoing therapy.
In the future my life will not be focused around this terrible
    event.
In the future I will be healed.

*Rev. Dr. Melinda Contreras-Byrd is the associate minister at Grant Chapel
African Methodist Episcopal Church in Trenton, New Jersey. She is also the owner
and director of The Generations Center, a unique mental health facility that meets
the holistic needs of men of color and all women, in Cherry Hill, New Jersey.*

A Protective Presence
by Rev. Dr. Susan Newman

Loving God,

I come to you seeking your protective presence. You've
promised that you would be a very present help in a time of
trouble. My troubling times have ended, but I am working

through releasing the memories that haunt me still. I am helped by a wonderful counselor, but I need the assurance of your presence. I need to feel the warmth of your arms around me. Leave me not, O God. Hide not thy face from me. When I call out, please answer me, hear my cry. Take the ugly faces away. Remove the anxieties and fears. O Lord, I know you are closer than hands and feeling, nearer than breath and breathing—teach my soul to rest in thee. I am assured of your love, and daily I learn to trust in thee.

Amen.

"When all around my soul gives way, He then is all my hope and stay."

—"The Solid Rock," a hymn

Rev. Dr. Susan Newman is the author of Oh God! A Black Woman's Guide to Sex and Spirituality *and* With Heart and Hand: The Black Church Working to Save Black Children. *She has served as the coordinator of the National Black Religious Summit on Sexuality.*

God Did It!
by Rev. Dr. Sharon L. Ellis

Heavenly and Most gracious God.
God of our weary years and God of our silent tears.
I come to You in Thanksgiving and in Praise.
Even in the midst of my pains and frustrations You are
    worthy of all Praise and Honor.
I thank You because You have searched me and You know me
    and You love me anyway.
I thank You because You are acquainted with all our ways and
    You love me anyway.

I thank You because there is nowhere that I can go that I
would be absent from Your love.

I praise You because You have brought me from victim to
victor.

You have brought me from a mighty long ways.

I praise You because I realize that I am fearfully and wonder-
fully made.

I praise You because I can now see my value as a Child of God.

I praise You because Your presence in my life has made me
whole.

There were times when I often wondered who really cared
about my pain and suffering.

My abuser told me no one cared and no one would help me.

But oh God, You have truly been my refuge and my strength,
a very present help in the time of trouble.

I know now that You have always been there.

I know now that You are my protector.

I will not always be free from the evil attacks of the world.

But I do know that evil will not have the final word and that
love will be my protector and justice will be my shield.

I know that whenever I am in trouble You will be there.

I felt Your presence in the still of the night as a violated
woman.

I felt Your healing balm as You rocked me in Your arms and
spoke, "You can make it."

I have come this far only because of Your mercy.

I have grown this strong only because of Your grace.

I feel so blessed to call You my friend.

I feel so honored to know that You are mine.

I praise You because now I know that I am more than a victim.

I am more than a survivor.

I am more than a conqueror.

I am healed and I am whole.

I have a song in my heart and joy in my soul.

I have wings like an eagle.

I have all of these things because of You, God.

You gave me all I needed to survive.

You gave me friends.

You gave me family.

You gave me counselors.

You gave me a pastor who cared.

You gave me a justice system to hold my abuser accountable.

You gave me understanding.

You gave me forgiveness.

You taught me how to let go and let God.

I will always praise You and thank You for this healing.

I will always remember that *"God did it"* for me . . .

Yes God, it is Your healing and unconditional love that has
sustained me.

It is Your healing and unconditional love that has restored joy
in my soul.

What I have now no one can ever take away.

In the name of my Creator I pray.

Amen.

Rev. Dr. Sharon L. Ellis is a survivor of domestic violence. A United Church of Christ ordained pastor, she is also an adjunct professor at McCormick Theological Seminary, a Chicago Police Department chaplain, and the founding pastor of God Can Ministries.

Prayer for Incest Survivors
by Minister Esther Catherine Huggins

Dear God, as I come before you, I bring the darkness of my troubled past and stand in the sunshine of your presence, where I know true love and acceptance. God, as I stand here, I represent many women with many experiences. Some have known the horrors of rape and some, like me, are survivors of incest. God, you know the unbearable pain, the unspeakable acts of violence, and you know the burden of sorrow, self-doubt, and misplaced shame.

God, you know that, like others, I lived a lie or told a lie to protect my tormentor. God, I thank you because you know the source and the reasons for my lie. I thank you because you have shown me compassion and let me know that I have no need to be ashamed. You know that I still have moments when fear, doubt and memories try to overwhelm me. But, when those moments come, I thank you for giving me the courage to speak the truth. I thank you for renewing my mind and giving me peace instead of guilt. I thank you for filling my spirit with love for myself and for others.

Wonderful Creator, I now ask for healing for the broken hearts and broken spirits of survivors who have been defiled by rape or incest. I ask for your divine touch to renew their minds and restore their faith in you and in themselves. I pray that you will send beautiful, caring souls into their lives to help them along the way, as you did for me. God, I ask that you teach them—as you taught me—how to trust again.

God, I ask for more determined souls endowed with love, strength, wisdom, compassion, and courage, who refuse to keep silent and who are willing to help.

Amen.

Minister Esther Catherine Huggins is the creator of a ministry for survivors of sexual violence, Sisters of Tamar. She is based in Washington, D.C.

A Du'a in Support of Survivors of Sexual Violence
by Dr. Debra Mubashshir

All praises belong to you, Allah. You are the Healer of memory and experience, of body, intellect, and spirit. Only the healing that comes from you leaves behind no ill. We ask your special mercy and compassion upon those who have been victimized, disgraced, and have survived. Deliver them, O Allah, from the grips of human and institutional oppression as well as the internal triggers that try to make them feel guilty or see themselves as less than you created them to be. Be to them the soothing balm that eases their pain. Grant them justice and peace. Remind them of their high value and worth to you. Surely, you are the Mighty, the Wise, the Renderer of justice. Hear us, as we call unto you. Admonish the evildoers and bring them to justice.

Dr. Debra Mubashshir is an assistant ~~professor~~ of religious studies at Beloit College in Wisconsin. A former Christian pastor, preacher, evangelist, teacher, and motivational speaker, Dr. Mubashshir made her transition to Islam in 1998 while completing her dissertation research on African Americans and Islam.

A Prayer of Unending Praise!
by Rev. Dr. Linda H. Hollies

Praise to the healing God
who forgives our sins and
delivers us from the searing pain of abuse.
Praise to the comforting God,
who provides a balm in Gilead,
and leads our wounded spirits to restoring streams.
Praise to the mending God, who stitches us,

anoints us with healing oil and sews back
together all that has been ripped apart by abuse.
Praise to the Beneficent God,
who crowns our heads with wisdom and
offers us the opportunity to be a part of
the healing process of our self and even
of our victimizer!
Praise to the creating God, who
made us, called us, gifted us, and
walks with us into new life in new ways.
Praise to the awesome God, who
loves us in the midst of our hating and hurting.
Praise to the Ancient of Days, who
saw us before our mother's womb,
knew the undeserved pain we would endure
and yet loved us enough to never leave us alone!
For the power and the glory,
God gets the praise.
For the awe and the mystery of healing,
God gets the praise.
For the chance to be made new
and to start all over again,
God gets all the praise!
Unto Jehovah-Jireh, our provider,
Unto Jehovah-Shalom, our present peace,
Unto Jehovah-Rapha, our constant healer,
we offer exuberant, ebullient, and enthusiastic praise!
And it is so!

Rev. Dr. Linda H. Hollies, a United Methodist clergywoman in Grand Rapids, Michigan, is an incest survivor and author of many books about spirituality for Black women.

Excerpt from *Baha'i Prayers*[2]

O God! Refresh and gladden my spirit. Purify my heart.
Illumine my powers. I lay all my affairs in Thy hand. Thou
art my Guide and my Refuge. I will no longer be sorrowful
and grieved; I will be a happy and joyful being. O God! I
will no longer be full of anxiety, nor will I let trouble harass
me. I will not dwell on the unpleasant things of life.

O God! Thou art more friend to me than I am to myself.
I dedicate myself to Thee, O Lord.

A Catholic Social Worker's Prayer
by Dr. Jamie T. Phelps

God our Father and Mother,
look with love upon the men and women,
both young and old, whose bodies, minds, and hearts
have been altered by the assault of sexual abuse and
  exploitation.

Their life is filled with doubt and mistrust.
Their life is filled with fear of touch and
  intimacy.

Most loving God, let them experience
your unconditional love through someone
who is a sacrament of your touch,
your embrace, and your faithfulness.

Send them someone whose healing touch reveals your love.
Send them someone whose loving embrace transforms fear
  into faith.

> Send them someone whose faithfulness overcomes their
> doubt and mistrust with your spirit of hope.
>
> We ask this in the name of Jesus, your Love incarnate and
> the life-giving power of your most Holy Spirit.
>
> Amen. Amen. Amen.

Dr. Jamie T. Phelps, O.P., an Adrian Dominican Sister, was a professional psychiatric social worker (M.S.W.) who worked for ten years as a counselor for abused and neglected children and adults in a private hospital and several public social work agencies in the Chicago area.

The Voice of a Silent Cry
Inspired by the Holy Spirit to Evangelist Portia Smith

Silence is not what you make it out to be,
Nor is it what you think.
But if you listen to my heartfelt cry or feel the pain that grips
    my heart,
then you would know that what you think you see is really
    not the big picture you see but what my silence says.
It's my past abuse.
It is more than I can bear.
The mask I wear is one I've come committed to and her
    name is "Silence."
Just like Tamar's cry, the cry of an incestuous fear[3] that has
    brought "Silence" to the front,
that says I'd rather be alone,
but the big picture is really saying:
Pray for the fear that grips my heart.
Silence has become the character of what you think I am,

but mental, physical, and emotional abuse has Silenced me
because of the agonizing pain of fear that still grips my heart.
Silence says don't tell that you have been stripped of your
  integrity, self-esteem, or feeling, that you are almost over
  the edge and giving up.
Suicide says this is the only way out.
But when I almost gave in to what Silence wanted, one day I
  heard a still, quiet voice that said:
My child, I've carried your loads.
Don't let Silence dictate anymore.
It's okay, for Time of Refreshing is present,[4]
the Spirit of the Lord is upon you.
Relax and know that I am God and that I am Jehovah-Jireh,
  thy provider,[5]
and the God that healeth thee.
For there is a balm in Gilead,[6]
for the wounds you have sustained, the great physician is
  present to comfort you in such a time as this,
that Time of Refreshing will overtake your spirit.
The Lord is saying to you:
My child, give me Silence.
Leave her at the altar and break out with praise and thanksgiving and let Silence know that:
No longer can you hold me in bondage,
but I'll shout the victory cry that I'm no longer a victim,
but now I can be a Victorious warrior in Christ Jesus.
Amen.
Amen.

Evangelist Portia Smith is a co-founder of Time of Refreshing Women's Support Group, which gives safe haven and emotional and spiritual aid to women in crisis, in West Palm Beach, Florida. She is also an evangelist at J.A.Y. Outreach Ministries.

Prayer and Chant
by Rev. LaVerne C. Williams Hall

Let us pray . . .

Spirit of the Living God, come by here, come by here, come by here.

We give you our thanks and praise for another day and ask that You lend Your ear and linger in this space for a little while down here.

Swaddle and cradle us in the comfort of Your embrace, touch us with Your healing and loving heart, breathe into us Your spirit of life and the pursuit of happiness.

Let the words of our mouths and the meditations in our hearts be acceptable in Your sight; allow us to utter prayerful words for those who inflict violence upon us.

To those of us who suffer from the brunt of the depression, degradation, and devastation of oppressive domestic violence in any way, shape, or form, license us with Your spirit of confidence, pride, self-esteem, force, and authority, so that one day we can all rise up as sisters in unity and unison, free and unfettered, dancing to Your joyful song of life.

O God, birth and breath of all generations, embrace this our plea, grant us Your incorruptible grace and keep us as the apple of Your eye.

And now to everyone, feast your eyes upon me, a child of

God and a living witness of God's tender loving mercies
and listen with your heart . . .

I am unique . . .

A treasure on a pedestal
admired, cherished, protected.

I am a cluster of precious jewels
more beautiful than rubies
true as emeralds
possessing the quiet brilliance of onyx
sparkling with the dust of nature
ringed with a rainbow of gold.

I am unique.

I am we
We am us
Us am we

We are One!

IusweI . . . IusweI . . . IusweI!
(Chanting together in unity)

Rev. LaVerne C. Williams Hall is the assistant pastor of Cherry Hill Baptist Church in Seattle, and the founder of Jemima Ministries, which helps women develop self-esteem, in King County, Washington.

A Prayer for Church Empowerment to Stand Up and Speak Out Against Domestic Violence
by Rev. Andrew L. Simpson, Jr.

O God, we know that it is past time for the Church (Your people) to stand up and speak out against all violence throughout the world. God, we need Your healing touch. We know that growing numbers of people in the world are born into environments of hatred and violence as victims, never to break free from their grip of death. As they are consumed by the inherent evil of hatred and violence, they pass the consequences of these evils on to others in the world. As we experience the violence of this world, we realize its awesome, transgenerational impact on us all.[7]

We know that abuse is not Your will for any of Your children to experience. So help us not to abuse Your Word to justify our violence toward one another, but to rightly use Your Word to bring healing, hope, and love to this world.

We pray that You would remove any feelings of guilt, shame, and embarrassment from victims of domestic violence, and that Your Word will call to accountability all victimizers of Your people.

God, we live in a society in which violence has become all too pervasive. Instead of it being a last resort in conflict, it has increasingly become the first option, and the first action. The consequences of domestic violence continue to devastate the very institutions we once cherished and in which we have often found our refuge.

O God, the world wants to know if the Church (Your people) has anything to say and any response to offer in light of this fact: That more than four and a half million women are victimized by intimate partner rapes and physical assaults each year.[8] God, we need Your strong Word of love and redemption that Your Church may be led into Your justice and righteousness and kept from becoming the center for judgment.

We pray O God, that You will help us to rethink what we are doing as leaders, privileged to serve You through our Lord and Savior Jesus Christ. Help us as a clergy and laity to break the "conspiracy of silence" surrounding the reality of domestic violence and its impact upon Your house, for this silence is really a strong form of denial and judgment.

We pray for sensitivity and compassion that only You can provide O God, in our exposure to, and handling of, the hurt, pain, agony, anger, and despair within Your house. We acknowledge our culpability in allowing domestic violence to have its free course in Your house and throughout the world. Surely if enough of Your people, who are called by Your name would stand up and speak out against this horrible reality, You would empower them to make substantive differences everywhere.

Call the Church (Your people) O God from its "safe position" in the middle of the status quo, to be the spiritual and physical reality it was established by Christ to be. Call us to boldness, daring, and risk-taking actions. Above all O God, empower us to transmit Christ's healing and reconciling love beyond our borders to a world so desperately in need of both.

Isaiah said, ". . . they that shall be of thee shall build the old waste places: thou shalt raise up the foundations of many generations; and thou shalt be called the repairer of the breach, the restorer of paths to dwell in." [9] We pray for empowerment O God, to participate with You in the repair of the breach of love, acceptance, and forgiveness. Empower us to unite as Your Church against this common enemy called domestic violence, that we may embrace the tedious yet rewarding task of rebuilding the lives of both the victims and the victimizers, and that together we may participate in the rebuilding of the broken institutions we once cherished, namely the home, the family, and the Church.

We pray this prayer in the name of Your Son, Jesus the Christ, and in the fullness of His resurrection lies our hope. A-men.

Rev. Andrew L. Simpson, Jr., is the senior pastor of Trinity African Methodist Episcopal Church in Kansas City, Kansas.

Path of Righteousness
by Ima Chayye Wise

Oh Most High God, Maker of All Things, Creator of
    Heaven and Earth, I Give Thanks for Your Divine Order.
I Give Thanks for being here, alive this day.
I have faith that my life is in Your hands, and that You are in
    control of everything, allowing every experience that I have
    had to be part of the mortar needed as You mold me into
    all that I am now and all that I am to be.
I pray that You will grant me serenity and peace, courage and
    strength and wisdom and understanding to go forth with Your
    beauty and light shining bright through me for all to see.

I pray for forgiveness and to be forgiven, as I know that none of us is perfect, but that You have a perfect and unconditional love in which I can always find comfort.

I pray for guidance as I strive to order my life on the path of righteousness and for direction as I do my best to walk humbly, in universal harmony each day.

I Give Thanks. Amen, selah.

Ima Chayye Wise is a leader of Beth Shalom Inc., a non-profit Hebrew Israelite community service organization in the Washington, D.C. Metropolitan Area.

A Preacher's Prayer for the Sisters and the Brothers
by Rev. Al Sampson

Dear God Father of our Ancestors
Eternally
We are ashamed of some Brothers' pathology,
Violating Sisters' minds and bodies
Left and right.
Brothers controlling, hurting, using their might,
Sisters be struggling, crying, "Let me feel free,"
Brothers' pain, weaknesses spilling venom on these Sisters'
    identity.
Dear God Father of our Ancestors
Eternally
We are ashamed of some Brothers' tragic pathology.
Sisters as you struggle with the awesome cutting pain,
God stop the Brothers from violating, raping sisters, again
    and again.
God grant Brothers and Sisters angels of protection,
The power of love—passion with direction.
Stop it Brothers, enough is enough.
Sisters need tenderness—Brothers are too rough.

Sisters are tired of holding bad memories of yesterday,
Sisters have nightmares and want dreams that will stay!
God of our Ancestors my prayer is for many unified
tomorrows.
While You heal God the Sisters' and Brothers' memorable
sorrows.
This prayer is to the Sisters for the pain they endure.
This prayer is to the Brothers that they get cured.
No rape should ever be our Sisters' eternal scars.
'Cause God fashioned our Sisters as our eternal stars.
Sisters are too sacred a gift, for our families need to stay
whole.
Sisters want Brothers to stop ruining their roles!
Sisters are our cultural treasure.
This violent act shocks them beyond measure.
Dear God Father of our Ancestors
Eternally
We are ashamed of some Brothers' tragic pathology.
God help heal the Sisters and Brothers of our race.
Eternally connected by Your Amazing Grace.
So Brothers watch inside the darkness of your heart.
Your sick behavior tears Sisters all apart!
So Brothers we close this simple prayer
To stop the tension and the strife
Remember, like you, Sisters only have one Life!"

*Rev. Al Sampson is the pastor of Fernwood United Methodist Church in Chicago.
He is also co-director of Operation Defense, a grassroots program created to protect
Black women in the wake of serial rapes that occurred on Chicago's South Side.*

Community Prayer of Confession
by Dr. Traci C. West

God of Abundant Love and Compassion,

We are sorry for the times that we have acted like the problem of sexual abuse and intimate violence is not very important to You.

We are sorry for the times that we have prayed to You about violence in the streets and forgotten to be concerned about violence in the home.

We are sorry for the times that we have been more worried about protecting the image of

"our" community, than about the need to investigate and stop the sexual violence that occurs here.

We are sorry for the times that we have ignored the anguish and increased the isolation of those in our families, in our churches, and in our neighborhoods who have been sexually abused and assaulted.

We are sorry for the times that we have suspected that something was wrong, suspected that someone was abusing a child, or that someone we knew had been raped, and decided not to get involved.

We are sorry for the times that we have not been paying enough attention to even notice a plea for help.

We are sorry for the times that we have known about a perpetrator of sexual assault and pretended it could not be true of our friend, of a church leader, of such a nice guy.

We are sorry for the times that we have known about an incident of sexual violence or abuse and shared it with others like it was a juicy piece of gossip.

We are sorry for the times that we have found reasons to
blame the person who was
victimized, instead of placing responsibility upon the perpetrator, where it belongs.

We are sorry for the times that we have turned away from
someone who needed to share a past experience of sexual
abuse or rape.
We are sorry for the times that we have felt embarrassed by
someone's pain, afraid of someone's pain, tired of
someone's pain.
We are sorry for the times that we have denied the truth of
someone's experience of sexual violation.
We are sorry for the times that we have blocked Your healing
power, instead of being instruments of it.

Forgive us, O God, for these sins against You.
We humbly repent.
Give us the courage and commitment:
to speak out, to reach out, to support,
to hold perpetrators accountable,
to respond to Your call to change our ways,
to leave our sinful denials behind and move into faithful
action.

Amen

*Dr. Traci C. West is an associate professor at Drew University Theological School
in Madison, New Jersey.*

Triumphant Affirmative Healing
by Rev. Dr. Atiba Vheir Vidato-Haupt

Eternal Spirit, Great Spirit, Father-Mother God
Holy Spirit of The Most High That Uplifts, Heals, and
Renews . . .

Infuse Your Holy Spirit in each cell and atom of My Being . . .

Uplift my spirit (each moment, each minute, today . . .
each day!)

Heal and Renew My Mind
Fill it with Your Peace That Passeth Human Under-
standing . . .
Infuse me with Your Peace . . .

Allow Your Inner Joy that flows
For I will not allow another to (eternally) snatch My Joy.

Heal, uplift, and *renew* My Spirit[10]
Heal, Uplift, and Renew My Mind
I am Open and Receptive to Heal and Renew
My Spirit, Mind, and Body . . .

ETERNAL Spirit, Father-Mother God, Most High Eternal
Creator
(Insert according to your spiritual/religious path)

Thank You for Your Divine Healing, Divine Protection, and
Divine Direction.

Affirm The Spirit of The Most High (within) that Sparks
Renewal.

Connect with the Healing Light of the Most High.

Envision Streams of Light moving into each cell and atom of your being from the crown of your head to the soles of your feet.

Move Forward and Claim *Triumphancy . . . Affirm . . .*

I am whole
I am peace
I am light
I am joy
I am whole

I am love
I am joy
I am whole
I am light
I am whole . . . renewed . . .

I am whole as a Daughter of The Most High . . .

Give thanks and affirm

I (insert your full name) affirm *I am whole* . . . Infuse Your Holy Spirit Most High . . .

Uplift, Heal, and Renew: The Energy around me . . .

Uplift, Heal, and Renew My Being

Protect My Being

Renew My Mind

Illumine My Vision

Direct My Vision

Renew My Body

Protect My Body

Renew My Senses
Protect My Senses. . .

Rev. Dr. Atiba Vheir Vidato-Haupt is the founder of Dove Healing Arts Clinical and Educational Holistic Wellness Programs and co-founder of Dove Center. She is a licensed holistic psychotherapist, ordained minister, reiki master, aromatherapist, and reflexologist in Washington, D.C.

Prayer for Peace[11]
by Rev. Terri Buffalo Star Gardner

Dear _____ (whomever you pray to, just as long as it goes up and not down):

I humbly come to You and ask for help in the ending of violence in our metropolitan area. Since You have made us all, we are connected in this web of life. I know that what affects my sisters and brothers affects me and the universe. I pray now that there can be peace and light in all the people's lives. That we can all work out our problems without violence of thought, word, or action. That we can take care with one another in our everyday lives and live with honor.

I pray for those who have been harmed by violence, for them to heal physically, mentally, emotionally, and spiritually from those events. That they can return to wholeness and balance in their lives, letting go of remorse, anger, and pain, turning that into the positive energy of compassion, understanding, and forgiveness for those who have harmed them.

I pray for those committing those acts of violence—for their emptiness and hurt to be healed.

I pray for the part of them that needs to harm others in order to feel good and powerful, for those who have lost their way, for those who must carry and use a gun to feel unafraid, for those whose anger rages out of control. I pray now for them to turn to You and get guidance on how to repair themselves to wholeness. That they know that You will take them for whoever they are and will walk with them. I ask that You give them the strength to look at themselves and choose to end the cycle of pain and violence. Give them the courage to seek help, accept responsibility for past actions, and make the choice to change their lives today.

Finally, I pray that this world can be a better place, starting with me. That I can assume the best in all people—not the worst, that I can have respect for all living things, and that I can make choices in my life that serve the highest good of all creation. I hold the thought of peace, joy, and beauty in all things every day. I ask that these prayers be answered in a good way, that no harm come to me or to anyone or to anything as a result of these prayers.

Amen.

Rev. Terri Buffalo Star Gardner is a minister at Gadohi Usquanigodi Native American Spiritual Center in Chicago. "Gadohi Usquanigodi" is Cherokee for Land of Miracles.

Overcoming Our Weaknesses—Sermon Excerpts on Domestic/Sexual Violence
by Rev. Bowyer G. Freeman

There are actions members of the clergy and the faith community can take in our effort to prevent violence against women. Many times we find it very difficult within our houses of worship to confront issues of domestic and sexual violence taking place within our congregations (whether Protestant, Catholic, Jewish, or Islamic).

It has been said, that for every one hundred persons within a congregation, you have a combination of every sin and malice known to humankind. If this assumption is true, there's someone within nearly every congregation, within every faith-based organization, who has had either a firsthand encounter with sexual/domestic violence or knows someone who has encountered sexual/domestic violence, either as a victim or perpetrator of said violence.

Many people who are members of a religious body, namely Christian or Jewish, have been led to believe that you just have to go along to get along. There is a general sentiment, that says if you are suffering from some sort of violence, perhaps you're just not being a good partner. Perhaps if you were a better wife or a better husband (yes, it's true. . . there are men who suffer from domestic violence as well), a better mate, this wouldn't be happening. The logic extends that perhaps there is something wrong with the victim, that this violence is precipitated through some fault of his or her own.

As we look at Judeo-Christian scripture, there are instances of sexual and domestic violence within the texts that give us insights as to how we can craft a twenty-first century response to this important issue. Scriptural references provide a window into some things we can do as a faith community to collaborate against sexual and domestic violence.

There is a passage of scripture in the book of 2 Samuel, chapter 13, that deals with this issue:

And it came to pass after this, that Absalom the son of David

*had a fair sister, whose name was Tamar; and Amnon the son
of David loved her. And Amnon was so vexed that he fell sick
for his sister Tamar; for she was a virgin; and Amnon thought
it hard for him to do any thing to her.*[12]

*One day a man by the name of Jonadab inquired of
Amnon and he said unto him, "Why are you, being the king's
son, so heavy in your countenance from day to day? Why
won't you tell me?" Amnon said unto him, "I love Tamar, my
brother Absalom's sister." Jonadab said unto him, "Lay thee
down on thy bed and make yourself sick and when your father
comes to see you, say unto your father, I petition you to let my
sister Tamar come and give me something to eat and dress the
food in my sight that I might see it and eat it at her hand."
So Amnon took the plan and he lay down and made himself
sick. When the king was come to see him, Amnon said unto his
father the king, "I petition you let Tamar, my sister, come and
make me a couple of cakes in my sight that I might eat at her
hand." Then David sent home to get Tamar saying, "Go now
to your brother Amnon's house and dress his food." Tamar
went to her brother Amnon's house and he was laid down and
she took flour and she kneaded it and she made cakes in his
sight and did bake the cakes. Amnon said unto her, "Bring the
food into the inner chamber that I may eat at your hand."
Tamar took the cakes which she had made and brought them
into the chamber to Amnon, her brother.*[13]

What transpired out of this series of events in the text is
that Amnon took his very own sister through coercion
and forced her to lay with him in an unwanted sexual
relationship. Amnon acted on his desires following the
recommendation of his "friend" Jonadab.

It's interesting to note that Jonadab was the son of
Shimeah who was David's brother. Therefore, Jonadab
was related to Amnon, Tamar, and Absalom as a cousin.

It was a family member who aided Amnon in his scheme to sexually violate his very own sister.

There are a few important points we can lift out of this passage of scripture. Points that can help the contemporary church and the broader community in this day and time. . . Amnon suffered from the fact that he did not have an ethical elder. His father, David, as you may recall from the scriptures, was King over Israel. David, we are told, was a man after God's very own heart, but David himself had "zipper trouble." He suffered from a series of sexual indiscretions. Amen.

Even though he was married, and even though he was king, David had a problem. One day while taking a rooftop stroll, overlooking his kingdom and the great wonders God had allowed him to rule, he saw a beautiful young woman taking her bath nearby. Her name was Bathsheba.

David commanded one of his aides to go and bring this beautiful woman to him. He wanted to check the sister out. When she came to him, she did let him know she was married to a man named Uriah, who happened to be one of David's Mighty Men of Valor, a member of the elite armed forces. (While David was at home eating grapes and figs and watching the local "sights," Uriah was out fighting a war for David and his kingdom.) That didn't stop David. He was so enthralled with Bathsheba that he forced himself upon her. Since he was King, you do know it was virtually impossible to say "no." In actuality what we see here is a rape. Some theologists have lain the responsibility of this act on Bathsheba, as though she played the seductress who enticed King David.

However, we must remember that David was the authority figure in this scenario. Bathsheba could not refuse the king and survive. Had she insulted the king, he quite possibly could have her head in a basket!

Out of this illicit relationship, Bathsheba becomes pregnant. David, realizing he has impregnated another man's wife, now ponders how he can "fix" the situation. What he does is conspire with others around him in order to devise a plan for doing away with Bathsheba's husband. David instructs his Army Chief of Staff: When the heat of the battle comes on, you take her husband and put him directly in the front of the battle, because when the heat comes down, we know that he's going to die and I won't have to confront him knowing that I have impregnated his wife.

According to this diabolical plan, Uriah ends up in the front of the battle. He is killed and Bathsheba subsequently gives birth to this child. But the child dies soon thereafter. Following a series of downward-spiraling events David develops a repentant heart and he brings Bathsheba into his house and takes her as a wife. More children are born of out this marital union. David also has other wives who give birth to children. One of these sons, named Amnon, exhibits similar behavioral/sexual habits of his father.

The point I'm making is that Amnon didn't have an *ethical elder*. We need ethical elders. We need them at every level of development, whether high school, middle school, elementary, or preschool level. Our children, even before preschool age, are watching what we do. We must have ethical elders who model for our children so they will know that violence is not the way. They will come to understand that you don't solve conflict by striking out. That you don't use power to abuse others, nor do you become powerful by abusing others. We need ethical elders within our community.

Not only do we need ethical elders, but secondly, we also need *positive peers*. Amnon revealed his story and his need and his interest to Jonadab, his cousin. Jonadab, being his peer, could have said, "Man, let's get you some help. You mean to tell me that of all the women in the world, you've developed an unhealthy sexual desire for your sister? Let's get you some help!"

Jonadab could have been a positive peer: "Man, let's talk this thing through. Come, let's pray about this. Let's work to get your life back on track. Get help so you can develop constructive relationships in your life."

But what did Jonadab do? Jonadab's advice went in the opposite direction. He said, "Listen, let me tell you how to get her." That's *sick*! We need ethical elders and positive peers who, when they know someone is perpetrating domestic/sexual violence against others in the community, will not turn their heads! We have to confront those involved in the issue. We must take risks. We must force the issue. We have to encourage offenders and the violated to get help. We need ethical elders and positive peers.

There are a few more things the religious community can do to help prevent this domestic violence: First, we can make our houses of worship "safe places." How often have parishioners gone to their minister to tell them about the hell they are catching at home, only to hear the minister respond in this manner: "Well, go home and just try to work it out." We have to listen to those who are experiencing violence, believe them, and respond proactively.

Second, our houses of worship can become centers of education. Congregations are excellent mechanisms for disseminating information about domestic/sexual violence.

Third, we *must* speak out. We must carefully examine scripture and begin to responsibly interpret texts, which address the historical reality that domestic/sexual violence does take place. We will not become less Christian, less Jewish, less Muslim, or less within any other religion because we raise the issue within the sanctity of our sanctuaries. We *must* speak out!

Finally, we must lead by example. Be positive peers and ethical elders. Offer space for organizations that are addressing the issue. Partner with others for existing resources. Partnering allows collaboration between the secular and the sacred community in order to create more impact on this issue.

Through my association with the health care arena here at Howard University Hospital, I have learned that the World Health Organization has defined "health" as "a state of complete physical, mental, and social well-being and not merely the absence of disease or infirmity." Those of you who believe and trust in a higher Creative Power, have expanded that definition to say that: "Health is the state of physical, mental, social, and *spiritual well-being* and not merely the absence of disease or infirmity." Much of what bothers us physically, mentally, and socially will be significantly reduced or eradicated altogether when we address the spiritual dimension of self.

Therefore, working collaboratively as community and congregation, we can help individuals reconcile wholeness within them. Once individuals are reconciled wholly/holistically within themselves, they are then able to reconcile in their relationships. Hopefully, what results is a reduction in the need to address the egregious issues of domestic/sexual violence.

Rev. Bowyer G. Freeman is the director of Pastoral Care Services at Howard University Hospital in Washington, D.C.

A Prayer for Spiritual Healing
by Dr. Gwendolyn Zoharah Simmons

Let us Pray
Bismillahirrahmanirrahim
(In the name of God, Most Merciful, Most Compassionate)

Oh ineffable God without form
without gender, without race.
Oh you great One who manifests as male and female
and imbues all forms with life, vitality, and intelligence.

Lift the veils of ignorance from your created beings.
Lead us away from our deep-seated desires
to make distinctions based on sex, race, colors, and class.
Lead us away from ingrained thought patterns of
hierarchy between men and women.

Lead your male creations away from their unnatural lusts for
land, women, and gold,
from their ideas of possessing and controlling women,
from their practice of assaulting women, sexually and
    physically.

Lead your female creations toward feelings of
self-determination, independence, and empowerment.

Lead both manifestations of You to
balance and harmony.
Lead both to an understanding of our divine origins and
    natures
and to the reality of our Real Identity.

Oh mother/father God,
lead us into harmony and light and
the complete disavowal of
egotism, greed, lust, miserliness, sexism, racism
and all the evil qualities and desires buried in our hearts.

May these impurities be burned from us by Your Radiant
    Presence
and may we radiate that Divine Light Form
from which we emanate
to the far reaches of our universe.

Ameen
(So be it. May He Make This Complete.)

Dr. Gwendolyn Zoharah Simmons is an assistant professor of religion at the University of Florida in Gainesville. She teaches Islamic studies, women and religion, and African American religious traditions.

NOTES

[1] Robinson, Lori. "Muslim Soldiers Reconcile Faith with U.S. Military Action," *The Crisis* (November/December 2001), 12.

[2] Abdu'l-Baha: Baha'i Prayers, U.S. edition, 151-152.

[3] 2 Samuel 13:13, 14, 20.

[4] Acts 3:19.

[5] Genesis 22:14.

[6] Jeremiah 8:22.

[7] The pronouns "you" and "your" following Deity have been intentionally capitalized for rhetorical effectiveness. The same applies in the use of "word." Where the term "the Church" is used, it is intentionally followed by the term "Your people" and vice-versa, to call us to our true divine identity. (Rev. Andrew L. Simpson, Jr.)

[8] National Coalition Against Domestic Violence. "Domestic Violence Facts."

[9] Isaiah 58:12. King James Version.

[10] To Heal, Renew, and Uplift is to change your vibratory rate. Vibrate above and

beyond the occurrence(s) of abuse. When one's energy rate changes, the mind and body rate is accelerated, and ultimately is changed in consciousness; i.e., the vibratory rate of an FM band station vibrates higher than an AM band station. To change one's vibratory rate is to move to a higher level, thereby facilitating the healing process. Affirm in the positive, give thanks to the Most High for the healing process, before it occurs, during and after . . . *Move from the space of terror to triumphancy!* (Rev. Dr. Atiba Vheir Vidato-Haupt)

11 The prayer should be said facing the east, preferably outside, with a small amount of tobacco or cornmeal in your right hand. After the prayer, drop the tobacco or cornmeal on the ground at your feet and say, "All my relations." These sacred plants given back to the earth mother are an indication of our respect for all life and thanks for the answering of our prayers. (Rev. Terri Buffalo Star Gardner)

12 2 Samuel 13:1–2. King James Version.

13 2 Samuel 13:4–10.

CHAPTER 8
RISK REDUCTION/PREVENTION FOR ADULTS

The sexual violence happening in today's Black community did not arise in a vacuum. Our violence is American violence. This country's very foundation is one of hundreds of years of brutality—the enslavement of Africans and the genocide of Native Americans. Since those barbaric beginnings, sexual violence has been an integral part of our experience in this land.

American culture continues to perpetuate sexual violence. It happens in every community, among every ethnicity, every race, and every economic bracket. According to the National Violence Against Women Survey, 20.5 million adults in the United States have been victims of attempted or completed rapes in their lifetimes. The report goes on to say that its figures likely underestimate sexual assaults.[1]

Experts agree that no accurate national survey or study examining sexual victimization exists—all of them underestimate sexual assault and abuse in the United States.[2] Over the last decade, only about 30 percent of rapes and sexual assaults were reported to police.[3] The most underreported violent crime, it is impossible to know how many sexual violations actually occur.

As with many social ills, African Americans are disproportionately affected by sexual violence. Black women are raped at a higher rate—nearly twice as high one recent year—than White women.[4] If our negative responses and survival mechanisms—victim blaming, suffering in silence, and even the denial of sexual violence in our community altogether—are as disproportionately high as the violence itself, combating this reality could be our greatest challenge.

Although sexual violence is ingrained in American culture, including in Black communities, it doesn't have to stay that way. Another violent crime of power perpetrated against individuals, racist mob lynchings, were at one time a part of American culture. (A lynching is mob murder with no legal sanction, usually by hanging or burning in a public, festive environment, although in U.S. history the participation of law enforcement officers was common.) If this form of oppression can be eliminated, why not sexual violence?

Like all successful movements, the end of mob lynching never would have come without the determination of individuals who struggled in ways large and small, on a national stage and, much more often, in their own small corners of the world. As essential as their effort was, the belief that their goal, however insurmountable it may have seemed, was possible.

Every woman and man can start with the belief that sexual violation can be stopped. You can take steps to reduce your own risk of victimization and to diminish the risks of assault and abuse that family, friends, co-workers, neighbors, and your entire community live with every day.

What is Sexual Violence?

A lack of understanding of what sexual violence is, who commits it, and why continues to leave adults of all ages vulnerable. From college students exploring their independence, to midlifers new to the dating scene after divorce, to church-going elders, everyone is a potential victim. The first step in risk reduction is understanding the problem.

In a recent Department of Justice study of campus sexual assault, *The Sexual Victimization of College Women*, about half the women who experienced completed rapes, defined as "unwanted completed penetration by force or threat of force," did not consider the incidents to be rape.[5]

Young adults aren't the only ones who don't comprehend the basic notion of having the right to control what happens to one's own body. Rev. Aubra Love, executive director of the Atlanta-based Black Church and Domestic Violence Institute, recalls a workshop she conducted a few years ago. "One woman said to me: 'How can he rape you if he's already married to you?'"[6] Far too many adults of all ages are unaware that they have a right to be in charge of what happens to their physical self.

It is incredibly common to think of a rapist as a gun-wielding, ski-mask-wearing, hardened criminal who breaks into the homes of single women in the middle of the night. Yes, perpetrators do rape strangers. While it is important to protect yourself from assaults by strangers, by no means are they your only threat. The National Crime Victimization Survey reports that almost two-thirds of sexual violence victims were assaulted by someone they knew.[7]

According to the National Violence Against Women Survey, nearly 8 percent of adult women have been raped by an intimate partner, defined as a current or former spouse, date, or live-in partner.[8] In the report on campus rape, 90 percent of survivors knew the offender, usually a classmate, ex-boyfriend, current boyfriend, co-worker, friend, or other acquaintance.[9]

Love consistently finds a lack of understanding when she explains to men what sexual violence against women encompasses. "Whether they're clergy, psychiatrists, or whatever the situation is, there's the initial reaction of shock and dismay and denial. A huge contingent of really good brothers of all races and cultures really don't know that this is a problem, even if they are participating in it," she explains. "Because if it's never been challenged, then they don't really know that it is a systemic problem in the lives of all women and girls."

According to Byron Hurt, a filmmaker and anti-sexism activist who conducts men-only workshops on violence against women, "It is very rare that someone would openly admit that it is okay to rape a woman. But, when you dig a little deeper, brothers will start to make all kinds of excuses to justify why women do get raped. It is very common to hear men say, 'If she didn't want to have sex, why would she be at my crib at two in the morning?'"

Many adults have never learned that people can want physical intimacy and affection without wanting to have intercourse. Even if a woman begins participating in foreplay with the intention of having sex, then changes her mind, feeling aroused does not give a man the right to have sex anyway. He may have an erection, but that doesn't mean he suddenly loses his ability to make decisions. Some men and women believe that men cannot control their sexual urges, but that is simply not true. Sex, forced after a woman has said no, is rape.[10]

Rape is frequently a component of domestic violence. In *Walking Proud: Black Men Living Beyond the Stereotypes*, George Edmond Smith places partner violence in an African-American context. "Abuse—verbal or physical—is a symptom of the powerlessness and desperate desire for control that many Black men feel. Women all too often bear the brunt of their angry mates' physical and emotional assaults."[11]

Rape happens when someone willfully disregards the rights and wishes of someone else, no matter what their societal status is. Some men justify raping strippers or prostitutes with the attitude that because of their profession they've automatically forfeited the right to control their bodies. Hurt says he no longer goes to bachelor parties because he has seen strippers treated abusively. Many prostitutes have a history of child abuse, so to rape a stripper or prostitute is to violate one of the community's most vulnerable members.

One definition of violence is an "abusive or unjust exercise of power."[12] Rape is violence involving the sexual body parts of the perpetrator, the victim, or both. Unwanted sexual contact, whether or not the assailant uses his physical strength, wields a weapon, drugs the victim, or articulates a threat, is rape.

Perpetrators, strangers to the victim or not, generally have access to consensual sex.[13] The falsehood that rape is simply a way of getting sex supports the myth that all rapists are crazed strangers starved for sex. In *The Date Rape Prevention Book*, Scott Lindquist spells out why men rape: [14]

- *Rape is about power. Men rape to get power over women. These men may feel powerless in their lives and so look for a way to increase their sense of self-worth by controlling and manipulating another "weaker" human being.*
- *Date rape or acquaintance rape is a violent act of control perpetrated not by a sick inhuman animal, but by an average guy who, given the right circumstances and the right frame of mind, may commit rape.*
- *Stranger rape is primarily an act of violence to control, in which the attacker attempts to humiliate and degrade the victim. The purpose of this kind of rape is to gain power through intimidation.*

Once you understand that rape is about power, not sex, it becomes easier to understand male-on-male sexual violence. It is true that sexual victimization in prisons is tragically frequent. It has been estimated that more than one hundred thousand inmates in U.S. prisons have been raped.[15] However, male-on-male sexual assault occurs throughout society, often as hazing incidents in all-male environments such as military training groups, fraternities, and athletic teams. Most men who rape other men are heterosexual.[16] Although it is rare, women can rape men.[17]

It has been estimated that more than 92,700 men are raped in the United States every year, not counting those in prisons and other group facilities. [18] Ten percent of sexual assault and rape victims are men.[19]

Misinformation Keeps Us All Down

Many Black women and men dismiss complaints of sexual assault as the irrelevant ravings of White feminists, despite the fact that African Americans are more likely to be sexually victimized than Whites. Violence against women and its foundation, sexism, are not just White women's issues.

Sometimes it is hard for people to accept things they don't experience themselves. For instance, some White Americans may think racism isn't a problem anymore because they have Black co-workers and neighbors who live quite comfortably. At the same time, even the wealthiest, most powerful African Americans are generally aware of racism's impact on their daily lives, from annoying slights to the possibility of violence. Money and status were irrelevant the day Danny Glover couldn't catch a cab, just as they were when Bill Cosby's son was shot to death in a hate crime.

Sexism is a reality in the everyday lives of women, including Black women, as racism is for African Americans. Black men earn eighty-one cents for each dollar earned by the average man. The average woman makes seventy-three cents for each dollar earned by the average man. Black women earn just sixty-five cents in comparison to that same dollar.[20]

Sexism is a problem for Black women and Black men, says Hurt, "because it limits us as a people, as a race, and does nothing to help eliminate the racism that we as Black men are so clearly opposed to."

Sexism distorts our perceptions of each other. "Treat a bitch like a bitch, and a woman like a woman," is a sentiment male sexual violence prevention experts have heard repeatedly. The idea that some women deserve to have their rights respected and others don't diminishes Black women's humanity in the eyes of some men. Whenever Black women are undervalued, disregarded or abused by Black men, particularly when they are violated physically, it can cripple their ability to have healthy relationships, to trust, to demand respect or even understand that they deserve it. Abused women develop a variety of problems, from mental illness, to obesity, to any number of diseases brought on by stress.[21]

Of course, children learn about relationships from the adults in their lives. Whenever girls and boys observe women mistreated in relationships, there is a chance they will mimic that behavior when they grow up. Sexist abuse in relationships can lead to a lifetime of personal pain for kids as well as the primary victim. "Grown men, many times, Marines, have cried openly in training sessions when talking about the pain of seeing their mother abused by their father or stepfather," Hurt recalls.

Sexism can even be used against men directly. "For example, when a man calls another man a 'bitch-ass nigger,' it is not just an insult, it is an attack on one's own 'manhood' as well as an attack on women. That comment suggests that you are not a man—you are weak like a woman—and it is an affront to many men because it is received as the ultimate putdown. This leads to senseless confrontation among men, which leads to violence, physical assaults, and murder, which leads many Black men straight to prison," Hurt explains.

Obviously, when men's violence against men causes physical and psychological damage, or removes men from their families by way of the criminal justice system, it directly affects their mothers and daughters, wives and girlfriends.

Perhaps nothing more clearly demonstrates the problem of sexism than the fact that women are by far the majority of sexual assault victims. We live with a constant awareness that it could happen to us. That's why blaming the victim is a common response. According to psychologists, people do not want to acknowledge that they are vulnerable so they rationalize that an assault happened because of something the victim did or didn't do, instead of blaming a perpetrator for committing a crime.[22]

One of the most common and harmful rape myths is the notion that women frequently falsely accuse men of rape or sexual harassment. Telling a story of victimization to police, lawyers, judges, even to family, can be a painful and demeaning experience that disrupts not just that person's life, but the lives of her family members. Although it happens, it is extremely rare that women go through this excruciating process without actually having been victimized.

The most recent figures available from the FBI show that 6 percent of rape reports were unfounded for the year 1999.[23] Unfounded reports are not just false allegations, but include cases in which the assailant can't be identified, the survivor can't be found, or the survivor decides not to prosecute or changes or omits details of her story, among other scenarios.[24] The figure commonly used by experts in the rape crisis field for estimating false reports is 2 percent, about the same rate as for other crimes.[25]

Another popular myth is that women want to be treated violently, that a man doesn't really love a woman if he doesn't use force with her. Some men think of forcing sex on a woman as being sexy. According to Love, it's no wonder some men think of violence as a normal part of a relationship. "Any man can make the choice to be violent because it is so heavily conditioned into male children. It's like, if all else fails, force your way. And sometimes, force your way so you don't have to deal with all else," she says.

When men are taught that sexual aggressiveness is a defining characteristic of masculinity, along with that comes the belief that they are not capable of controlling their bodies once sexually aroused. This attitude denies men the understanding that they are at all times multidimensional—spiritual, intellectual, emotional, as well as physical—beings. Instead, it gives them the understanding that they are sexual brutes, the very stereotype used to oppress Black men during and after slavery.

"The impact of historically generated myths and stereotyping in the minds of Black men cannot be underestimated. Black men are indoctrinated early by their parents and peers, and often adopt these subliminal messages without even realizing it," writes Smith. "Compound the [obstacles unique to Black men] with an outpouring of critical public opinions that classify Black males as lazy, sexually charged, and violent and the stage is set for the end result . . . an angry Black male with nothing to lose. He yields to the pressure of fulfilling public expectations."[26]

Black men are demonized while White men are excused for their violence. "It is incredible how the media irresponsibly presents images of violent Black and Latino faces to the world. Sexism and violence against women transcend race. It happens in all communities regardless of socioeconomic conditions. And by focusing on Black men as violent sexual predators, it gives White men a pass and does not allow us to deal with the culture of violence that raises many men in this country to beat, rape, and sexually abuse women," says Hurt.

Sexual violence is a universal reality. It is a problem for women and men. These myths allow the Black community to live in denial. They prevent us from making our communities and ourselves safe.

Get Informed! Get Involved!

In order to diminish the risk of sexual abuse and assault for everyone, including yourself, spend some time breaking down rape myths and learning about how rape harms victims and the entire community. By all means, don't go it alone. Simply by reading this book, you are probably better informed about sexual violence than most people you know. There is a plethora of ways to continue to boost your level of knowledge and make sure your community gets up to speed, so that together you can make your world safer than ever.

Arrange for professional prevention educators to teach groups of adults the truth about sexual violence and empower them to get involved in anti-rape activities. To find one, call a rape crisis center or your state coalition against sexual assault. Experts say single-sex groups are particularly effective, and advise choosing a workshop leader of the same gender and racial background as your group if possible, preferably someone who can address both racial and gender oppression as factors of sexual violence. You might want to ask them about the possibility of bringing a survivor along, as a survivor's personal story can be a powerful learning tool. Any setting where adults can gather and communicate respectfully is an appropriate space for learning, healing, and growing together.

The place where adults spend most of their waking hours, at work, can be a great training site. Some companies and government agencies sponsor enrichment activities for employees during the lunch hour or after business hours. Contact your human resources office, Employee Assistance Program, or union to get them to invite a professional educator. Nonprofit organizations and educational institutions can contact the Oakland-based Todos Institute to schedule a specialized training anywhere in the United States.

On most college campuses, students and faculty should find opportunities for learning about sexual violence risk reduction through counseling centers, health service offices, or student life offices. Numerous colleges and universities, including several historically Black institutions, have begun developing safety and survivor service programs through federal Violence Against Women Act grants. Howard University, LeMoyne-Owen College, and Southern University are among the Black schools offering culturally appropriate services. If your campus lacks adequate sexual violence prevention resources, lobby for workshops through dormitory staff, a dean, or concerned professors. Ask your student government or other student groups to arrange trainings.

African Americans have a strong tradition of service. Have your NAACP or Urban League chapter, civic group, volunteer organization, sorority, or fraternity bring in an educator, as well as add anti-rape efforts to their regular agenda. Together with fellow members, lobby the headquarters of your organization to make sexual violence a priority on its national agenda.

Encourage your investment club, alumni organization, or book club to take part in an anti-violence workshop. David Robinson, the community service coordinator at Women Organized Against Rape in Philadelphia, says he often gets requests for presenters from parenting and fathers' groups. And Mary Ann Jones, prevention and education coordinator of the Oakwood Center of the Palm Beaches in West Palm Beach, Florida, reports teaching adults at nontraditional locations including religious crusades and revivals, health fairs, music festivals, and social circles and clubs. She also reaches folks with her message by promoting workshops as an opportunity for them to learn to reduce the risk of violence in their children's lives. Adults will often broach the subject for their kids' sake, even if they won't do it for themselves.

Many houses of worship make excellent settings for sexual violence prevention training. Just be sure that the host institution is open to the philosophies of the prevention educator. Unfortunately, leaders of some churches and mosques still lack a sufficient understanding of assault and abuse, and may prevent a workshop from being productive.

Invite a rape crisis center prevention educator to speak to women's and men's groups. Muslims can invite an expert for a Friday khutbah in your mosque. Make sure the leadership and staff participate so that they become optimally prepared to respond to congregation members in cases of crisis.

Another option is to seek out the services of faith-based educators. The Oakwood Center of the Palm Beaches and the Dinah Project in Nashville both provide church-based sexual violence prevention services. In addition to group workshops, The Black Church and Domestic Violence Institute will provide your congregation with a Sunday sermon. It also hosts a national conference on violence against women, *This Far By Faith*, open to people of all faiths each February. For church members active in their denomination or conference, request that sexual violence education be put on the schedule for regional and national meetings, and get the issue added to the list of national ministries.

With a group or on your own, find out about participating in anti-rape activities in your community such as a Take Back the Night rally, an anti-rape educational event held annually nationwide and usually sponsored by rape crisis centers. Film screenings, live performances, and art exhibits that deal with sexual violence are great learning opportunities. Such activities will likely be even easier to find during April, Sexual Assault Awareness Month, and October, Domestic Violence Awareness Month.

Performance art and film can be valuable education tools. Survivor Salamishah Tillet and her sister travel around the country staging their multimedia performance piece *A Long Walk Home*. Another African-American survivor, Aishah Shahidah Simmons wrote, directed, and produced *No! The Rape Documentary*. Black actors Blair Underwood and Tommy Morgan, Jr. produced the video *Sister, I'm Sorry*, to foster healing between the sexes.

If you decide to conduct a sexual violence prevention workshop without hiring a professional educator to lead it, you have a lot of research to do. Discuss with your group what you hope to achieve, then meet with a sexual violence expert about your goals and how best to accomplish them. Contact the National Sexual Violence Resource Center to find out about age-appropriate curricula and other resources. Also call your state coalition against sexual assault or a rape crisis center to find out if they have materials you can use. Check with these sources for information on avenues for activism against sexual violence. The National Advisory Council on Violence Against Women has developed the *Toolkit To End Violence Against Women*. It provides information on organizing in a variety of group settings.

Be prepared to support survivors, as they are likely to be found among any group of women. Some may never have discussed their assault or abuse, or even understood that they were violated. If someone does disclose an assault, direct her to the appropriate rape crisis or domestic violence center. If she's not ready to go, make sure she knows how to contact them. If the assault just occurred, encourage her to report the crime to the police and get a medical exam.

Most importantly, urges Los Angeles Commission on Assaults Against Women associate director Leah Aldridge, "Continuously remind the victim that it's not her fault, that she's not alone, and that there is help out there when she's ready to receive it." If you have access to the people who will make up the survivor's support system, provide them with encouragement and information about support services so they can become as helpful as possible. Suggest that they take advantage of counseling at a local rape crisis center as well, should they need further support.

Following is a list of action items you can use alone or with a group to work toward wiping out sexual violence:[27]

- Volunteer at your local rape crisis organization.
- Host a fundraiser for an anti-rape group.
- Donate money to local, state, or national rape crisis organizations.
- Recognize that no one ever asks or deserves to be raped.
- Don't blame rape victims for the violence perpetrated against them.
- Don't use words, like "bitch," "ho," or "freak," that send the message that some women deserve fewer rights and less respect than others.
- When you hear a rape joke, explain that it is offensive and harmful in the same way that racist jokes are.
- Know that silence does not equal consent.
- Take responsibility for your sexuality; don't let it be defined by your partner, the media, or anyone else.
- Don't use alcohol or drugs to get someone to have sex with you.
- Men: Become an ally to the women in your life—do not participate in sexist behavior by objectifying or stereotyping women.
- Women: Take a self-defense class.
- If someone you know behaves abusively toward his girl-friend or wife, tell the abuser what changes you want him to make and why. Make him aware of organizations that help men stop violent behavior, such as Men Stopping Violence in Atlanta and Men Overcoming Violence in San

Francisco. If he commits a crime, report it to the police. Be sure to do this in a way that does not endanger you!

- If you think someone is being abused, make sure she has domestic violence or rape crisis hotline phone numbers. Let her know you are available to take her to a crisis center or shelter if she wants to go.
- Start an anti-sexual violence project through your community, social or civic group, mosque, church, or workplace.
- Start an anti-rape organization.
- College students: Let faculty and staff know you want to have rape prevention programs on campus.
- Teach your children, friends, parents, and peers about the myths and realities of sexual assault.
- Find out what your local K-12 school board's policy is on sexual violence prevention and anti-rape education and get involved. If it is not proactive enough, change it.
- Men: Be a leader in men-only settings. Whether one-on-one or in groups, talk with other men about what sexual violence encompasses and why it is unacceptable.
- Get in touch with your local chapter of the National Organization for Women and find out if they have any ongoing anti-rape efforts you can support.
- Lobby your local, state and federal legislators to pass legislation that will produce more anti-rape education or that supports survivors in any way.
- Start a court-watching program in your jurisdiction to monitor trials and help improve fairness for survivors in the criminal justice system. Contact the NOW Legal Defense and Education Fund in New York to get a copy of their "Guide to Court Watching."
- In April, attend a Take Back the Night rally.
- If you have been a victim of a sexual assault either by a stranger, acquaintance, or intimate, know there is help out there. Seek it.

Reducing Your Risk[28]

Self-defense classes are an excellent way to build confidence and self-esteem while learning simple but very effective techniques for crisis situations. Shop around for high-quality instruction. Ask people you know if they've taken self-defense or personal safety training. Call rape crisis centers and martial arts schools to find classes. Many local government recreation departments offer inexpensive self-defense classes at community centers. Try looking in your local phone book under self-defense programs. If cost is a concern, be sure to ask if the program offers sliding-scale fees based on students' level of income.

Visit the locations and view a class in progress. Ask questions about exactly what skills you will learn. If possible, choose a class in which you can actually practice the skills you are learning with a trained instructor dressed in protective gear. Self-defense training can be offered as a single workshop session or a series of classes that take place over weeks or months. Find the most comprehensive training you can fit into your schedule and budget. Refresh your skills with a new course every year.

People study various martial arts, like karate and tae kwon do, for all kinds of reasons, including self-defense. Personal safety is more than the ability to defend yourself physically against attackers, be they strangers, acquaintances, or intimates. You may want to commit to studying a martial art that covers a wide spectrum of safety issues, including mental and spiritual components. Ask yourself what goals you want to achieve, and compare your answers with the benefits of these disciplines according to instructors, books, and Internet resources. Again, you should shop around to find a school that suits your needs.

A simple self-defense strategy that everyone can follow is to always be aware of your surroundings. Attackers look for an easy target, for instance someone who is daydreaming and can be caught off guard. When going to a new place, be it a neighborhood across town or a house party across the street, go with someone you know.

When you travel alone, carry as little as possible. Trying to handle too many objects creates just the diversion attackers look for.

In the event that someone tries to assault you, it is very important to try to stay calm. Are you going to be nervous? Of course, but you need to assess your options as quickly as possible. Your primary goal should be to get to safety however you can. One key strategy is calling attention to yourself. Yell "no" loudly and repeatedly. In your loudest voice, scream for the attacker to stop what he is doing and leave you alone. Shout as loudly as possible, whether or not the assailant is someone you know, that he is bothering you and that you need assistance, because some people will not intervene if they think that a couple is together consensually and having a fight. Even if you don't think people are around, yell loudly because it may scare the attacker away. Some safety experts advise yelling "fire" instead of "help."

Even if you are trained in self-defense tactics, do not try to have a boxing match with your assailant. Do not stick around a second longer than you have to. Do whatever you can to incapacitate him long enough to get far enough away from him that you are no longer in danger. Stomping on his foot with your heel and kneeing him in the groin can both be effective techniques. Run to a populated area. You may never have considered flat shoes a self-defense tool, but they can be key to your safety if you should ever need to take off running. Avoid high heels when you will be alone or in unfamiliar surroundings.

To be as self-assured and secure as possible, learn to use some other safety tools. Most women carry many items that can be used as a weapon, like keys, pencils, and combs. In an emergency situation, you can use them to jab an assailant in the eye to stun or disable him long enough for you to get away. How effective they are depends on your preparation and confidence in using them. Many self-defense classes will train you to use such items. If it isn't part of the curriculum, request that it be included.

A cell phone can also be a lifesaving self-defense tool. Carry your phone on a belt-clip when possible as opposed to inside a purse, so that you will have quick, easy access to it in case of an emergency. Noisemakers are another great safety aide. Carry a siren-sounding personal alarm or whistle on your key chain. If you have to walk in a potentially unsafe environment, carry it in your hand. And keep a flashlight in your car and at home. You can shine the light in an attacker's face to keep him from seeing well momentarily or use it to hit him in a sensitive spot like the nose or throat.

Most weapons have the potential to do you more harm than good in the event of an attack.[29] If you ever have to use one, a one-second hesitation can be all an assailant needs to disarm you and possibly use your weapon against you. Anyone who carries one needs to be prepared to use it with confidence.

Pepper spray is a lightweight, inexpensive self-defense product that can be carried on a key chain. It should contain 10 percent oleoresin capsicum, a derivative of hot peppers. It is used by spraying the attacker's face directly from up to six feet away. It will produce a burning sensation in the eyes, causing them to close, and will make breathing difficult, disabling your attacker for twenty minutes or more. Mace or tear gas produces similar results, but is considered less effective. If not used with accuracy, or if the wind blows the spray toward you, you will, of course, be disabled instead of the attacker. If the assailant is wearing glasses, these sprays won't do you much good unless you can aim at an angle that will get it into his eyes.[30]

About the size of a package of cigarettes, a stun gun will disable an assailant by zapping him with thousands of volts of electricity. Close proximity is necessary in order for the electricity to make contact with the assailant's skin or through a thin layer of clothes, and the charge must be maintained for at least five seconds before he will collapse. Another electrical device, a taser, can cause someone to temporarily lose control of his body. When ejected, its probes, which are connected to fifteen-foot-long wires, will attach to his clothes. Both of these weapons require pinpoint accuracy. Anyone who buys them must get training in order to use them effectively. Shop for these products in gun stores.

A gun can give you a feeling of security. But keep in mind that if you are the least bit unsure about your ability or willingness to use it to cause serious bodily harm during an attack, don't carry one. You may feel scared and panicked during an assault and any hesitation to use your weapon can allow your attacker to use it against you. You should also be aware that a gun kept in the home is much more likely to injure or kill for a family member than an assailant.[31]

If you do decide to buy a gun, stun gun, or taser, call your local police department to find out if there are any laws or restrictions about carrying them in your jurisdiction. Once you have that information, it is essential that you get trained and refresh your skills regularly. Gun stores often sell a variety of self-defense products. Some have on-site training or can refer you to a gun range for instruction. If your skills get rusty, that weapon is nothing but a liability.

If someone does attempt to assault you, try to diffuse an attack with verbal self-defense. Even that is a skill that should be practiced in self-defense training. Your highest priority is to get to a safe and secure place. Remember, fighting or using force of any kind should be an absolute last resort.

Safety Tips[32]

At Home

- If you live alone, make it a regular part of your routine to let someone know you arrived home safely. If you live with someone and you know that you will not be home at your usual time or you are going to take a detour before coming home, call and let them know.
- If you live alone and you will be arriving home at night, be sure to leave lights on in your home. Attackers love nothing better than a dark residence. Leaving a television or radio on will also give the impression that there is someone awake inside.
- Alarm systems are great! If you can't have one installed for

whatever reason, put a security company's sign in front of your home or on the door or windows to give the impression that you do have an alarm system.

Socializing

- Know who you are going out with. Let someone know where you are going. Go on blind dates with another couple or a group of friends.
- Dress in a way that will enable you to move fast if you have to.[33]
- If you are going on a one-on-one date with someone you don't yet know well, meet him in a well-populated, well-lit place. Do not go anywhere that is isolated.[34]
- At a bar or club, get your own drink or accompany a guy buying you a drink to the bar. If you leave it unattended, don't go back and get it. Get a new one. If someone did add a date rape drug, you probably wouldn't be able to see, smell, or taste it.
- Always take money with you in case you feel the need to end a date or leave a party so you won't have to depend on anyone to get you home.
- Before you start any intimate activity, let the person know up front what is acceptable to you and what is not. If you know that you do not want to have sex, inform the other person so that there are no unrealistic expectations.

Transportation

- Have your keys in your hand and ready. Don't get to your car and then fumble around in your purse to find them.
- Look inside your car before you get in. The back seat or floor of your car is a good hiding place for attackers.
- As you are getting in your car, lock the doors before you close yours to prevent someone else from getting in.

- When putting infants or toddlers into their seats, try not to turn your back completely. Step inside the car so that you can at least see what's happening around you until children are safely in their seats.
- When you park in a public lot or garage, above ground or below, refrain from going to your car alone, especially at night. Also avoid waiting for public transportation alone at night. If you have to take the subway late in the evening, sit as close to the conductor as possible.
- If you must work late and your workplace does not have a security guard to escort you to your car, call someone to come and meet you when you get off.

Everywhere

- Be aware of your surroundings at all times.
- Walk confidently. Act like you know where you are going even when you don't.
- Follow your instincts. If a man walking down the block makes you nervous for some reason, cross the street, enter a store, or stay in your car until he gets far away. If you get an inexplicable unsettled feeling around a co-worker, avoid being alone with him. If you notice that a date is inappropriately affectionate, tries to put you down, insists that you drink a lot, or disregards your boundaries in other ways, take a cab home instead of riding alone in his car. Feeling a little silly for following your gut is a small price to pay for ensuring your safety.

Self-defense strategies and safety tips are important for women but these guidelines do not prevent sexual violence. Designed primarily to protect women from attacks by strangers, the least common type of sexual violence, they simply reduce the risk of assault.

Unlike in the anti-rape campaigns of years past, today's activists place the main responsibility for preventing sexual violence on men.

They don't want men to protect women so much as they want men to teach other men not to rape.[35] Perhaps the most important sexual violence prevention strategy is for men to help each other understand what constitutes a sexual violation and that such behavior is unacceptable. On the basketball court, in the barbershop, at the office, in class, at the fraternity meeting, at the club, in church, at the mosque—men must make a commitment to speak out against sexual violence in conversations with other men. If friends and acquaintances condone the disrespect of women or encourage sexual aggression, enlightening them may be a challenging task. Summon your strength and courage to lead them to healthier beliefs and behaviors.

NOTES

[1] Tjaden, Patricia, and Nancy Thoennes. *Full Report of the Prevalence, Incidence, and Consequences of Violence Against Women: Findings from the National Violence Against Women Survey* (Washington, D.C.: U.S. Department of Justice, National Institute of Justice, November 2000), 14-15.

[2] "NCVS' Crime Statistics Obscure a Clear Picture of Sexual Assault Says the NSVRC," National Sexual Violence Resource Center press release, 19 June 2001; available at www.nsvrc.org/p061901.html.

[3] Rennison, Callie Marie. *National Crime Victimization Survey: Criminal Victimization 2000* (Washington, D.C.: U.S. Department of Justice, Office of Justice Programs, June 2001), 10.

[4] Rennison, Callie Marie. *Criminal Victimization in the United States, 1999: Statistical Tables* (Washington, D.C.: U.S. Department of Justice, Office of Justice Programs, January 2001), Table 5.

[5] Fisher, Bonnie S., Francis T. Cullen, and Michael G. Turner. *The Sexual Victimization of College Women* (Washington, D.C.: U.S. Department of Justice, National Institute of Justice, December 2000), 8, 15.

[6] Love, Aubra. The Black Church and Domestic Violence Institute, telephone interviews, 1996-2002.

[7] Rennison, *National Crime Victimization Survey: Criminal Victimization 2000*, 8.

[8] Tjaden, Patricia, and Nancy Thoennes. *Extent, Nature, and Consequences of Intimate Partner Violence: Findings from the National Violence Against Women Survey* (Washington, D.C.: U.S. Department of Justice, National Institute of Justice, July 2000), 9.

9 Fisher, Cullen, and Turner, 17.

10 Lindquist, Scott. *The Date Rape Prevention Book: The Essential Guide for Girls and Women* (Naperville, Ill.: Sourcebooks, 2000), 4.

11 Smith, George Edmond. *Walking Proud: Black Men Living Beyond the Stereotypes* (New York: Kensington, 2001), 108.

12 *American Heritage Dictionary of the English Language*, Fourth Edition (Boston: Houghton Mifflin Company, 2000), 1921.

13 W. .te, Aaronette M. "Talking Feminist, Talking Black: Micromobilization Process in a Collective Protest Against Rape," *Gender & Society* 13, no. 1 (February 1999), 96; Ledray, Linda E. *Sexual Assault Nurse Examiner Development and Operation Guide* (Washington, D.C.: U.S. Department of Justice, Office for Victims of Crime, 1999), 79.

14 Lindquist, 5, 58-59.

15 Human Rights Watch. *No Escape: Male Rape in U.S. Prisons* (New York: Human Rights Watch, 2001), 130, 371.

16 Scarce, 17.

17 Ledray, 80; Snyder, Howard N. *Sexual Assault of Young Children as Reported to Law Enforcement: Victim, Incident, and Offender Characteristics* (Washington, D.C.: Bureau of Justice Statistics, July 2000), 4, 8.

18 Tjaden, *Full Report of the Prevalence, Incidence, and Consequences of Violence Against Women*, 13.

19 Rennison, *Criminal Victimization in the United States, 1999: Statistical Tables*, Table 2.

20 "Women's Vote Center Focuses on Equal Pay Day," in Democratic National Committee website [cited 30 July 2002]; available at www.democrats.org/wvc.

21 See note 11 above.

22 White, 96.

23 U.S. Department of Justice, Federal Bureau of Investigation. Uniform Crime Reporting Program Return A Master File, 1999.

24 Lonsway, Kimberly A. "Unfounded Cases and False Allegations" in Violence Against Women Online Resources website [cited 31 July 2002]; available at www.vaw.umn.edu/FinalDocuments/Investigate/ParticipantManual/Allegations/AllegationsMOD.htm.

25 See note 22 above.

26 Smith, 114.

27 Some of these action items appear in the California Anti-Sexist Men's Political Caucus publication "Fourteen Ways You Can Begin to Stop Rape Today" in California Coalition Against Sexual Assault website [cited 30 July 2002]; available at www.calcasa.org/involved/involved_action.html.

28 Unless otherwise specified, the primary source for information in this section is an interview by the author with Marcia Chisolm, an instructor at the Dennis Brown Shalin Wu-Shu Academy in Silver Spring, Maryland.

29 Dyer, Gerri M., ed. *Safe, Smart and Self-Reliant: Personal Safety for Women and Children* (Rockville, Md.: Safety Press, 1996), 200-205.

30 See note 21 above; Pelton, Robert Young. *Come Back Alive: The Ultimate Guide to Surviving Disasters, Kidnappings, Animal Attacks, and Other Nasty Perils of Modern Travel* (New York: Doubleday, 1999), 58-61.

31 See note 21.

32 See note 23.

33 Lindquist, 31.

34 See note 24.

35 Ohlson, Kristin. "Be a Man," *O: The Oprah Magazine* (October 2002), 286.

CHAPTER 9
RISK REDUCTION/PREVENTION
FOR CHILDREN AND TEENS

As adults we are responsible for safeguarding our young people to the greatest degree possible. This is no quick, easy task. It can require us to unlearn entrenched ideas and accept some painful and frightening new ones. We will have to talk about things that we may never have been comfortable talking about before. Not once, but repeatedly, in different ways, over time.

In this world, no one can guarantee an abuse-free childhood for any young person, but much can be done to strive toward that goal. By equipping yourself with the information in this chapter, you distinguish yourself as a brave, mature, compassionate leader. You demonstrate a commitment to creating the safest environment possible for your most valued treasure, your kids, not to mention your community. Congratulations for taking the first step.

Children

Sexual violence has been described as a "tragedy of youth" because the majority of sexual victimizations reported to law enforcement nationwide are crimes against minors.[1] A Department of Justice report examining child sexual abuse over a five-year period shows that in two-thirds of sexual violations reported to law enforcement, the victim was younger than eighteen. In one-third of cases, the victim was younger than twelve. One out of seven victims was younger than six.[2]

Naturally, violations of children are direly underreported because some victims are too young to understand that what happened was a crime, to have the vocabulary to describe it, or even to have learned to talk. Sexual abuse happens to children as young as infants.

The sexual abuse of children takes many forms. Sexual abuse can occur without physical contact, when someone inappropriately exposes his or her genitals to a child. Having a child look at sexual pictures or toys, or watch or listen to sexual acts, is a form of abuse. Talking about sex with the intention of shocking or arousing curiosity in a child is a form of sexual violation.[3]

Physical sexual victimization includes fondling a child's genitals or touching a child with one's genitals, penetrating a child's mouth, anus, or vagina with a body part or object, and photographing or filming a child for pornography. When one father hired a prostitute to introduce his ten-year-old son to sex, he was sexually abusing him.[4]

Don't make assumptions about who abusers are or what they look like. As the Catholic Church's revelation of sexual abuse by priests in epidemic proportions has made clear, sexual abusers can be among a community's most esteemed citizens. They can work in any profession and have any economic status. Most people who sexually abuse children are adults, but they can be children as young as or younger than their victims. According to the report *Sexual Assault of Young Children as Reported to Law Enforcement*, in cases of victims younger than six, 40 percent of perpetrators were younger than eighteen. Most offenders are men, but they can be women. Females accounted for 6 percent of offenders of juveniles in the study.[5]

As with adults, it is essential for children to know how to reduce their risk of victimization by strangers. However, strangers are the perpetrators in even fewer child sexual abuse cases than in instances of adult sexual victimization. The same Department of Justice report estimates that strangers were the victimizers in only 7 percent of child sexual abuse cases reported to law enforcement. Ninety-three percent of juvenile sexual assault victims knew their perpetrator.[6] Three-quarters of victims younger than twelve are girls and one-fourth are boys.[7]

Some abuse is perpetrated using physical size and strength to overpower a child, but many offenders simply misuse their position of authority to victimize kids. Predators also lure children with things they want or need, like candy, clothes, food, toys, affection, or attention. Children can be abused without being overpowered or tricked simply because they don't understand that what is happening to them is inappropriate.

In a house full of visitors during a family reunion, one seven-year-old girl was playing with a cousin she'd never met before, a girl about her age and size. The two slept side-by-side in sleeping bags on the living room floor. As part of their "play," the visiting cousin instructed the girl to lick her between her legs. If this child had been empowered to say no to something she didn't understand or feel comfortable with, and taught about private body parts, this abuse might have been avoided.

If a lack of information can leave kids vulnerable to victimization by other children, their level of vulnerability to adults, who they are taught to blindly respect and obey, is staggering. If never explicitly told by the main authority figures in their lives that there are exceptions to that rule, they are left defenseless if abuse is attempted.

"I have a son and I made rules very early. For example, I told him that he doesn't have to hug or kiss someone if he doesn't want to—even if that person is a close family member," says Mary Ann Jones. "I teach him how to trust his gut and also that good people can do very bad things. I also have taught him about privacy. I would do the same with a girl."

As soon as kids are old enough to communicate verbally, it's important to impart the message that there are private parts of their body that no one is allowed to touch, the parts covered by their underwear, and that they should never be asked to touch someone else's private parts.

Kids must also be informed that they alone control their bodies, and have the right to say no to any unwanted attempts to touch their private parts. Let them know that the only exception may be a doctor helping to make sure a child is healthy, but that even a doctor must have a parent's permission to examine a child. Present this information in a balanced, nonthreatening way by including in your discussion what positive touches are, like hugging, bathing, and tickling, and how they feel.

Experts advise that children be taught correct names for each part of their body to help instill a respect for their entire physical self. Using created names like "wee-wee" instead of "penis," or "pocketbook" instead of "clitoris" and "vagina," sets the stage for ineffective communication about the body.

An excellent way to start informing your children about staying safe is to read with them an age-appropriate book on the topic. Use it as a basis for discussion and allow them to ask questions about what you've read. Like any other subject, for information to take root and be remembered over time, it needs to be discussed and reviewed. The lessons will mean even more coming from the most credible adults in a child's life, parents, grandparents, or guardians, than from the stranger who gives one presentation at school.

There are also videos available, such as the one included in the Good Knight Child Empowerment Network's Family Security Kit. Research other resources for teaching children in a nonthreatening way about personal safety by contacting a rape crisis center, the Committee for Children, the Safer Society Foundation, the National Crime Prevention Council, or the National Sexual Assault Resource Center.

Essential to creating an overall safe environment for children is fostering comfortable communication with trusted adults. If kids do not feel they can discuss with you whatever questions or thoughts come to mind, they may go without important information. With openness as a characteristic of your everyday conversations, your child will already be in the habit of speaking freely when it's time to talk about personal safety, or should anything negative happen.

Be honest with yourself about how approachable you are. If you feel uptight or anxious discussing this subject, what you say may come across in a negative, frightening manner. Your comfort level can greatly influence how receptive your child is to the information you are sharing. If you are uncomfortable discussing parts of the body or safety issues, practice what you will say alone or with another adult until you are at ease with the words and concepts you'll use.

Tell your child that if anything inappropriate is ever done to her or in front of her, she should tell you or another trusted adult immediately so that you can make sure she is safe. Explain that she should never keep a secret about something that caused bad feelings or pain.

If a child ever hears a news report, or even a rumor, about child sexual abuse, use it as a learning opportunity. Reinforce that it was not the victim's fault. After one boy had been abducted from the woods near his middle school and sexually abused, one set of parents made the incident the primary topic of discussion at a family dinner. Their oldest son, who was around twelve at the time, a schoolmate of the victim, learned about the crime at a school assembly.

"We shared additional information and told them how we would want them to handle themselves in that situation. And we got their feedback: what they thought he did wrong, how they would have handled themselves differently, questions that they had," says Chaye Wise, a mother of three. "It's very important as parents that you make sure that children really understand what you're saying. When I say to them, "Run and yell," I see one thing. They may see something totally different. And if you don't allow them the opportunity to give it back to you the way they see it, putting it in their words, you don't know that they're thinking that you mean run around in circles and yell as opposed to run away from the person and yell."

It is also important to tell kids that children who are abused are still loved by their family and friends, although people who hurt children sometimes prevent them from telling trusted adults by threatening that their parents won't love them anymore. "It is very important to teach our children that they are not bad because someone does something bad to them," says Jones. "Children often feel that if a 'good' person does something bad, then it must be their fault."

Although the vast majority of child sexual abuse is perpetrated by someone a child knows, it is also crucial to teach your child not to go anywhere with a stranger. Explain that adults who seem nice, who might even give away candy, toys, or other gifts, sometimes harm kids. Let them know that if a stranger wants to take them somewhere or tries to give them a ride for any reason, they should yell "no," do whatever it takes to get away from that person and run to other people who can help. Then they should tell an adult they know and trust.

One mother, a domestic violence survivor, applied to her children lessons she learned in a self-defense workshop for women. She explained that if anyone ever tried to touch their private parts, they should yell "stop" or "no" as loud as possible. And when her children were three and four, she made use of commuting time in her car by having them practice screaming. "The goal was to be louder than the next person," says Schuyla Goodson-Bell. "I wanted them to become comfortable with being loud and not feeling afraid, because a lot of times, if you're always quiet, when it's time for you to scream you can't even do it because you're not used to your voice."

Your responsibility to keep your children safe extends beyond personal safety lessons. Make sure their school, day care, and other environments they frequent are safe before they get there. "It takes a lot of talking to people about where are your young people in day care, and how is it going for them there, and what do you like about it, and do you feel like they're safe. Doing our research, basically, like we would if we were buying a car, by talking to the people who actually are using the services," reports Nell Myhand, program director at Todos Institute.

Find out if the administrators at schools or day cares take steps to ensure an abuse-free environment, such as doing police background checks on employees and volunteers, and offering violence prevention training so that staff can recognize signs of abuse. If you do not know families with children in attendance there, ask to be referred to parents of currently enrolled kids to get their impressions about the environment's safety. Be present as much as you can in your child's school, on field trips, and at extracurricular activities to monitor staff and safety procedures.

The following is a list of signs that can indicate sexual abuse in children.[8] If you notice any of these serious physical symptoms, take your child for a forensic medical examination right away. See Chapter 1 for more information on exams.

- Constant scratching or rubbing genitals
- Sores on the genitals or in the mouth that may indicate a sexually transmitted infection
- Recurring urinary tract infections
- Discomfort or pain when sitting or walking
- Blood stains on underwear or swelling or bleeding from the genital or anal areas
- Significant increase in bathroom use or pain when urinating

The following is a list of behaviors that sometimes result from sexual abuse.[9] None of these is a conclusive indicator. They can all be signs of other issues. If you observe one or more of the behaviors on this list and are concerned about the possibility of sexual abuse, consult a rape crisis center expert about whether you should pursue a medical exam or crisis counseling for your child. You can also call the toll-free National Child Abuse Hotline for more information.

- Compulsive, ongoing masturbation
- Bedwetting by a child who is potty-trained
- Extreme lack of hygiene or cleanliness

- Persistent sexual play or mimicking adult sexual behavior
- Drawings of sexual acts or images
- Age-inappropriate knowledge of sex
- Wearing unnecessary layers of clothing
- New desire for seclusion
- New fears of particular places or people, or of going to a doctor
- New extreme desire to please everyone
- Nervousness and withdrawal from ordinary hugging
- Compulsive lying
- Excessive crying
- Withdrawing from family and friends
- New moodiness
- Change in appetite
- Changes in school performance or behavior
- Significant increase in headaches
- Inability to sleep through the night or nightmares
- Return to babyish behavior
- Depression or anxiety
- Decreased self-esteem
- Hostility and irritability
- Running away
- Suicide attempts or other self-destructive behavior

Children who have been sexually abused often do not tell anyone because of fear, embarrassment, shame, or a lack of understanding that they were violated. (See Chapter 1 for more information on barriers to disclosure.) If you suspect that a child old enough to talk has been abused, calmly ask if someone touched her inappropriately. Assure her that she is safe, loved, and not to blame for the victimization. If she does disclose abuse, let her know that she did the right thing by telling you. Remain calm and contact a child protective services agency or the police.

Group Education

Personal safety instruction that takes place in schools and other group settings for elementary-age kids is intended to convey the basic concepts of good touch and bad touch, and the right to control what happens to their bodies. By exposing as many children as possible to safety information, you are helping to make your entire community safer. Group presentations by sexual violence prevention experts will be the only opportunity many children have to learn about this subject. And by making sure your child's school schedules prevention education sessions every year, you will reinforce the lessons you teach at home.

Find out if your child's teacher or school administrator plans to bring in an expert. If not, offer to help make arrangements. Work with the PTA to ensure that professional educators are brought in to teach children at every grade level. To find prevention educators near you, contact a local rape crisis center or your state's coalition against sexual assault. Some YWCAs also have sexual abuse risk reduction programs.

If teachers and administrators are uncooperative, go to your school board to find out its policy on prevention education. If there isn't one or the one that exists is inadequate, work with people in your community to establish one. Attend school board meetings and write letters to representatives with other concerned community members until you succeed in getting safety education in your child's school.

But don't think you have to limit prevention to school. "I think we should talk with our children everywhere—the school, church, classroom, playground. We have a pandemic problem and need to remove the cloak of shame and secrecy," says Jones. Potential settings for prevention education include scout troop meetings, community centers, Sunday school, sports practices, Boys & Girls Clubs, Tots and Teens, apartment-complex recreation rooms, Jack & Jill, day care centers, and anywhere else that children gather.

Teens

Sexual violence against teens can take any of the forms of victimization that happen to adults or children—any unwanted sexual activity including voyeurism, acquaintance rape, incest, stranger rape, and indecent exposure. A perpetrator can be someone she just met or someone she has known her whole life. He can be a classmate or co-worker, a first-time date or long-term boyfriend. As with people who sexually abuse children, perpetrators of sexual assault against teens are often people who take advantage of a position of authority and trust to manipulate and coerce young people into sexual activity. A perpetrator can be someone a teen looks up to, like a pastor, coach or teacher.

One fifteen-year-old boy who was sexually abused repeatedly by the leader of his Boy Scout troop lived in an emotionally abusive household and consequently had low self-esteem. As is typical, this predator exploited the needs of his victim—in this case, the boy's need for affirmation and encouragement. One of the many reasons the survivor did not report the abuse was because the perpetrator was the only person feeding his emotional needs.

Much teen sexual assault happens in the context of dating violence. "I can't tell you how many letters have been slipped to me as a prevention educator that say, 'I didn't want to have sex, but then my boyfriend just did it. Is that rape?'" says Jamie Lee Evans, who taught sexual violence prevention at San Francisco Women Against Rape.

And like every other community, the Black community is not free from incest. Despite African Americans such as Oprah Winfrey and Donnie McClurken publicly sharing their stories of victimization, we pretend it doesn't affect us by making jokes about "inbreeding" White families. Any relative can sexually violate a teen. One fifteen-year-old girl was raped once by a cousin she'd known all her life. Another survivor was physically and sexually abused by her father from age four to twenty-three. Cases of incest vary as broadly in severity as other sexual victimizations; however, the trauma caused includes the deepest betrayal of trust imaginable, significantly complicating the healing process.

Of National Violence Against Women Survey respondents who are rape survivors, nearly one-third of women and nearly one-fourth of men were first raped between ages twelve and seventeen.[10] Traditionally, sexual assault prevention training has been directed toward girls and women. As potential victims as well as bystanders who may have the opportunity to help someone in danger of assault or abuse, it makes sense for boys to become as well informed as girls. Both have vital roles to play in risk reduction and creating a safe community around them.

Sexual violence risk reduction for teens incorporates an increased level of responsibility for their own safety in comparison to risk reduction strategies for young children. Of course, it is never a victim's fault when a perpetrator decides to force unwanted sexual activity on her or him. According to Jones, "Sexual violence will stop when perpetrators stop victimizing. There is no 100 percent [foolproof] method by which a potential victim can protect herself." Teens have, however, reached an age that requires them to make decisions that can increase or decrease their personal safety. They will make decisions about whether they will respect others and demand respect for themselves.

Adults' Role at Home

With less control over the environment of teens than that of younger kids, and teens' increased exposure to potential dangers, adults face a growing challenge in helping young people stay safe as they get older. In order to remain relevant and useful, personal safety information must transform in age-appropriate ways as young people mature. To be proactive in reducing their risk of victimization, teens need increased knowledge about healthy friendships and romantic relationships, sex, the concepts of consent and sexual violation, as well as self-defense. If they don't hear these messages repeatedly over time, misinformation from ill-informed peers and the media can undermine what you've already taught your kids at home.

One child safety strategy that does not change in the teen years is the need for open communication with parents. At this stage, it's more crucial than ever. Get in the habit of talking freely day to day with your teen about anything and everything. "Just talk to your young person and know what's going on. Don't badger, don't hound—talk," recommends Shanterra McBride, director of education and programs at The Empower Program, a nonprofit educational organization in Washington, D.C. If you don't have a track record of listening to their everyday concerns, she says, "When something does happen and you want your young person to talk to you, why would they?"

In an open relationship, teens are more likely to feel comfortable telling you with whom and where they spend free time. You can discuss their decisions and guide them toward making positive, safe choices. What you say can help young people steer clear of dangerous people and situations, and by speaking frankly and honestly, you will teach them communications skills that will help them stand up for themselves and stay safe.

One way to fit quality conversation time into your family routine is to eat meals together. Not always an easy task with the busy schedules of parents and youth, eating together at least one day each week without the television on can become a valued habit both parents and teens enjoy. Also invite your teens' friends to your home and spend time interacting with them. Meet their parents. Attend school and extracurricular activities and spend as much leisure time together as you can.

Research has shown that teens who have positive relationships with their parents tend to delay their first sexual intercourse longer than those who do not.[11] Delaying sexual activity is important because many teen sexual assaults happen in situations that begin with some consensual activity. Any intimate situation lacking mutual respect and emotional maturity—concepts many adults still have trouble with—is potentially dangerous.

Young people who are more involved in school and extracurricular activities are more likely to delay their first sexual encounter longer than kids who are not active.[12] Activities that give teens opportunities to create and achieve things they enjoy and are good at help them build self-esteem. High self-esteem makes young people more likely to steer clear of potentially abusive situations as victims or perpetrators. Encourage your kids to participate in school clubs and athletic teams, Boys & Girls Club activities, or any other well-supervised community or school activities that interest them.

What Teens Should Know

Healthy Relationships and Boundaries

As teenagers, kids begin to establish some independence from parents and discover who they are as individuals. One of the ways they accomplish these tasks is by forming new friendships and relationships. It is important for young people to develop healthy, platonic friendships. It's through those relationships that they'll learn to build the foundation necessary for maintaining a balance of power and mutual respect in any relationship. "With same-sex friendships, you have to have boundaries, because anyone can take advantage of anybody," says McBride. "Boundaries are just feeling like you can say what's on your mind. It can be as small as, 'I always spend the night at your house. Can you spend the night at my house?' 'I always let you borrow lunch money. I don't feel comfortable in doing that.'"

Boundary setting for both genders is a crucial skill during the teen years. During this formative period, even the most self-assured young people are developing self-esteem. Many teens seek the approval of kids at school and in the neighborhood. Peers don't just impact clothes and music choices, but can significantly influence how young people view themselves.

It is not uncommon for a young person to stay in a relationship that is abusive because of the status it gives her among her peers. "Having a relationship in high school is the coolest thing in the world," explains McBride. "[Teens] really look at stuff that's going to be more acceptable for other people. When it's just a friend, they don't really care how he looks. But when it comes to a boyfriend, hey, everybody needs to think he's cute. So you begin to compromise your standards because you try to please everyone else."

Peer pressure can also influence kids to exhibit abusive behavior, prevent them from trying to stop abusive behavior happening to someone else, or simply lead a teen into being pressured to have sex before she's ready. Pay attention to how your children and their friends communicate with each other. Do they talk in a friendly way? Do any of them frequently insult others? Do they make encouraging comments or hurtful jokes at someone else's expense? Do they compromise or does one of them insist on getting her way?

If you notice your child behaving negatively with friends, talk about your concerns. Often such behaviors are a way to cover up emotional wounds or insecurities. Get to the root of his or her reasons for hurtful words and deeds, and explain that such behavior will have long-lasting effects on the target. If teens are behaving negatively because of peer pressure, encourage them to choose more positive friends and put them in different environments, like a new church youth group or community activity, so they can meet other young people. Ask friends and family about activities their young people are involved in that may be appropriate for your child.

Help your teen understand that in any relationship she has the right to be treated in a way that makes her feel safe, at ease, and good about herself. If your child is being mistreated, even if it is simply a matter of being the brunt of too many jokes, again, talk about the behavior concerning you. Help her think of things to say and do to avoid or curtail negative interactions with other kids. Practice such conversations with him in role-plays at home. If bullying, harassing, or teasing is a frequent problem, meet in person with the staff supervising your child to make known your expectation that the behavior will be stopped. Teachers and administrators are often most responsive to parents who go out of their way to show concern and be involved in their child's development.

Recognizing abusive patterns is a significant step in avoiding unsafe relationships. Many girls believe abusive relationships only happen to adults, even when they are being shoved around, struck, or emotionally abused. Verbal and emotional abuse frequently escalate into physical and sexual violence.

When your child starts dating, be on the lookout for the following signs of abuse: a boyfriend or girlfriend who is possessive, controlling, or extremely jealous, has violent outbursts or a history of unhealthy relationships, has too much influence over your child's decisions, blames others for his or her own mistakes and problems, insults or manipulates your child, encourages your child to keep secrets, or has caused your child to withdraw.[13]

Discuss with your teens the kind of relationship they want. Have them describe their dream date and ideal relationship. Ask how he or she would demonstrate respect, physically and verbally. How would he demonstrate trust? How would she want to be treated? Then discuss the qualities of healthy relationships listed below.[14]

Teens are more likely to have a healthy relationship if both partners:

- feel good about themselves. Each individual recognizes that he or she is as valuable and lovable as any other human being.
- do not rush to build the relationship. It takes time to develop even platonic friendships.
- behave responsibly at home and school. Neither partner gets in trouble a lot or does things that are potentially dangerous.
- communicate honestly. Each partner can admit when he or she is wrong and can disagree with the other in a respectful way.
- maintain their independence. Partners have their own interests, express themselves freely, have some separate friends, dress however they want, and don't feel like they have to change who they are to please their partner.

- are kind to each other. Each encourages and supports the other emotionally, and never tries to embarrass or belittle the other.
- are trustworthy and trusting. Neither partner is suspicious or jealous of the other's friends.
- compromise. Partners take turns going places each likes. When there is a conflict, they talk it through without doing or saying hurtful things. Partners agree to ask for advice from elders they both trust.
- agree not to have sex, or at least to wait until they develop deep trust and respect, and get to know each other well.

Consider obtaining additional resources on this topic, such as the Center for the Prevention of Sexual and Domestic Violence's multicultural curriculum on healthy relationships for use in classrooms, community groups, and religious settings. The National Coalition Against Domestic Violence has resources on dating violence.

Encourage teens to avoid relationships with people who are many years older. For a teenager, it can be exciting and flattering when someone who seems mature and has more money than most kids is interested in him or her. Apparently many such relationships exist—national statistics indicate that half of teen moms got pregnant by adult men.[15] However, such relationships naturally have an unbalanced power dynamic. An older man or woman will have a disproportionate share of power and influence by virtue of experience, including sexual experience.

The example set by adults in their lives is a major influence on teen relationships. If a young person has seen a woman insulted, pushed around, or worse, by a spouse or boyfriend, explain why the behavior is inappropriate and what its effects may be. Go out of your way to regularly expose your child to adult couples and friends who treat each other with respect and kindness. If you are in an unhealthy relationship now, your child could have no better example to learn from than to see you take the steps necessary to best care for yourself, be that going to counseling, working through self-help books, or if necessary, leaving an abusive relationship.

Gender Roles

"I recently visited a local high school here in Mobile where I spoke to a group of ninth and tenth graders regarding sexual assault issues," says Shae Timmons, training coordinator at Contact Mobile, a rape crisis and social services agency in Alabama. "We had finished discussing the cycle of violence when a young man said to me that all relationships followed that same pattern because girls liked to be treated in such a manner."

Just as young people learn positive behavior in relationships, dangerous misinformation about male and female roles in relationships can be instilled early. Explains Myhand, "Right away, there's an 'Act Like a Man' box that starts getting built for boys: Be tough, don't cry, suck it in, love sports, prove your manhood [by having] lots of women. The 'Act Like a Lady' box, on the other hand, is: Be nice, be soft, go along, don't be too smart, be hard working, care for everybody first if not to the exclusion of yourself. And so we start getting trained into those roles no matter what's inside of us."

Masculinity stereotypes can be harmful when boys apply them to interactions with girls. For example, when the concept of masculinity is linked to excelling in sports, boys may learn that the more aggressive and competitive they are, the better, and that winning is everything. If those ideas are applied to exploring their blossoming sexuality, negative consequences could result.

Some girls have learned to think of sex as a means of getting or keeping a boyfriend, as opposed to being an expression of love that results from a well-established emotional, spiritual, and intellectual connection. For doing the very thing boys are encouraged to do, acting on their sexual feelings, girls are sometimes labeled "freaks" or "hoes." Such names send the message that some girls don't deserve to be respected and valued. Girls who defy their gender role as passive, polite, and soft-spoken by expressing anger or refusing a boy's advances, might be treated as if they are behaving inappropriately, seen as unfeminine, and called derogatory terms like "bitch."

These gender roles can, not surprisingly, lead to unwanted sexual activity. "They say, 'I felt like I may as well do it because I'm already here.' They didn't want to do it, but they felt that they should go ahead and do it because if they didn't the guy was going to talk about them or the guy could get mad. I hear a lot of that," says Shanterra McBride, of her work educating junior and senior high school girls. When she explains to students that they do have a choice about whether or not to have sex once in an intimate situation, many teen girls disagree. They believe they should be "taking care of him instead of taking care of themselves," McBride says.

Both boys and girls are taught to equate money with power. If a boy pays for a date, buys a girl an outfit, or pays to get her hair or nails done, the false belief that she "owes him" can lead to unwanted sexual activity. Money buys sexual activity only from a consenting prostitute. Until a mutually respectful relationship develops, by each paying their own way, a dating couple will not have to worry about unrealistic expectations based on money.

A good resource for examining gender stereotypes in an African-American context is popular music. While many contemporary artists promote healthy images in their songs, it is impossible to listen to a hip-hop, R & B, or pop radio station for long without hearing sexually explicit lyrics. Likewise, you can't watch a music video channel without seeing those lyrics acted out or being bombarded with images of women whose only role is being sexual. It's been estimated that 57 percent of women in music videos are partially clothed, twice the percentage of men.[16]

Talk to teens about the messages and roles in songs and videos. Analyze men's and women's appearance, and get them to think about how those depictions may influence people and how they compare to real life. Together, discuss a book or watch a film about gender roles, such as the documentary film *I Am a Man*.

Sex Education

"The majority of us got our sex education from our partners," says Evans about colleagues and girls she has taught. "We didn't even know what we wanted to say yes to. And if you don't know what you want to say yes to, you don't know what you want to say no to."

Teens' bodies are maturing and their hormones are racing. It is natural for this age group to begin having romantic and sexual feelings, and to begin acting on them. Some adults do not want to teach young people about sex for fear it will encourage them to become sexually active. But studies show that school sex-education programs that include information on contraception either delay or have no effect on the initiation of sexual activity.[17]

Being knowledgeable about sex, whether or not they are having it, is essential in order for teens to respect and care for their bodies, and to make the safest choices. It is also important because abusers often target the most naive kids who are easiest to manipulate.[18]

Instead of letting teens' peers, the media, and an occasional sex education teacher determine what and how they learn about sex, why not instill in your teens your own values about sex? Approach sex from a holistic perspective, addressing the positive role it can play in a mature, committed relationship. If teens learn only about the dangers of pregnancy, sexually transmitted diseases, and the prevalence of sexual assault, they may feel too intimidated to ask questions about sex or share what's happening in their relationships. Let teens know it is natural for them to be curious about the changes their bodies are undergoing, and about intimate relationships. It may help to remove the stigma from the topic by letting them know you were curious about sex and relationships at their age.

Be sure to dispel common myths, such as blue balls (the falsehood that males must have sex once they get an erection or else they will be in pain) and boys' inability to control their sexual urges once they've been aroused. Before having these conversations, take some time to make sure you are prepared by reading about sexuality yourself. If you still have unanswered questions, consult your doctor for accurate information.

Again, a great starting point is an age-appropriate book. At a public library or bookstore find books your teens can read on their own or videos you can watch together, about the parts of the body, reproduction, and the spiritual and emotional aspects of sex.

Among the sex education resources available are informational brochures from the Sexuality Information and Education Council of the United States or Planned Parenthood. You can also obtain the National Black Women's Health Project's sexuality education video for girls called *Tell Me What's Going On . . . My Body, My Self, My Life.* For sex education in a group setting, get *Teaching with SEX, ETC.: Articles & Activities,* a manual with forty articles and corresponding activities designed for educators who work with teenagers.

The Black Church Initiative of the Religious Coalition for Reproductive Choice will send you free of charge a seven-week faith-based sex education curriculum for teens. They also have a curriculum for adults to help you boost your knowledge and comfort level for discussions on healthy sexuality. For more faith-based resources, contact the Center for the Prevention of Sexual and Domestic Violence.

Monitor your teen's entire media intake, not just videos. Even if your child's viewing is carefully monitored, chances are they are hearing about sex and violence in the media from friends and classmates. More than half of television programming contains sexual content.[19] During prime time, the proportion rises to two-thirds.[20] Sex in the media is often shown outside the context of loving, trust-filled, committed relationships, which glamorizes casual sex and devalues emotional and spiritual connection and commitment. Combine such influential images with peer pressure, and it's no wonder many teens wind up in potentially abusive intimate situations before they are ready. Watch television and movies with your teen and discuss the images and situations that occur. Ask questions about choices that characters could make to reduce their risk of violence.

Consider involving your teen in a rites of passage program, an African-centered process that fosters cultural awareness and the development of social and personal responsibility for teens transitioning into adulthood.[21] Talk to the leaders about the agenda, and ask specifically about what is taught regarding gender issues. If the program sounds as if it will enrich your kid's development, enroll him or her. Check with churches, independent Black schools, and community organizations to find one.

Consent and Communication

"No" always means "no." "No" never means "maybe." "No" never means "yes." If your teens learn nothing else about sexual assault risk reduction, make sure they understand this message clearly. To consent to a sexual activity means that you agree to participate, that you give permission to your partner to engage in the activity with you. If someone does not want to participate in sexual activity, or if they are not sure if they want to participate, they have not consented.

"The particular myth that perpetuates sexual violence that I hear is when a girl sends mixed messages to a guy by kissing, rubbing, and touching him, if she gets him turned on and he gets an erection, then she definitely wants to have sex. Or she's asking to be raped," says Timmons.

Boys and girls need to be informed that at any stage of physical arousal, anyone has the right to change his or her mind about continuing with sexual activity, and that everyone, no exceptions, is capable of controlling his or her own body and stopping the activity. Both partners are responsible for making clear what they do and do not want to happen, and for respecting the other's wishes.

McBride regularly encounters a lack of understanding about what constitutes sexual violation when teaching high school girls. "When we ask them about consent, they don't ever know what that means. They think about rape when they think about somebody jumping out of the alley. They never think about the stuff that can happen between you and your boyfriend."

Because girls are often socialized to be timid and soft-spoken, they may object to sexual activity in a corresponding way. Because boys are often socialized to be aggressive, particularly in their pursuit of sex, when they continue sexual activity despite being told no, they may not understand that disregarding her wishes amounts to violating her. Some boys even interpret vocal objection to sexual activity as playing hard to get.

Anytime teens place themselves in intimate situations in which one or both parties lack an understanding of consent and respect for their partner, it is a potentially dangerous situation. Make sure girls and boys know that the only way to be sure that their partner wants the same thing is to talk about it. Teach your teenage boys and girls to encourage their dating partners to articulate what they want to happen and what they do not want to happen, as well as to verbalize their own wishes, so they can ensure that they do not miscommunicate.

Let them know that communicating their wishes with actions, as well as words, is critical. Body language and tone of voice can be even more important in communicating a message than words.[22] Because so many boys have learned to misinterpret what girls say and do, girls have to get their message across as clearly as possible. That means they cannot afford to worry about being polite when they say it. They should speak in a strong, confident tone, and their body language should support whatever is being said.

Group Education

Just as should be done for younger kids, arrange personal safety training for teens in group settings. For this age group, school often feels less than safe emotionally and physically. For some teens, going to junior high or high school is an outright threatening experience every day. School remains a crucial setting for teaching young people about personal safety.

"Students are used to this environment as one for learning. This is also where they receive most of their peer influence and where the stage is set for most of the inappropriate behavior, especially sexual harassment, which can often lead to the bigger issues—sexism, sexual assault, etc.," says Christopher Watson, a sexual assault prevention educator at Southwest Texas State University's Hays-Caldwell Women's Center.

As with elementary schoolers, make sure your children's junior high and high schools arrange personal safety presentations for students. Help schedule the presentations if necessary, again, by contacting a nearby rape crisis center or state coalition against sexual assault to find educators. Even better, if a school or youth organization has financial resources to contract someone to teach an extended curriculum or train its own teachers to implement a curriculum, such as that of Washington, D.C.'s Empower Program, look into that option. Check with the National Sexual Assault Resource Center and the National Crime Prevention Council for educational resources.

For anti-violence information and training designed for male groups, including help for teen boys who are abusive toward girls, contact Men Stopping Violence, Men Can Stop Rape, Men Overcoming Violence, and the Family Violence Prevention Fund about their youth programs.

Think outside classroom walls for teens too. "I've held workshops with my younger cousins and niece in my home around the kitchen table," says Phyllis Harris, director of education at the Cleveland Rape Crisis Center. "I've provided workshops for incarcerated youth, Midnight Basketball programs, and public housing communities." In addition to settings listed in the children's section that are relevant for teens, presentations for this age group can be done for academic clubs, sports teams, cheerleading squads, marching bands, job sites, block parties, summer camps, and anywhere teens can come together and communicate respectfully and openly.

Choose a professional prevention educator to whom your kids can relate. "Make prevention education culturally, gender, and age specific to build credibility. It is okay to request someone of African descent to speak to a group of African-American girls," advises Harris. "If the staff person does not fit the demographics of your audience, don't stop there. Many prevention education programs have a speakers bureau of trained volunteers who may be better suited."

If you cannot find a Black educator in your area, be flexible. Your highest priority should be finding someone who cares about young people and is knowledgeable about sexual violence. When contacting rape crisis centers or other local violence prevention agencies about scheduling a presentation, inquire about peer educator programs. Some teens will be more receptive to the information coming from someone close to their own age.

Many experts agree that it is beneficial for girls and boy to be separated by gender during prevention education workshops. Single-sex environments are more likely to foster open, honest discussions. Of participants in her all-girl workshops, Harris says, "They generally share more of their experiences and ask more questions."

Boys are more likely to think of the information as being targeted toward girls, even though they are also vulnerable to abuse. Boys should be addressed as potential bystanders who want to stop violence before it starts, not as perpetrators.

"Girls and women tend to have thought through these kinds of issues way more than men have, so when a boy or a man says something that seems way off base, I can challenge him in a way that would be considered male bashing if the same challenge was issued by a girl or woman. Sad but true," says Byron Hurt, an anti-sexism activist and filmmaker. "Boys and men already feel targeted and defensive when you talk about rape or any form of gender violence. Most young boys have never talked about these issues with a man leading the discussion, and I think that breaks down layers of defensiveness."

Jones says she discusses victimization in greater detail in single-sex workshops, where participants are more likely to disclose abuse. However, she does make use of mixed-group settings when she has certain goals in mind. "With co-ed groups, we can facilitate exchanges between the sexes about appropriate behaviors and how experiences might make a person feel. For example, we might ask a boy what he would do to get a girl's attention. He might say that he teases her or exhibits a behavior that might be considered sexual harassment. Then we ask the girls how a particular behavior makes them feel. They then can explain to the boys that certain behaviors embarrass them or hurt their feelings," explains Jones. "We can also demystify sexual violence and discuss how it affects both boys and girls."

There's at least one circumstance in which the gender of the educator and group can differ. Says Jones, "Sometimes we have young men talk with the girls. One of our consultants is a former athlete, and he conveys to the girls what boys do when they respect you. I think it's important for them to get the message from males and females."

Having survivors share their experiences can be among the most powerful learning experiences. "When an audience sees someone that looks like them or someone they look up to, it helps to destigmatize rape and increase sensitivity," explains Jones. "I believe experts are those who have been impacted. People listen to messages that come from the heart—they remember."

Professional sexual assault prevention educators vary in their opinions about untrained adults doing the teaching. "Bring in an expert!" urges Los Angeles Commission on Assaults Against Women associate director Leah Aldridge. Non-experts can mean well but without training may still reinforce myths or blame victims by suggesting that a girl who wears a skimpy outfit, gets drunk or high, or places herself in an intimate situation is at fault for being assaulted, instead of blaming the perpetrator for his decision to rape. They also may be unprepared to handle disclosures of abuse or assault should they come up.

Watson considers the credibility and trust that an already familiar teacher or group leader has with teens to be an asset in any prevention education workshop, even if they have no violence prevention background. However, they must be willing to put in time and effort to learn about sexual violence issues.

If you do decide to teach a group of young people about sexual violence on your own, consult an expert who can help design your curriculum and point you to age-appropriate resources. Discuss your goals, common student questions, reactions, and challenges you may face. Spend some time talking through your beliefs and assumptions about sexual violence, who perpetrators are, who victims are, how it affects individuals and communities. Attend a workshop for adults on the topic. Take a self-defense class. Remember, if you are ill prepared, you could do more harm than good.

Make sure teens understand the concepts they are learning by encouraging them to ask questions and engage in dialogue with the presenter. Allow them to share experiences of having witnessed various kinds of violence, against boys or girls, and the spiraling effects it can have.

Honesty and openness are key. Says Watson, "Being real just means not using complex vocabulary, and speaking from one's own experience. The presenter should refrain from 'preaching' to the group and [should] validate a youth's opinion, while providing alternative ideas."

NOTES

[1] Tjaden, Patricia, and Nancy Thoennes. *Full Report of the Prevalence, Incidence, and Consequences of Violence Against Women: Findings from the National Violence Against Women Survey* (Washington, D.C.: U.S. Department of Justice, National Institute of Justice, November 2000), 35.

[2] Snyder, Howard N. *Sexual Assault of Young Children as Reported to Law Enforcement: Victim, Incident, and Offender Characteristics* (Washington, D.C.: Bureau of Justice Statistics, July 2000), 12-13.

[3] Detroit Police Department Rape Counseling Center. *Sexual Abuse—A Threat to Our Children* (South Deerfield, Mass.: Channing Bete Co., 1995), 3.

[4] Smith, George Edmond. *Walking Proud: Black Men Living Beyond the Stereotypes* (New York: Kensington, 2001), 177.

[5] Snyder, 8.

[6] *Ibid.*, 10.

[7] *Ibid.*, 4.

[8] Neuman, Erica. "Signs of Child Sexual Abuse" in Sex Ed Mom Archive of

Oxygen website [cited 23 July 2002]; available at www.oxygen.com/experts/ sex_ed_mom/sex_ed_mom_20010823.jhtml. "Protecting Our Children" in Women's Coalition of St. Croix website [cited 23 July 2002]; available at www.wcstx.com/childabu.htm.

9 See note 7 above.

10 Tjaden and Thoennes, 35.

11 Office of the Surgeon General. *The Surgeon General's Call to Action to Promote Sex ʻal Health and Responsible Sexual Behavior* (9 July 2001), 7.

12 *Ibid.*

13 "Early Warning Signs For Parents" in Teen Dating Violence section of Melrose Alliance Against Violence website [cited 30 July 2002]; available at www.maav.org.

14 "Building a Healthy Relationship" in Women's Coalition of St. Croix website [cited 23 July 2002]; available at www.wcstx.com/hlthyrel.htm.

15 Latimer, Leah Y. "R. Kelly and the P Word" in BET website [cited 20 September 2002]; available at www.bet.com/articles/0,,c3gb2682-3344,00.html.

16 Lamb, Yanick Rice, et al. "Talking to Our Girls about Sex?" *Essence* (March 2002), 144.

17 Office of the Surgeon General, 11.

18 Neuman.

19 Office of the Surgeon General, 8.

20 See note 15 above.

21 "Creating and Supporting The Village to Raise the Child" in The Rites of Passage Institute website [cited 24 July 2002]; available at www.ritesofpassage.org/rites.htm.

22 Lindquist, Scott. *The Date Rape Prevention Book: The Essential Guide for Girls and Women* (Naperville, Ill.: Sourcebooks, 2000), 78.

CHAPTER 10

RESPONDING TO OPPRESSION:
Attitudes and Solutions in the Black Community

People who want to eradicate sexual violence, to comprehensively eliminate the aspects of our society that perpetuate sexual assault and abuse, must untangle the problem from its roots. A look at the history of the sexual victimization of African Americans and their struggles against it will help illuminate African-American attitudes about sexual violence today. The experiences and advice of women and men already on the path toward a rape-free society will inspire and, hopefully, propel you into action.

"We need to talk honestly about the vulnerabilities of both Black men and Black women historically and now," says Aaronette White, a psychologist and resident scholar of African-American Gender Studies at Wilberforce University. "There's a connection between the rape of Black women during slave times and the present. We need to make a connection between false charges against Black men during Reconstruction up until now. At the same time, we have to emphasize how rape, in particular, disproportionately negatively affects women, without having to bite our tongues, [and recognize] how it's hurting all of us."

The roots of the sexual victimization of Black people on American soil extend back to our arrival in North America. The same collective mindset that supported the enslavement of an entire race of people legitimized the routine sexual exploitation of Black women.

Rape has never been a matter of sexual desire. In the landmark book *Women, Race and Class*, scholar Angela Davis wrote, "Rape was a weapon of domination, a weapon of repression, whose covert goal was to extinguish slave women's will to resist, and in the process, to demoralize their men."[1] Raping Black women was an integral part of controlling and reproducing free labor, and consequently, of U.S. economic development.

It is impossible to know exactly how many Black women were raped during slavery. But enough of a historical record exists to know that it was commonplace. It was so prevalent that nearly 50 percent of people of color in antebellum cities like St. Louis, New Orleans, and Baltimore were of mixed race.[2] According to historian Darlene Clark Hine, "Virtually every known nineteenth-century female slave narrative contains a reference to, at some juncture, the ever-present threat and reality of rape."[3]

The rape of enslaved Black women reached perhaps its most pathological extremes when slavers decided to "breed" more slaves. Periodicals ran articles about the best conditions for breeding slaves, a popular conversation topic.[4] One-third of enslaved people on U.S. President James Madison's plantation were younger than age five, an indication of intentional breeding. One freed African, James Roberts, described a plantation he'd lived on where fifty to sixty Black women were reserved for the sexual access of White men only. The plantation owner could sell racially mixed children for more money than non-mixed children.[5]

According to White, whether or not breeding was systematic is peripheral. "Black women were used sexually in a number of ways. Sometimes the masters let their sons sleep with Black women for their first sexual experience. Sometimes the masters would let their friends who were coming there just for a party go out there and get one of the women. And we know that they were raped by their masters and that they were forced to sleep with Black men," explains White. "The point is that they had no sexual autonomy. And that is the injustice, that Black women did not own their body. Period."

Black women simply did not have the right to not be violated. An enslaved girl named Celia was repeatedly raped from the time she was acquired by Missouri farmer Robert Newsom in 1850. Five years later, she was in her third pregnancy when she resisted another rape with force, killing Newsom. Though state law indicated that a woman was justified in killing a man trying to rape her, a judge ruled that the law did not apply to Celia because she was a slave. She was hanged.[6]

Sadly, emancipation didn't make Black women safer. "Unfortunately for southern Black women, Reconstruction escalated the degree of violence, especially sexual violation, to which they might be subjected. Slave women were prey to the abuses of their owners, but with Emancipation, White men as a race rather than slave owners as a class viewed sexual trespass as a privilege, a right that might reinstitute White supremacy," says the encyclopedic volume *Black Women in America*.[7]

Whites used methodical violence, including organized gang rapes, to wipe out Black gains made during Reconstruction and maintain economic and political dominance.[8] Burning homes and churches and raping women were frequent practices of Ku Klux Klan terrorism of Black communities. Rape was a tool of terror just as lynching was.

The White-created myth of Black women as hypersexual, animalistic creatures had always been a justification for their rape. So deeply imbedded was the belief, that South Carolina Senator Cole Blease said early in the twentieth century, there was "serious doubt as to whether the crime of rape can be committed upon a Negro."[9] The parallel myth of Black men as oversexed beasts took firm root during the Reconstruction period. The protection of White women, who were supposedly endangered as the objects of Black male lust, was a main justification for epidemic lynchings.

During slavery, hundreds of White abolitionists were lynched. Immediately following the end of slavery, lynchings of Black men flourished as a result of White conspiracy theories about Black rebellions, and to suppress Black economic and political empowerment. Once African Americans' post-slavery aspirations toward equality had been squashed, the "political invention" of the Black rapist brute became the most effective justification for lynching Black men, writes Angela Davis.[10]

Crusading African-American anti-lynching activist and journalist Ida B. Wells-Barnett presented one of the first analyses to accurately link the lynching of Black men and the rape of Black women. White men, she explained, unjustifiably victimized Black men for false charges of sexual crimes, while raping Black women with impunity. She estimated that more than ten thousand lynchings occurred from 1865 to 1895 alone.[11] Many of the Black men hung or burned to death were castrated as well. Some Black women were tortured and killed, although fewer than men, for reasons including resisting sexual assault or publicly naming White perpetrators.

"The myth of the Black rapist of White women is the twin of the myth of the bad Black woman—both designed to apologize for and facilitate the continued exploitation of Black men and women. Black women perceived this connection very clearly and were early in the forefront of the fight against lynching," wrote Gerda Lerner in *Black Women in White America*.[12]

Sexual victimization of African-American women reached far beyond the brutality of Klan terrorists and lynch mobs. Well into the twentieth century, one of the few wage-earning opportunities available to Black women who had to support their families was working as domestics, often live-ins. For many women, this meant increased exposure to sexual abuses.[13]

The Legacy

This legacy of violence and sexual victimization affects every member of society, but Black women continue to bear more than their share of the fallout. African Americans today can be very empathetic about the subject of sexual violence, but, says Neil Irvin, director of community education at the Washington, D.C.-based organization Men Can Stop Rape, "Some of the historical interpretations of our sexuality get in the way of us having a unified voice."

African Americans have not made addressing sexual assault and abuse a collective priority. "Because people have been so ashamed, if this is something that has happened to them, that it's not something that's pushed [as an issue]. It's not something that families want people to know that their daughters have experienced. It's not something that husbands want people to know, that their wives or their daughters have had this experience, so it's under the rug. For so many hundreds of years now people are not getting the kind of support that they need," says Ruth Sallee-Gresham, a race and gender equity consultant with the Ohio Department of Education.

Sallee-Gresham witnessed many manifestations of this legacy while working at universities. She recounts a 1971 rape at the University of Illinois, Urbana-Champaign, where she was a residence hall director. Two African-American male students raped an African-American female student. "I called campus police and explained to them that there had been a rape in the building. I had the student with me. And the first question [from the White officer] was, 'Is she Black or White?'" Sallee-Gresham says. "I was stunned and I said it doesn't matter. Just send someone." He likely asked the question because of the lasting racist notion that the importance of sexual victimization varies depending on who the victim is.

Says White, "There is this idea that Black women's rapes are not as important as White women's rapes. That's not just my opinion. The facts are such that the highly publicized rapes tend to be the rapes of White women. And then too, there is this notion that Black women are not as pure as White women and that comes back from slavery and the idea that ideal womanhood is a White woman." These racial biases are institutionalized to this day. "Black women's rapes are taken less seriously in the criminal justice system," White adds. "Recent studies have shown that judges generally impose harsher sentences for rape when the victim is White than when the victim is Black, and that the behavior of White jurors shows a similar bias."

The perpetrators in the University of Illinois case were never punished. "There was a really ridiculous response from the community," says Sallee-Gresham about the students' peers of both sexes who tried "to make a big joke out of it."

Thirty years later, there is still a tendency among African Americans to trivialize sexual victimizations of women, particularly in cases of acquaintance rape. Says White, "It's important to acknowledge the sexism in the Black community, that a lot of sexist notions about Black women run rampant, even within our own community."

Cassandra Thomas, senior vice president of direct services for the Houston Area Women's Center, agrees. "We don't put as much emphasis on the lives of women in our community as we do on the lives of men," she says. "Certainly a big issue is that as women, we tend to just say if it happens, just move on. We don't make as big a deal about it as we could."

When Sallee-Gresham was the assistant director of student and staff development at Ohio State University three years after the University of Illinois assault, some eight Black members of an athletic team gang-raped an African-American student. The perpetrators were not punished, Sallee-Gresham believes, because of the cachet afforded athletes as well as the trivialization of assaults against Black women.

In this case, protesters, primarily White lesbian students, held a sit-in in the president's office to demand that the perpetrators be punished. "I remembered that just the week before there had been a gang rape over in one of the fraternity houses on campus. It was all-White. It was a White female who had been gang-raped. Nobody said a word," Salee-Gresham recalls. "I was uncomfortable because it really made it look as if the only rapists were Black men."

The overlooking of White men's violence against women deepens the enduring myth of the Black rapist. Racist notions about Black sexuality affect the treatment of both women and men in today's criminal justice system. "We do need to raise that question of how Black men are prosecuted more, they're falsely charged more, and they get harder sentences than White men [for sexual assault]," says White.

The ignoring of White male violence isn't just bad for African Americans. "If [White] girls and women continue to be warned only about the danger Black male perpetrators represent, they will continue to be more vulnerable to assault by White male perpetrators, who statistically are much more likely to assault them," states Joseph Weinberg, a Wisconsin-based sexual violence educator. He continues, "If boys and men continue to be taught that Black males are the predominant perpetrators of sexual assault, White male perpetrators will be discouraged from understanding their behavior as assault."[14]

As has been the case throughout U.S. history, sexist and racist oppression are inextricably linked. The rape myths of White male innocence and Black male guilt are reciprocal notions that help reinforce White privilege. Says Weinberg, "I believe that racial inequality and the stereotyping of people of color—racism—is the single largest element in the creation and maintenance of rape culture."[15]

Ohio State University's president responded to protesters by providing funding for self-defense classes. When Sallee-Gresham noticed that no students of color were attending, she took a few out to lunch to explain the importance of the workshop. They promised to attend that evening, and got as close as the hallway of the session, but walked away at the last minute. "They didn't give me a reason, but when I looked down the hall, I could see that there was a bevy of Black brothers down the hall. And so I approached them and I said, 'I don't understand. This could happen to your mother, your sister, your girlfriend, your wife, your aunt, your grandmother.' And they said, 'No, we'll take care of our women,'" she recalls.

Their attitude bears out yet another historical legacy. "In a context in society where certainly you have the idea that men should be in charge, you have Black men who internalized this patriarchal message that Black men have to be in control of their women, in control of their communities, and not the notion that Black men and Black women together can control them," says White. "They almost are [pleading] that they be allowed to be the same kind of patriarchy as White men instead of criticizing the entire system in a revolutionary way."

In another case of rape in a university setting, White shares her own story of sexual assault. As a senior, White was told by a high-ranking African-American administrator that he had selected her to accompany him on a research trip in an African country, and that she needed to come to his apartment for language lessons. After the first lesson, he suggested they get accustomed to sleeping in close quarters. "Gosh, am I acting like a prude? I mean, come on, this is an administrator. He's not going to bite me," she recalls thinking. "And then he just attacked me."

When she confided in another African-American university official, she was told, "You can't say anything. He's the top Black administrator at this predominantly White university. They're not going to believe you anyway because you were over there. Students flirt with administrators all the time. They're going to say you were flirting with him."

Says Thomas, "We still buy into several myths. [As] strong Black women, we just can take whatever and move on. And the other one is that we have to take care of men. If we take care of men, then we're not going to report men who are violent."

These myths harm not only women, but the entire community. "It eats away at the unity that we need to fight racism. It breaks down the camaraderie that we need to pull together," says White.

The oppression of Black men is given priority over the oppression of Black women. African-American women survivors end up doing what's best for Black men without regard for what's best for themselves. Black women are less likely to report sexual violation than other women for many reasons, including sexist victim-blaming and centuries-old racist stereotypes about Black sexuality. It all adds up to a tenacious conspiracy of silence.

Each of the crimes recounted above occurred when the anti-rape movement was in its infancy. While mainstream America and the African-American community have become more knowledgeable and empathetic about rape, these attitudes are still alive and well.

Beginning in the late 1980s, a string of particularly brutal sexual assaults brought these all-American legacies of sexism and racism into the limelight. Silence, at least for a moment in history, was broken.

In November 1987, fifteen-year-old African-American Tawana Brawley was found, smeared with feces, racist and sexist slurs written on her skin. She said six White law enforcement officers raped her. A police officer who fit a description she had given killed himself shortly after she was found. A grand jury met for seven months to determine if there was probable cause to prosecute. In a highly charged political climate, Brawley's lawyers advised her not to cooperate with the investigation. With no testimony from the victim or her family, the grand jury decided not to indict the suspects in October 1988.[16]

In April 1989, several Black and Latino boys gang-raped a White woman who was jogging in New York City's Central Park. She was beaten and left for dead. Six were charged with rape and assault. In August 1990, three boys were convicted in a jury trial.[17] In March of 1990, five White members of St. John's University's lacrosse team and one White member of the rifle club used alcohol to facilitate the gang rape of a Black female college student. Three were acquitted in a 1991 trial and three later plead guilty to reduced charges bargained down from original felony charges.[18]

Historically, highly publicized rape trials in the United States have involved interracial crimes. Then along came two intraracial cases that exposed enduring wounds of sexism, classism, and racism of the mainstream and within the Black community more publicly than ever before.

A White woman, Patricia Bowman, accused William Kennedy Smith of raping her on Easter weekend 1991. Over the following months, the prosecutors found several other women who acknowledged being a victim of rape or assault by Smith. A member of arguably one of the most elite White families in United States history, Smith was found not guilty later that year.[19] And in July 1991, heavyweight-boxing champion Mike Tyson was accused of raping an eighteen-year-old Black woman. He was found guilty in February 1992.[20]

Although much of the discussion these cases generated was steeped in racist and sexist myths and stereotypes, ultimately they did spur more open dialogue about sexual violence nationwide. "It just had such a tremendous impact," says White. "It allowed women to start talking about it more. And by doing that you raise the consciousness of women."

History of Anti-Rape Activism

Throughout U.S. history, there have been African American-led grassroots efforts and small-scale acts of resistance against sexual victimization. According to Davis, Black women's club members held one of the first organized protests against sexual victimization in the late 1800s.

Tera W. Hunter's book *To Joy My Freedom*, lists several examples of African-American men organizing shortly after the Civil War ended to stop sexual violations of Black women by White men in cities such as Savannah, Richmond, and Mobile. Hunter also mentions a Black women's effort in the early 1900s to pass a law against incest and to hold batterers accountable for violence against women and children in their own community.[21] And of course, individual women resisted and fought sexual violence in their own creative and resourceful ways.

But the period of heightened activism known as the anti-rape movement would not happen for many decades. Says Janelle White, director of the University of New Orleans's Women's Center, "When the anti-rape movement started in the seventies, it really was about social change and challenging the institutions that contribute to violence against women." Out of this movement, rape crisis centers were born, which have shifted focus from politics to health services. Now, more than nine hundred of these facilities serve survivors nationwide.

The anti-rape movement and the women's movement were predominantly White and middle class. However, Thomas challenges the belief that feminism was irrelevant to African Americans. "The anti-rape movement came out of the women's movement. And the women's movement was reactivated because of the civil rights movement," she explains. "So the truth is that we owe where we are now to the civil rights movement. Had it not been for those ordinary people doing activist work and showing us that ordinary people can make a difference, then women probably would not have begun to do what they did."

Some Black women activists understood quite early the need to participate in various movements at the same time. One of those women is Loretta Ross. The third African American in the country to direct a rape crisis center, she ran the D.C. Rape Crisis Center from 1979 to 1982.

"As we [women of color] entered this process, we always brought with us an understanding of the fight against racism and the fight against colonialism and the fight against apartheid being very much a part of the fight to end violence against women. And I think that's what conceptually and ideologically distinguished us from the [mainstream] movement to end violence against women," says Ross, now the founding executive director of the Atlanta-based National Center for Human Rights Education. "That broader movement rarely offered a critique of the American system. They [White feminists] just didn't like that fact that some of them were victimized by it."

The women's movement never embraced the issues of people of color. Says Aaronette White, "The mainstream feminist movement has not talked about some of the racist rape myths that make rape in the Black community a much more complex situation to understand."

A dramatic example of this split began in 1975. Joanne Little was tried for the self-defense killing of a White prison guard who had raped her in a North Carolina jail. She was supported by African-American organizations and women's groups and was acquitted. She went on to support a Black man on death row in Florida, Delbert Tibbs, falsely accused of raping a White woman. White women in the anti-rape movement were reluctant to support him, despite Little's appeals. All charges against him were dropped three years after Little's trial.[22]

Thomas recalls, "It became, 'Well, either do civil rights work or do women's work.' And for a Black woman there isn't that separation. You have to do both. So that moved lots of African-American women out of the women's movement."

According to Ross, "One of the things that really failed to materialize, at least to my satisfaction, is an affirmation and confirmation of the leadership of women of color in the movement." Without diverse leadership, women of color have not had the institutionalized power to ensure culturally relevant programs and a broadened focus to address factors other than sexism that contribute to sexual violence. "But that doesn't mean that we failed in any way because I think that even without that institutional transformation, every community of color now recognizes violence against women as a problem. And so we had considerable political impact even though we had very little institutionalized power," she says.

That mainstream anti-rape organizations have continued to be majority White doesn't mean African-American women stopped organizing against sexual violence. At the height of the women's movement, there were a handful of Black women's activist organizations that included sexual violence on their agenda, including the Combahee River Collective and the Third World Women's Alliance, which developed out of the Student Non-Violent Coordinating Committee. The ideologies and philosophies of the anti-apartheid movement and other anti-oppression movements converged to form what was referred to as Black feminist thought.

Black women did not form anti-rape organizations because women of color could not afford to be single-issue activists. Says Ross, "You found a lot of allies, for example, in the Committee to End Sterilization Abuse, which was largely Black, Latina, and Native-American women coming together around reproductive rights. But that also meant that they came together around violence against women."

Recommends Aaronette White, "Ultimately, more than likely, Black people are going to have to do what they've always done, and that is form our own anti-rape movement, but then form coalitions with more established movements at critical junctures."

Community Solutions Today

In the era of sit-ins and freedom riders, everybody knew the country was in the midst of a civil rights movement. While there may not be nationally recognizable signs that a movement against sexual violence is transpiring today, anti-rape efforts are going on all the time. There are African Americans across the country who refuse to be satisfied with the advancement of rape crisis centers. They are addressing and organizing against sexual violence in culturally relevant ways in order to create social change.

Just what is meant by social change? According to social change expert Lawrence H. Mamiya, a professor of religion and Africana studies at Vassar College, it is "an attempt to bring about change in people's attitudes and in institutions and behavior, through either reformist means or sometimes revolutionary means."

Mamiya lays out the primary steps of social change. Consciousness-raising is the first step, often occurring after a personal experience with the phenomenon. Community organizing, frequently a long-term process, is the second step. "You need to gather first of all those people who have been oppressed by a certain issue. They will form the core group that will try to mobilize others," he says. "And community organization also involves bringing in as many community groups as possible on the issue."

The coalition should then agree on specific goals and come up with various strategies to achieve them. A critical ingredient of your plan should be getting media coverage in order for the message to reach enough people to garner momentum for the cause.

Sexual violence in the Black community is an even more complex issue to organize against than racist enemies. "Part of the problem with sexual and domestic violence is that they involve people within the community," he says. "That makes it difficult. It is easier to mobilize people when you have a target like the [Ku Klux] Klan or the government or city hall or the police."

Challenging? Definitely. But hardly impossible. Following are two successful cases of anti-rape grassroots organizing within the African-American community.

Taking on Mike Tyson[23]

In February 1992, boxer Mike Tyson was convicted of raping a Black woman, Desiree Washington, in St. Louis during the weekend of the Miss Black America pageant in which she was a contestant. During the trial and appeals process, sexist and racist attitudes about African Americans and sexual assault were asserted by lawyers trying the case, and commonly made in national and local media, including some African-American media outlets. African-American leaders who had vigorously defended Tawana Brawley attacked Desiree Washington, assailing the credibility and trustworthiness of Black women.

Despite testimony from Black women that Tyson had groped and verbally disrespected them during the weekend of Washington's assault, and a defense attorney's acknowledgment of this behavior during the trial, prominent African Americans insisted that Tyson was the victim in the situation. They circulated petitions calling for leniency and held prayer vigils on his behalf. They also accused Washington of being complicit in another White racist attack on a Black man.

A group of five Black feminists along with an informal organization of women who worked at a St. Louis university wanted to do something to address what they saw as profound misunderstandings in the Black community about rape. They decided to educate their community with an anti-rape campaign. An additional goal of the group was to encourage African-American women to speak out about rape. The women realized they could reach a significant portion of their community by producing a newspaper ad. It was to be modeled after the 1991 ad placed in *The New York Times* and six Black newspapers by African-American women in support of Anita Hill during the Clarence Thomas Supreme Court confirmation hearings.

The first task of the St. Louis organizers was to assess and interpret the situation in a way that would mobilize support for their position. Group members took on various tasks, including monitoring local talk shows for common comments, obtaining *Court TV* videos of Tyson's trial, and gathering current rape statistics. In reviewing the collected information, three primary themes emerged. First, the Black community believed in a White conspiracy against Black men that used Black women as pawns. Second, whether or not an assault actually happened, African Americans should not publicly air dirty laundry. Third, a pervasive lack of understanding of rape, its victims and perpetrators, existed within the community.

They then drafted a statement countering rape myths with facts and explaining the race, class, and gender dimensions of the sexual violence problem. The women set about getting one hundred Black women to lend their names in support of the statement, which would be published in a newspaper at the time of the appeals decision, giving them about a month. Their most successful recruiting strategy was giving presentations at all-women social gatherings and organization meetings. At these events, the women introduced the topic by singing relevant songs and reading poetry. They often found themselves in the middle of rap sessions at which women told of their own painful histories of sexual assault and abuse. Of the 112 women who supported the statement, ninety-two allowed their names to be printed.

The ad ran in the free, high circulation, Black weekly newspaper, the *St. Louis American*, on April 15, 1993. With significant positive responses, the organizers decided to reprint the ad with men supporters' names listed. They agreed that Black men should take responsibility for the emotionally challenging work of explaining and debating sexual violence issues at all-male gatherings. Male activists collected the names of 148 male supporters. The ad ran in the same newspaper with a total of 240 African Americans' names on October 21, 1993.

As a result, a Black columnist at St. Louis's largest mainstream newspaper interviewed the organizers for an article about their work and the issues it presented. More importantly, the initial effort transformed into a one-year-long education campaign, an unplanned consequence of the ad. Organizers continued to hold women's and men's groups on the topic, and to teach community groups about rape prevention.

Ending a Chicago Nightmare

The St. Louis case developed at the conclusion of a high-profile trial of a world-famous athlete. Very different circumstances triggered a triumphant grassroots organizing effort in Chicago almost a decade later: ongoing serial rapes—receiving too little publicity—in working-class neighborhoods. Between May and August of 2000, nine sexual assaults following a similar pattern took place on the South Side of Chicago. Young Black women who used public transportation were robbed and raped near bus stops. The assaults started up again in March of 2001.

Says community activist Elizabeth King, "The serial rapes were like my September 11. They were a terrorist act of an unimaginable magnitude that had a life-altering effect on the people in my community and changed my world forever."

As a consultant she had the time and flexibility to devote several months to organizing Black women to help stop the rapes. "I made a choice that this is what I want to do, full-time, right now," says King, who grew up on Chicago's South Side. "My mom's living at ground zero where these rapes are happening. Boom. I'm doing this."

For eleven years, King had periodically organized roundtables, which she defines as a collective of community leaders that focuses attention on a critical issue and pools resources to create solutions. She initially decided to form a citywide roundtable to address the crisis. She started collecting basic facts about the case by calling local television news programs and police. She quickly distributed a leadership roundtable proposal for money and in-kind donations to four institutions. None were willing to support her effort.

When she heard that two more rapes had been committed, she narrowed her proposed roundtable's participants to Black women, and invited every Black woman in her rolodex to attend the initial meeting. This time, the Chicago Department of Public Health Office of Violence Prevention, headed by an African-American woman, chose to provide a meeting space, supplies, and other in-kind support. Forty women met at the Black Women's Leadership Roundtable in June 2001. Their mandate was to create a collaborative solution to address at least one solvable element of the immediate problem, the serial assaults known as the bus stop rapes.

Churches represented by the organization Black United Methodist Pastors established a two thousand-dollar reward for tips leading to the capture of the rapist. "One of the main things that our group thought that we could do in an action-oriented way [was] raise some funds and bring that up to at least ten thousand dollars," says King. "If we're going to put a price on the value of a Black woman's life or dignity, let it not be two thousand dollars."

Roundtable participant Terri Gardner, then-president of Soft Sheen/Carson Products, spearheaded the contributions group of the roundtable, which raised an additional eight thousand dollars. The roundtable aired public service announcements about the reward on

Black and youth format radio stations. That fundraising effort spurred the FBI and local institutions to contribute to the fund, which reached twenty-five thousand dollars.[24]

Says Courtney Avery, a roundtable member and program director of the Sexual Assault Prevention Initiative of Chicago's Mayor's Office on Domestic Violence, "Our original goals at that time were to get the word out and put pressure on officials in the city of Chicago about what was being done about the bus stop sexual assaults, because it seemed like they were laying by the wayside." She recalls Black community members' frequent comparison of police handling of this case to a similar one. From April through June of 2000, a serial rapist assaulted seven Asian women and one Latina woman. By August of the same year, the FBI caught the perpetrator in the Philippines.

Recalls King, "The roundtable was the impetus for a group of Black women to meet with the superintendent of police, the top cop in the city, and say, 'We're frustrated, we're scared, and we're concerned. And what are you doing?' I think that really changed the position of the bus stop rapes on the docket. It began a dialogue about concerns and an exchange of key information that empowered every Black woman in the city."

Out of that meeting, King developed a relationship with the superintendent of police, which helped facilitate the funneling of information about the case to the Black community. The roundtable obtained sketches of the assailants immediately after they were revised and distributed them through members. Two Black women police detectives, the highest-ranking Black women in the department, became part of the roundtable.

When Gardner, a minister of a Cherokee spirituality, decided she wanted to do a cleansing and clearing ceremony at the crime sites to help bring about a resolution, the roundtable was able to get permission from the police, ensuring that they didn't interrupt the ongoing investigation and that police didn't interrupt them. Gardner also created a Prayer for Peace Day. More than two hundred faith communities in Chicago were invited to pray for peace in local communities, with an emphasis on ending violence against women.

Another major contribution to the effort was a communications tool. The roundtable launched the website StopTheAssaults.com, where users could file anonymous crime tips, access a rape crisis directory, and get updates about the investigation.

King says she was also determined "to raise Black women's voices and visibility on the issue of the bus stop rapes in an effort to help stop those rapes. We were a small—but don't underestimate us—part of keeping the issue out there. Black women are usually cast as voiceless or followers or unempowered or victims. The roundtable helped keep empowered images of Black women out front as proactive crisis managers, community leaders, and experts on a crisis that uniquely affected us."

The Black Women's Leadership Roundtable was only one of many multifaceted, concurrent grassroots efforts. While King was gearing up for the Black Women's Leadership Roundtable's first meeting, Rev. Al Sampson, a well-known civil rights activist in Chicago, was creating Operation Defense, which he calls "organizations within organizations committed to developing strategies to advocate for women who are being violated."

Along with Black United Methodist Pastors, Sampson started holding weekly community awareness forums in his church about the rapes. Representatives of community institutions as wide ranging as the Nation of Islam, the YWCA, and the Black Women's Leadership Roundtable, attended. Elected officials, police, and news reporters, were among those who shared information about the case with the community.

"Once we found out what the issues were, and what the inherent problems were, we were then able to talk about a strategy in terms of how are we going to now expose this as a crisis," says Rev. Felix D. Burrows, Sr., president of the Chicago chapter of Black United Methodist Pastors. Sampson held a press conference blasting the police for their handling of the case. "It put us in conflict—which is what we wanted—with the police department, causing them now to do their job," says Burrows.

Says Sampson, "We had shown that first and foremost there were White detectives controlling the information gathering on the cases, but they were trying to relegate it to robbery because they didn't place the value on the sisters. It wasn't until we started hollering that we want Black detectives who know the neighborhood, who know the people, that they broke that kind of process up. Then we went and challenged the FBI." Sampson sent a letter requesting that the FBI become involved in the case.

Operation Defense created several unique initiatives to help women stay safe and also maintain the media's focus on the case. They recruited African-American motorcycle clubs to drive through the areas of the rapes at night to deter more assaults. They offered free self-defense classes for women in churches, and they made available an escort service of men to accompany women who had to use public transportation at night.

Perhaps the most important element was daily television news coverage of Operation Defense and the other Black groups working in coalition to get the crimes solved and ensure African-American women's safety. "We were really dominating the news," Sampson reports.

A total of sixteen Black girls and women, from age fourteen to twenty-three, were raped. Three suspects were apprehended on September 5, 2001. "I think the case would have not been solved at all. Or they would have been caught in the act at some later point down the road," says Burrows, if not for Operation Defense.

"The roundtable achieved some level of success in raising Black women's voice and visibility during the bus stop rape crisis, and contributing in its own way to the resolution of the crime," says King. "I think [Operation Defense] played a very critical role. I think everybody who stepped forward played a really critical role in the whole thing."

Social Change Strategies

The anti-rape movement, like other progressive social movements, has gone mainstream. "There's a part of it people feel real comfortable with now, that every survivor should get some kind of services. But I think if it gets more political than that, there's a discomfort because it means that we're challenging power," says Janelle White. "So we're putting a Band-Aid on the problem. If you're a social movement, you want to address: What can we do to change the society in which we live so women don't have to face rape, so girls don't have to be abused?"

Loretta Ross agrees that a society-wide paradigm shift needs to happen, from simplifying sexual violence as unrelated incidents of assault, to "looking at it as a social problem that requires a broad-based social solution, not just individual therapy for men who need anger management counseling."

One initiative that attempts to create that solution is Incite! Women of Color Against Violence, a national activist organization that supports grassroots organizing in an effort to eradicate all types of violence against women of color. Formed in 2000, the organization sponsors activist institutes around the country to create community-based solutions to violence against women and communities, including alternatives to the criminal justice system. The group held a national conference, themed "Color of Violence: Building a Movement," in 2002, bringing together 1,600 participants, 95 percent of whom were women of color. Another is planned for 2005.

For women interested in independent activism or in starting a chapter of Incite!, you can get a detailed organizing packet, which includes information on how individuals and groups can contribute to the anti-violence against women movement. You can also contact an Incite! activist for guidance and support for your work.

King's Black Women's Leadership Roundtable did not end with the arrest of the perpetrators of the bus stop rapes. It continues to serve the Chicago community as a multifaceted communications network. Most recently, members have performed court advocacy for the serial rape survivors, created a traveling forum and been interviewed by various media outlets to keep the community informed about a new serial-rape crisis. They have also hosted Black Women's Dinners, which provide the opportunity for women to talk about their issues in a supportive atmosphere. The roundtable has continued to develop its relationships with activists and law enforcement and shared its experiences with Latinas facing a similar crisis.

Do not feel that you must be part of an organization to contribute to social change. Take the example of Daniel Whitner, an Atlanta dentist. When he heard reported on the local news that a thirteen-year-old girl had been gang-raped by as many as twenty African-American boys and men, he came up with actions to affect the individual survivor and the collective community.

"I said, 'Well, someone should respond to this because we need to tell our brothers and sisters that this is not proper behavior in our community, and we won't tolerate this type of behavior in our community.' That message had to be sent," he recalls. So he approached Concerned Black Clergy of Atlanta about helping him organize a prayer vigil. Local television and print media covered the event. In addition, he made a personal donation of one thousand dollars to the victim's family.

Whitner tried to wait for community leaders to speak out about the egregious crime. As a matter of fact, he waited about two months before he realized he had to speak out. A dentist is just as capable as anyone else of working toward the eradication of rape in the Black community.

Sexual violence has never placed high on the agendas of national Black leaders or mainstream African-American organizations, with the exception of sporadic incidents involving racially motivated assaults. "As far as I know, at the beginning of the [bus stop rapes'] media coverage, no one besides Rev. Sampson spoke out loudly, clearly, and publicly on the issue," says King. "Certainly among the questions I asked myself when I heard the news about the bus stop rapes was 'Where are the Black community leaders during this time of crisis?'"

Whitner urges that constituents demand more from leaders. "Be sure that when our community leaders are addressing problems, that we include that in their agenda," he says. "Organize yourself with people who feel the same way and address it to the community leader, to the political leader of neighborhood organizations." Try an email or letter-writing campaign or petition drive, and demand to meet with your community leaders about how fighting sexual violence will figure into their mission.

Informing your peers about the importance of incorporating anti-rape activities into community organizations and institutions is key. Says Burrows, "What I would recommend as a first thing is that there has to be a commitment to community awareness. Community education has to be done through your pulpits, it has to be done through your block club meetings. Almost inundate the community with this issue."

"We need to have open forums within our churches and other institutions to honestly address sexual violence against Black women. This includes dialogue about what rape means within our community and how we can collectively address this very serious concern," says Helen Neville, Black Radical Congress organizer and a professor at the University of Illinois at Urbana-Champaign. "The key here is to get community people to identify this as a serious problem that they are willing to work to eradicate."

Avery recommends assessing the needs of your own community "by talking to social service organizations, law enforcement, medical personnel, and citizens in that community. Also check to see if there's an existing program that provides comprehensive rape crisis services." Not only can these experts assist throughout your awareness-raising process, they can help you brainstorm goals. You will be able to determine what kinds of campaigns or protests are best suited for you, and what resources in your community are available to support your work. Seek out experts in grassroots organizing who can help you formulate strategies and goals for your anti-violence work.

"I have helped to get some organizations to make this a piece of their agenda. I'm constantly on the NAACP [chapter] here to put a little focus on women and not all the focus on men," says Thomas. "Black organizations need to be having this on their agenda and doing something." Although she has not been satisfied with their efforts, Houston's NAACP chapter has made a step in the right direction by starting a support group in the Black community for women who have been sexually abused.

Sallee-Gresham, who had helped organize a rape prevention education program at Ohio State University, brought the program to the Columbus Urban League in the 1980s. It is the only Urban League chapter with such a program.

According to rape prevention specialist Qiana Williams, the program is designed "to increase attention, awareness, and response to violence against women in the African-American community. We do this through education within schools, churches, and community organizations." The program receives slightly more than 1 percent of the Columbus Urban League's resources. Williams is its sole employee. While it is significant that the program has survived more than a decade, the lack of funding devoted to it indicates its priority level.

King felt disappointed by the lack of response she got from local civil rights organizations, fraternities, and sororities while organizing the Black Women's Leadership Roundtable. "It appeared to me that too many of the well-established, respected, traditional, mainstream Black organizations had no way for concerned citizens to contact them, access their help or services, let alone partner with them to act in the case of community crises," she said. But her persistence has paid off. "We've kept on networking for contacts and now, for example, the Chicago Pan-Hellenic Community Action Council is an important partner in the roundtable."

If you are a member of a community or civic organization, urge other members and its leaders to take action. Suggest hosting a fundraiser for a local rape crisis center or activist organization to get reluctant peers involved in the issue. Or perhaps your organization will consider launching a permanent sexual assault awareness program to serve your community.

Avery also recommends working with your state coalition against sexual assault to monitor legislation. "Within the Illinois Coalition Against Sexual Assault is a public affairs committee that monitors any laws that affect victims of sexual violence. They welcome people outside of the rape crisis center to participate on that committee." Investigate the possibility of participating in, or creating, a court-watching program to ensure fair treatment of survivors by monitoring trials.

Be sure to target your spiritual home. Meet with your minister about ways to address sexual violence within your congregation. After Burrows learned that a young woman in his church was being sexually abused by her stepfather, he started a health and wellness ministry. Through the ministry, church members and friends learn about various health topics, including sexual assault and abuse. Also, encourage your minister to become familiar with womanist biblical literature and begin to incorporate anti-abuse messages in sermons.

Don't allow the topic to get relegated to being a women's issue. "There needs to be space for Black men to challenge one another on their own levels of sexism: In what ways do they reinforce sexist behaviors at home, the job, in the community? In what ways do they challenge such behaviors? What can they collectively do within their own communities to address the concern?" says Neville. "We need to get men on board with the goals of the project. They need to feel like they can be part of the solution and not just the problem."

Says Irvin, "It's important for anyone, particularly men and men of color, to give them opportunities to participate in a way in which they feel comfortable doing so. Whether that be attending a rally or vigil, or whether that be helping on a mailing. Whether that be attending some kind of presentation or workshop. Provide as many options and try to make them as inclusive to men participating as they can possibly be. Because the problem is so big that I don't think any one answer is a solution, I think obviously it's going to take many different types of solutions. Provide those for the community."

NOTES

[1] Davis, Angela Y. *Women, Race and Class* (New York: Random House, 1981), 23-24.

[2] Berry, Mary Frances, and John W. Blassingame. *Long Memory: The Black Experience in America* (New York: Oxford University Press, 1982), 118.

[3] Hine, Darlene Clark. *Hine Sight: Black Women and the Re-Construction of American History* (Brooklyn: Carlson Publishing, 1994), 38.

[4] White, Deborah Gray. *Ar'n't I a Woman? Female Slaves in the Plantation South* (New York: W.W. Norton and Company, 1985), 31.

[5] Wyatt, Gail Elizabeth. *Stolen Women: Reclaiming Our Sexuality, Taking Back Our Lives* (New York: John Wiley and Sons, 1997), 13.

[6] Hine, Darlene Clark, Elsa Barkley Brown, and Rosalyn Terborg-Penn, eds. *Black Women in America: An Historical Encyclopedia, Volume I* (Bloomington: Indiana University Press, 1993), 703.

[7] *Ibid.*, 247.

[8] Hunter, Tera W. *To Joy My Freedom: Southern Black Women's Lives and Labors After the Civil War* (Cambridge: Harvard University Press, 1997), 33.

[9] Berry and Blassingame, 115-116.

[10] Davis, 183-184.

[11] See note 9 above.

[12] Lerner, Gerda, ed. *Black Women in White America: A Documentary History* (New York: Vintage Books, 1992), 193-194.

[13] Hunter, 106.

[14] Weinberg, Joseph. "Rape and Racism: Issues for Educators," *Teaching Sexual Ethics: The Joseph Weinberg and Associates Newsletter* (January 1998), 8.

[15] *Ibid.*, 1.

[16] "The Truth About Tawana Brawley," in Abuse/Incest Support website [cited 24 July 2002]; available at incestabuse.about.com/library/weekly/aa121997.htm.

[17] McFadden, Robert D., and Susan Saulny. "Prosecutor seeks the Reversal of Convictions in the Jogger Case," *The New York Times* (6 December 2002); and Flynn, Kevin, and Jim Dwyer. "Reconsidering Other Verdicts in the Jogger Case," *The New York Times* (2 December 2002).

[18] Fried, Joseph P. "St. John's Sex Abuse Case Ends With Plea Bargain," *New York Times* (12 February 1992), B3.

[19] Sanday, Peggy Reeves. *A Woman Scorned: Acquaintance Rape on Trial* (New York: Doubleday, 1996), 210-221.

[20] Steptoe, Sonja. "A Damnable Defense," *Sports Illustrated* (24 February 1992), 92.

[21] Hunter, 34, 138.

[22] Davis, 174-175.

[23] White, Aaronette M. "Talking Feminist, Talking Black: Micromobilization Process in a Collective Protest Against Rape," *Gender & Society* 13, no. 1 (February 1999).

[24] Strausberg, Chinta. "Sampson, Obadela Hail FBI's $10,000 Rape Reward," *Chicago Defender* (5 July 2001), 4.

PART II
SURVIVORS' STORIES OF HEALING

Four wonderful souls share their stories of healing here. Audrey is a domestic violence survivor. Christopher is a child sexual abuse survivor. Marta is a survivor of acquaintance rape. And Audree is a survivor of stranger rape. They have achieved varying degrees of healing in different ways.

They decided to tell their stories because they wanted to inspire and encourage as many survivors as possible. If you are a survivor, you may recognize some of their feelings, thoughts, and behaviors. You will certainly be reminded that you are not alone in your struggle to heal. They offer their stories not as the best or only way to heal, but to give you ideas about healing by explaining what has worked for them. I hope these stories will encourage you to continue striving for the peace and well-being that everyone is capable of achieving.

Please be aware that reading about the assault or abuse of someone else can be traumatic, depending on how far along you are in your healing process. Although the stories here do not generally go into extreme detail about the assaults themselves, feel free to skip over the paragraphs describing the violations if you are concerned that it might be harmful to you.

These survivors have told their stories because they want to contribute to the healing of families and communities as well. Whether you are supporting a loved one who has been victimized or are simply concerned about the tragedy of sexual violence in your area, these stories can help you understand how sexual assault and abuse impacts individuals and their communities.

The decision by Audrey, Christopher, Marta, and Audree to share their triumph over terror is a special gift for us all. To these magnificent guides helping us navigate our way to truth and wholeness, thank you and may God bless you.

AUDREY'S STORY

Surviving child abuse can be challenging on its own, but Audrey has overcome even more than that. For fourteen years she was married to a man who abused her emotionally and physically. As is the case for many who experience domestic violence, rape was part of the pattern of victimization she suffered. Since summoning up the courage to divorce her husband and press criminal charges against him, Audrey has been immersed in healing work—for herself and others. This community-oriented mother of two with a healthy sense of humor tells us how her commitment to healing has paid off handsomely.

As part of my work I do stress management workshops, often in high schools and colleges. Sometimes I'll ask people, "What's a source of stress for you?" Some young ladies will raise their hand and say, "My boyfriend, he doesn't do the things that I want to do. We always have to do what he wants to do." When I was that age it was, "Look, we're either going to do some things that we both like to do or you get lost." It was just cut-and-dry. How I ended up so different in the marriage, I don't know. That self-esteem dwindled down to zero.

I am from a small town named Mound Bayou, Mississippi. Family life was simple; we raised cotton and soybeans. My dad owned a couple hundred acres of land and farmed it all with my five brothers running the farm equipment and the three girls working the fields. I am the seventh child.

I don't have a lot of memories of my childhood because I was molested. I don't know who molested me. At one point I was so intensely focused on trying to remember, and then I realized it's just not that important. It's more important that I accept that it happened and deal with it.

When I started dating during high school, those relationships were pretty much normal. If there was any hint of abuse, it would have been me being the aggressor. I was angry at the world. Angry about the abuse. Angry about not being able to tell people. Possibly angry because I felt that folks should have known even if I didn't tell them.

At seventeen I left home for Delta State University, about nine miles away. Even though it was so close to home, it was exciting to be out on my own. It was nice to be away from what I considered to be the source of my issues. And it was refreshing to be able to see different things, talk to different kinds of people, not just folks that lived right there in Mound Bayou.

I was one of those kids who was at the head of the class all through school, and that was just boring. Nobody liked the smart kid in class. So you kind of wanted to not be smart so that you wouldn't be the outcast. But I was also hell-bent on not wanting to need other people's approval. So I wasn't the kind of person that would join a sorority. I just kept saying, "I don't have this need to belong. I don't need you. I don't need your approval. You need mine."

I wasn't really into the party scene. I went to some of the games. I went to the dances, different meetings. I just went to see what was going on, but I didn't have this great excitement about being out there. Looking back, maybe my aversion to joining groups was some form of self-imposed isolation: "If I belong, if I join, somebody might figure out my secret."

My leisure time was spent reading—I used to sleep with books in my bed. I read a broad variety of genres, except romance novels. They were just too far-fetched, from where I was coming from. My favorite author was Maya Angelou. Not because she was also sexually abused as a child, which she wrote about in *I Know Why the Caged Bird Sings*, but because of her struggle after she left home, finding her way in the world. She was strong-willed and strong-minded. She went through a lot of crap. And she went through some guys who weren't good for her. And she had her son. Just that common struggle that many women go through.

It was at Delta State that I met the "sperm donor"— my daughter's nickname for my ex-husband and her father. By the way, I don't discourage her from saying that. Some people say, "Don't say ugly things about your father." When people do that, they are negating your feelings. They're invalidating you and how you feel. So when she says "sperm donor," I don't care. I actually laugh because it's just funny. It pretty much sums up what he was good for.

Anyway, we met in a class we both were taking. I can't remember for the life of me which one. I was a freshman and he was a senior. I think he spoke to me first. He asked me something about a test that was coming up. We ended up studying together, and went to movies and dances together.

My first impression was that he was quiet and unimposing. At the time, I did not know he was one of the star basketball players. What I liked about him initially was that he wasn't a judging person. He didn't judge you by where you came from or what you drove.

An early sign of what was to come was his aggressive behavior toward men around us. But if you don't know it's a sign, then you think, "Oh, now here's a person I can depend on who will be there when I'm in my time of trouble." The knight-in-shining-armor thing. I didn't think, "If this is how he acts with the waiter or the guy who's flirting with me, this is also how he will act with me."

His father was an alcoholic and was abusive to his mother. I didn't know that at the time of our marriage. When I met his father, I just thought he was the most wonderful person in the whole wide world until after we were married and spent one weekend there. His dad came in drunk, wailing and, as my kids like to say, scandalizing the neighborhood. It was acceptable to my husband that men do that. One day when my husband and I got in a fight and my mother-in-law was there, she said, "Pete hit me in the nose and broke it one day," as if to say, "This shit happens. This is normal. This is not bad." I loved this woman until that day.

My family kind of liked my husband at first, but as that relationship progressed, I think they started seeing things that I was ignoring. Like he was a loner. Wasn't very talkative. Didn't mix or mingle well.

I decided to get married basically because I got sick. I've got a kidney problem, and at that time it was giving me a lot of trouble. I had to drop out of school mid-semester the fall of my sophomore year. And so I guess internally the fear of having to go back home where all the bull crap is was just unthinkable. And the only other thought was to latch on to this person and get away from there. We got married in my hometown in May of 1979. He was twenty-three and I was nineteen. My daughter, Kristina, was born in April of the following year. My son, Gary, came along three years later.

We started out with an occasional tiff here and there. Actually, now that I think about it, within the first six months we had one big falling-out. It was never a one-sided, beat-Audrey-to-death kind of thing. He's got some stab marks—scars I gave him. In some instances, I would start the fights. Rid myself of the not-knowing when it's going to happen to gain control. Let me tell you one of my major issues. I'm a control freak. I've got to be in control, not of other people, but of things that affect me. And him being the kind of person who had this need to control other people, we would constantly be at odds.

The fights started over anything, "There's too much salt in the food." So the next time I'd put none in there. He'd still say there's too much salt in the food. There didn't have to be a real issue. It would just be that something was bothering him and since he was too chicken shit to deal with it, he'd put it on me. Whatever came to mind was justifiable to him. It was usually something extremely silly. Plus the fact that I'm not a person to hold my tongue about a whole lot of nothing. "Too much salt in the beans? Don't eat 'em." "You don't like the way I iron your shirt? Iron your own damn shirt." At the height of the physical violence, we fought maybe once a week, sometimes more, but at least one day a week something wasn't right.

It started out as verbal putdowns, which always led to physical altercations due to the fact that I am *never* at a loss for words. The fights would always end up with me being hurt more—he is six foot four and I am five foot three. No matter how hard we fought or what was said, he would always come back and apologize and bring gifts. I suppose that thinking the shit would change—I'd never forgive him, but would say it was okay. I never trusted him after the first incident. I just somehow figured I had married him and would have to stay in the relationship.

The physical abuse escalated to sexual abuse probably two or three years after we were married. It was as if he thought, "Oh okay, so if I hit you, I can't break you. Let me try something different. Let me take it to another level." So I got real used to numbing my entire person—physical, mental, emotional, even spiritual. He took the abuse to another level and I took the reaction to another level.

I started realizing, "This ain't going anywhere. You've got to make some changes." It got past the physical abuse, the sexual abuse. It got to the "I am going to kill you, and before I kill you, I'm going to kill your kids and make you watch" stage. He was saying it in those exact words. "I will kill your mother, your sister, if you run to somebody's house. I'll kill them." At some point when a person tells you that, you don't know whether they're joking or not.

When it got to that level, I thought, "Okay, there's something that you've got to do, but you can't just get up and go because you might not survive." One of my brothers lived in San Antonio, Texas. I started sending him money to put in a savings account for me. I started working above and beyond the call of duty at my job. At that time, I was a teacher assistant in an elementary school so I started this mentoring program for children, probably because I needed a mentor. In the process, I met a whole lot of people, including the state representative who offered me the job I have now.

I started listening to what my husband would say. If he'd sit down and watch TV and say, "Oh, I hate a woman who smokes," I started smoking. "I hate a woman with short hair," I cut my hair. This was: "Everything that you don't like, I am going to be, so you will get the hell away from me."

And so he finally moved out one night. He cleaned out the bank account and took all of the car keys and the cars. I had all the locks changed. That was 1988. It was my daughter's birthday. She hates her birthday.

Six years after we separated, he started to realize, "She's not coming back. She's actually serious about staying out there on her own." He offered me all kinds of things. "I'll buy you a new car." "No thanks. I'll just ride in this raggedy piece of junk I have." "I'll buy you a new house." "That's okay. I'll scrape by." When he moved out, he took all the furniture. We slept on the floor. I didn't care if he took mine because for me it was: "Everything you take that reminds me of you gives me less reminders." But to take the furniture from your kids and have them sleep on the floor?

It was most violent after we were separated and he'd come to my apartment and rape me in the middle of the night. He'd always threaten to hurt the kids if I resisted. He would tell me that no one would believe me, or that I would be a burden to my family if I talked to them or asked for help. He always used the word "love," which really almost destroyed my faith in the concept. Although intellectually, I knew what he was saying was not true, emotionally, I started to internalize it and believe what he said was true. And, of course, there was the usual, "no one will want you with two kids" strategy. My self-esteem was null and void, so I swallowed that crap too.

When he came back one time, I called the police. They came

over. They talked about the ballgame. Patted each other on the back. "Okay bro, see you later. Be cool. Take it easy on the old girl." Then he comes back empowered.

He wouldn't break in. My kids had keys. They'd come in with the baby sitter and he'd come take them somewhere, like maybe to McDonald's, and then he'd go to Kmart with them and buy them a toy. So while he's buying toys, he's making copies of keys. In those five or six years, I had to change the locks at least ten times. At least. I'm talking locksmiths coming in charging you eighty bucks a shot. And me making six hundred dollars a month, paying four hundred in rent. Imagine.

The beginning of the end came when he raped me on June 27, 1994, just before I was to go to night class. I was back in school at Southern University in New Orleans and I was dead serious about finishing, going to school at night, working during the daytime in the same job that I have now. He started doing things like having my telephone cut off, rerouting my mail, picking up all my bills. He canceled my car insurance. He canceled my health insurance. I mean, he just did all kinds of things. I had not changed back to my maiden name and I realized then that was a big mistake. See, the Mr. and Mrs. thing in Louisiana gives a man a lot of power. A whole lot of power. You can just walk in the post office and say, "I am so-and-so and I want to do this, that, and the other."

I had talked to a lawyer about going ahead with this divorce. My attorney said he was going to have my husband served with divorce papers. I kept saying, "If you have him served and I haven't said something to him about it, just the same way he gets that shock, that surprise, that's the way he's going to surprise me and he's going to do it on my job. I'm going to have to tell him." The lawyer said, "I would let him get shocked." Well, that's a man's point of view. He's not the one getting his butt kicked around the house.

So I went over to his house on my way to night school to tell him, and he raped me. That was the last time because after that I pressed charges. I knew that if I didn't pursue legal action by pressing criminal charges, the abuse would never end. I already had an attorney for the civil actions—child support, separation, divorce. The D.A.'s office handled the criminal case. I gained this wonderful rapport with them. These people were looking at me like, "This woman works in the community. She volunteers. She's got two small kids. This is a model citizen. We've got to help this lady."

He was arrested for rape and imprisoned. Bond was set at half a million dollars! My "sperm donor" implicated himself on several occasions during the proceedings to the point where onlookers in the courtroom were guffawing at his attempts to hoodwink the attorney. The legal proceedings, which began in July 1994 and ended in December 1994, wore me out. I had to miss work. My niece or Terry, my present husband, had to accompany me to the proceedings so I wouldn't psyche out. Seeing him over and over kept me physically ill. I just had to start believing that God would help me persevere. He did.

My sister lived seven houses away from me. At that time, my kids and I were staying with her. It was very helpful. And once my brothers found out what happened, they wanted to do the cowboy thing. That was very validating. It was just nice to know that somebody thought that what he did was unacceptable. My mother was very supportive. She lived three hundred and some miles away, so we ran up a lot of folks' phone bills. She was financially and emotionally supportive. Then there was a sister in Atlanta who took the kids for a couple of weeks just to give them a breather.

I felt cheated when the D.A. allowed him to plea-bargain, yet I understand they wanted to be sure to get him convicted of something. I feel his sentence was much too lenient, but am grateful to the Jefferson Parish District Attorney's Office for trying to help me solve the situation. They were very serious with him. Even the judge warned him never to appear before him in court again or he would throw the book at him.

He pled guilty to aggravated battery and was found guilty of stalking. He served about nine months in prison—compare that to a lifetime of rebuilding—and was warned to never come near me again. During his prison stay, I filed for child support. I also obtained a lifetime restraining order, which is worth only the paper it is printed on since I can't count on him following it. There was nothing to split up since he had taken everything.

Just before he was arrested, he was working as a crane operator. His supervisor held his job for him until he got out of jail. After he got out of jail, he quit his job as soon as he found out that his wages would be garnished for child support.

I am still dealing with the magnitude of what happened. Healing for me began on June 27, 1994, because it was then that I finally realized that I had to do something to bring the situation to an end. The lingering effects are many. I spent years checking doors and windows all through the night. I try never to allow myself to get hemmed up in traffic or at the drive-thru at fast-food places. I lock my Ford F150 truck door constantly and keep it filled with no less than half a tank of fuel. I still have nightmares of being raped. I still check the doors sometimes. I have to look at tall, slim men twice before breathing. I feel sad that my children have no closure with their father. I still fly off the handle occasionally. Back me in a corner and you may not survive the counterattack.

Still, I haven't let what happened keep me down. I did everything I could think of to help stop the pain, and I kept one thing in mind, Marilyn Van Derbur Atler's saying: "You have to do your work." And I did it.

I started counseling at the YWCA rape crisis counseling unit across the river from New Orleans in Gretna a couple of months after the last time I was assaulted. I read every self-help book I could get my hands on. I watched videos of survivors. I wrote poetry (and still do!). I journaled. Journaling mostly allowed me to express a lot of the things that I felt, as opposed to keeping it in. And the more you express it, the more you're able to accept and deal with it.

I used self-help books to understand just exactly why I felt or why I did certain things: why I stayed, why I put up with it. And also to find out that there are a whole lot of other folks going through the same thing. I liked *The Courage to Heal,* and one called *Allies in Healing,* and another called *Beginning to Heal. The Anger Workbook* is also really good.

Therapy helped me in many of the same ways as reading the books. I attended individual therapy with a psychiatrist and board-certified social worker as well as group counseling off and on for about five years. Feeling like you're the only person going through this makes you feel ashamed because then you think, "There must be something wrong with me." Being able to hear other people talk about how they felt, what they'd gone through, and what issues came up because of what had happened helped a lot.

I try to help other survivors by telling my story through poetry readings on sexual assault and child abuse. That and my job help me heal. As the executive director of the Jefferson Youth Foundation, I am always doing something for someone else. I administer programs for at-risk children, facilitate parent support groups, write grants and run creative writing and poetry workshops, organize poetry readings, and lead stress management workshops.

My career has been an amazing blessing in another way. I met my current husband about a year before the trial because he was a board member of the organization that I applied to for this job. Our relationship is challenging. There's a lot he has to deal with, although things have gotten better. He had to deal with my nightmares almost as much as I did because he was there going through them with me. At one time I was going to counseling three days a week, twice a day. It was just wearing me out. Working and being a parent on top of everything else was just overwhelming. And, of course, all of it took me away from home. And so he'd ask me to address that, and sometimes I didn't like being asked. Also, there were times when my anger was misdirected at family. So our marriage has been very challenging but well worth the challenge. We tied the knot on September 21, 1997.

The sexual violence almost destroyed my sexuality—I thought of sex as a power tool, did not want anything to do with it. In fact, I looked at it as something men would never get from me, just to show them I was in power. My sex life is still in the healing phase. I still have issues when it comes to dealing with the act itself, especially if I have to discuss intimacy with my husband. I think sex is okay, sometimes even great, but on occasion, somewhere deep down, I still have to keep reminding myself it's not a bad thing.

The most significant part of my healing process was learning to love me again. Now I know how to make myself feel really, really good. When I started doing stress management classes, I basically did them for myself. I had to know all the things that one should do in order to reduce stress, like breathing exercises and actual exercising too. Exercise boosts the level of endorphins—natural chemicals in the brain that affect mood. We've got this big gym set up in the house so I do a bit of weight training and try to walk two to four miles a day on the treadmill.

A lot of laughing and joking also causes your endorphins to overproduce, making you feel great. I make sure that I surround myself with people who are happy and jolly and know how to laugh. I get emails with jokes sent to me every day from www.ivillage.com and free daily joke sites so all day I'm looking at something silly.

I'm a water freak. I like showers and baths, so I take great pains to stretch them out while using aromatherapy candles in the bathroom. The scent of lavender is very calming.

I think of my healing as a way of life. I see no end to the personal growth I wish to make and to the pain I wish to lessen. I think I've grown professionally to the point where I interact with people in a much more positive manner. I have raised my self-esteem from the gutters. I have learned to help the community by using action instead of just complaining about the issue. Right now I would describe myself as strong yet tender, grown yet embracing the child within, giving yet cautious, and intelligent yet willing to learn more. And forever a child of God.

Though I never lost faith in God, I was angry with Him for a very long time. We have since reconciled. I have been reaffirming my faith in God, and I stopped the blaming. At first I was saying, "You're supposed to be all-powerful, all-knowing, and all that good stuff. I just don't see any reason You would let this happen." I started realizing that the negative things people do are man's handiwork, not God's handiwork. We don't have to do them. We just make that choice. I had stopped going to my church, St. Joseph the Worker, for a very long time, and had just started going back around the time that I graduated from Southern University.

For families of women in abusive relationships, I want you to: Be supportive. Be supportive. Be supportive. I can't say that enough. Be supportive regardless of whether she decides to get out at this time or not, because that will ultimately help her make the decision to leave. It will give her an alternative. Help her make the decision by offering her as much information as possible. Don't dictate to her. Don't tell her she's right or wrong.

The first thing I tell women is: You don't deserve it. It is not your fault. You deserve better.

Make a plan. Seek out professional help because no layperson can do all that needs to be done. A professional can explain much more than Joe Blow can about what you're going through, why you're going through it, and what you can possibly do to get out of it.

Put money aside. Put aside as much as you can filter out of that household without being noticed. Put it with someone you can trust because when you do decide to go, there's a great possibility that that person will try to freeze all your assets. I'm going from experience here. If a person will hit you and throw you into a wall, most assuredly they will not give you any money to walk away from it.

Explain to the kids that this is not an appropriate thing that is going on and you are working on getting them out. It's very important that kids understand that this is not cool.

Don't blame yourself, regardless of what he says to you. "You made me hit you." That's not true. Nobody makes anybody do anything. He chooses to hit you. Realize that he has a problem. And it is not a problem that you can solve. I've learned not to even use the word "change" unless you are talking about yourself.

Women, we've been conditioned to think that cute, dainty, prissy is the only way to go. It's okay for a woman to get angry. It is okay for you to be angry about this. Do not allow yourself to suppress the anger because that further binds you. If you get angry enough, you'll make something happen.

Christopher's Story

Sexual violence is a tragedy for women and men, girls and boys. Men reaching out for help in the wake of such a crime face some challenges very similar to those of women survivors. Additionally, our culture's notions about sexuality and masculinity present some unique issues for male survivors. Christopher, a young man in the early stages of healing, shares his pain and his great strides toward wellness.

I was raised primarily by my mother. My father moved to the West Coast when I was three. Aside from six months that we lived with one of her boyfriends, it was basically just me and her.

My father considers me to be his special child because I'm his oldest male child. We are as close as you can be with someone who lives three thousand miles away. When I was growing up, we talked on the phone once a month, less often during some stretches. I didn't know any different so it didn't really bother me that much. I knew that there were other kids out there that had both parents, but my mother's presence in my life was so profound. She was basically both mother and father to me.

Of the kids in my neighborhood and family, I was one of the more studious ones. I got really good grades. I knew how to read when I was two. One of my mother's best friends used to be a teacher. As I understand it, from the time I was born they shoved flash cards in my face.

My mom and I moved around a lot to different apartments and houses, all in Baltimore. She was living in the house where I live now for the last eight or nine years of her life, until she passed away from cancer. I've been living here with my aunt and my cousin since then.

To be honest, the sexual abuse I experienced as a child didn't really change my personality much. I tried not to allow any outward notion that there was anything wrong with me. Basically I was a pretty shy child anyway. I tried not to be different than I always had been. It worked pretty well because nobody ever knew. My mother never knew.

When I was five, I think my next-door neighbor, a little girl of about the same age, was being abused. Looking back, she knew a lot about sex at the time. We would be in my yard and she would want to fool around. It would start with kissing and then it went to hands down the pants. We altogether skipped rubbing against each other through our clothes. We would be rubbing our genitals against each other. That's as far as it got.

We'd be riding our bikes, and then, bam, let's do that. It would seem very adult because she would say things like, "Let's make love." Maybe something happened to her or she saw something that she was trying to mimic. It happened more than a couple of times. It went on periodically however long we were living there, for at least a year.

There's one thing that really sticks out in my mind. She had a cousin who was younger than both of us. She was like, "You should see this." She knelt down on her knees, maybe two or three feet away from him, and he peed in her mouth. At that point, I knew this was just nutty. This is off-the-wall. Even at age five I knew. I wish I could go back in time so that I could say, "Just stop all this because it's crazy." I never told anybody this. It was so out there I didn't want to even admit that I had ever seen it.

From there we moved into an apartment that was part of a house with my mother's boyfriend, probably for financial reasons. I was eight. It was a very unhappy situation for both of us. He would come home late. He may have been messing around on her. In my view, if he wasn't emotionally abusive to her then I don't know what he was. I just knew that she wasn't happy and as a result I wasn't happy either. That wasn't the only reason, though.

One of his sisters had some disease that made her very limited mentally. She was thirty- or forty-some years old, but she had the intellect of a child. I had my own room in the attic. As far as my mother knew, she would come upstairs and we'd play with my toys.

At first she just made me fondle her and then she got me to perform oral sex on her. That happened a few times. One time she tried to make me have intercourse with her, but it just didn't happen.

I just tried to live life in a way that didn't acknowledge that it was happening. It would happen and it would be over and then I would just be Chris again. I remember one time saying to myself, "This just didn't happen. This never happened."

I didn't want to say what had happened to me because at first I kind of just went along with it. Because of my history, it just didn't seem like there was anything wrong with it. But after a while I felt like I shouldn't be doing this. I didn't want anybody to know. I figured I just wouldn't put up a fight and it would be done. I didn't ever try to stop it. There was just really nothing I could do.

Something else happened once. You know how something can happen and you can only remember bits and pieces of it? You can see certain things but some other things your mind just won't let you recall. I keep wanting to tell myself that I made this up. I keep saying, "This is probably your imagination," but the way I feel when I think about it, I don't think anybody can convince himself to feel that way. I feel frustrated and confused. Frustrated because I have a need for the truth, for a moment of total clarity about what happened, and confused because the lack of clarity brings doubt.

As best I can remember, here's what happened. This was after we moved out of the apartment with my mom's ex-boyfriend, so I would have been eight or nine. My mother wanted to play cards with friends, old friends from way back in the day. So we went over to this house and she was with them, chilling. Since it was a grown-up thing, kids had to go, so they took me to another house.

I remember there being a girl there who had to be in her early teens. I was in the room with her for a while, and then she took me to this other house. It was really late and for whatever reason, I just didn't feel comfortable trying to sleep in there. And there was some man there. I can kind of see a face, but as far as a name, I can't remember. I remember him wanting me to sit on his lap, and he wanted to put his hand under my shirt. By then I knew this wasn't kosher. He said things like, "I want you to be my little girlfriend." And I just knew this isn't good.

When I tried to push away, I remember him choking me almost to the point where I thought I was going to pass out. When he stopped that, I tried to reason with him. I said, "You don't have to do this. I'll convince my mother or one of my cousins to do what you want." And he said that wasn't what he wanted. I tried to get to the phone and call somebody, anybody. It was one of those wall phones, rotary phones, and he took that thing and he hit me with it. I remember when he hit me my mind was half really, really sharp and half really, really woozy. The really sharp part acknowledged the fact that that really hurt, really bad. He might have hit me with the phone or his hand again. I just remember going down and pretty much begging for my life. For a while I thought I was going to die.

At that point I was kind of out of it and I didn't really try to fight anymore because I didn't want to get hit by the phone again. I remember being carried or dragged. I think I was conscious for some of it. I remember being in a room where it was really hot. I was raped.

I can't describe how much it hurt. I tried to force myself to go to sleep because it hurt that badly. I remember being asleep and then waking up and wanting to go to the bathroom. I wanted to wash my face off, but I couldn't because he said I had to stay in that bed, right there. I remember going to sleep again and then being woken up and it happening all over again. By then I just wanted to go home, I just kept on begging, "Just take me home." The only thing I remember from that morning was finally being allowed to wash my face and being told not to tell anyone or he would kill me. Whoever came to get me, when they asked what was wrong with me, I said I was playing and I fell and hit my head on a doorknob or something like that.

Somehow, for the next ten years I pushed all these things out of my mind. My mother made life so happy. I was doing Little League, going on trips. I actually remembered some of that stuff the day I was baptized. I was thirteen. Everyone was looking at me and I thought to myself, "Oh my God, they know." That very phrase just popped into my head. I don't know why I thought that, I just thought they knew what had happened, and it wasn't a very good feeling.

Aside from that it was natural that it just never came up. Nobody ever spoke of my mother's ex-boyfriend's house. It was always out of sight, out of mind, except for the day I was baptized. And at that point, I said, "You know what, I am not going to think about this at all." And then I consciously put it out of my mind and it just didn't come back up.

In retrospect, I can see how the abuse affected my thinking. I remember one time—I think in fifth grade—some kids were playing tag. My best friend ran up the sidewalk and pulled me in front of this girl. She ran into me—I was a pretty big child by then—and fell down, hit the ground. She just kind of sat there with this really blank look on her face. When she was sitting there, I was very scared because I didn't know what was wrong with her. I didn't know how badly she'd been hurt. The best idea I could come up with to prevent getting in trouble was to offer her sex, which I thought would placate her. I felt that if I were in a situation where I was faced with bad consequences, I could avoid it by giving sex. In my mind, that's how I'd come out of other negative situations.

For the most part, through middle school and high school, I was just a regular, average, everyday kid, with the exception of my mother having cancer. I had just turned thirteen when she was first diagnosed. I had to grow up fast and help take care of her. I did have a childhood, but it wasn't like a lot of other folks' childhoods from that point on. Having gotten the best grades in school and all that good stuff, it was expected of me to be really mature.

I went to college when I was eighteen. That was my first time away from home. I was lonely for stretches there. I met women over the web. I met women in person. The only way I related to some of these people was through sex. It was a way to get people to like me because I had never really been promiscuous before then. Once I was away from my comfort zone, I guess, I just got out there. I used it as a means to make friends. It was also about not wanting to be alone. I was emotionally worn out from having been through all the stuff with my mother.

And then, because of something a friend told me, I wasn't able to block things out of my mind anymore. I was nineteen before I really understood what had happened to me. It was surreal. I'd met this young lady online. We were just friends. And one night we were online talking when she just came out and said to me, "Chris, I was raped." No one had ever said that to me before. At that point I didn't know how to process it.

She told me a day or two after it happened. I got really silent because I didn't know what to say. I asked her to tell me how it happened. I did have the sense to tell her it wasn't her fault. I didn't just come out and say, "Oh yeah, that happened to me too," because I was in denial about it. Instead I told her, "I'm so sorry. That's terrible." But the more she said, the more what had happened to me kept creeping back into my mind.

We talked again a day or two later, and the feelings started to stir. I guess what caught my attention the most was her describing the feeling of being trapped and not being able to fight back. That stirred up a lot more feelings inside me than thoughts. We were talking about it another time and she told me that a cousin had been abusing her sexually since she was very young. I kind of just blurted it out then: "Well, it happened to me too." I told her about the woman who molested me but I didn't tell her about the man at all.

Because of the combination of my mother dying and these awful memories creeping into my mind, I was feeling completely torn down. I'd already done terribly in school. My first year was just a complete and total disaster. My grades came home and my mother wasn't even mad. She was completely confused because I graduated in the top ten percent of my high school class.

I felt guilty for having those feelings then. I felt like, "How can I be concentrating on anything other than my mother?" She had sacrificed so many things for me to have the opportunity that I had. I felt that I was being selfish by even thinking about anything else other than my mother and my schoolwork. I owed my mother a debt, to go to school and do well. That was the only thing she ever wanted for me and I didn't think that thinking about some things that had taken place more than a decade ago, no matter what their impact on my life, was appropriate.

I have not been able to come to terms with the fact that I hid this so much. I made up a lot of stories to cover for a lot of these things. When it came to almost anything else, I could talk to her. I just elected not to tell her about this stuff. Maybe it was my feeling guilty about it happening period, but I feel guilty about not having told her. I can't tell my father because he's old school.

My friend helped me come to grips with it. She said, "If there's any way you can, tell your mother." This was a Saturday night. I decided to come clean about everything. I went to bed at 2 A.M., and that morning, I got a call at about six saying that my aunt was on the way to pick me up because my mother had taken very ill. That's all that anybody would tell me. When I got back home, my mother had suffered liver failure and had gone into a coma. Her eyes were open but she wasn't responding, she couldn't speak. I don't know if I ever will forgive myself. I missed that chance to tell her how much I hid and lied to her. The very day that I had decided to tell her what happened was the very day that I missed my chance to tell her forever. It stings because, unlike being abused, it was my choice.

After my mother passed, I went back to school. I went through the motions second semester of my sophomore year but things just got worse. I was probably going to lose my scholarship anyway—a full ride, baby, all the way through. I just wanted to get away from there.

Some friends told me that they only saw me when I would be going to class. Other than that, I would go to the dining hall—that was the only time that they would see me unless they came to my room. As a matter of fact, I was in my room so much that I watched every news broadcast I could, from four in the afternoon to eleven at night. I watched *The Simpsons* and wrestling too. I actually did study, surprisingly enough. And I had a whole lot of movies on tape. The news was a way for me to feel like I was at home, but everything else was an escape for me. I played a lot of computer games. That was an escape too. I told only a handful of friends what I was dealing with. Everyone else would be like, "What is wrong with him?"

I didn't want people to see me sad. I didn't want to be the one who spoiled everybody's good time. Thinking about my mother made me sad and it was hard to hide that. I just wanted to be alone as much as possible. I didn't want people to see that there was something wrong with me because then they might ask me what was up. I didn't want anybody knowing everything that was bothering me.

So I left. It was a mutual decision between me and my aunt. She thought I should come back home and I agreed. College had a lot of bad memories. I did not want to be in that room anymore.

I went back to school in Baltimore and started working, which was even more of a disaster. Academically, that year was worse than anything that ever happened at my first college because I just flat out stopped going to class. I didn't want to face the world because of memories of what happened to me as a child weighing down on me.

When I first went to college, I didn't have any problems having sex, but after remembering everything, some things became difficult.

I don't do oral sex that well. I don't want to feel like I'm being selfish but it's just hard to do. One girlfriend kept on asking me and asking me to do it, and once I started doing it, I felt like I did way back when: trapped, hurt, paralyzed almost. After I finished, I just lay on her couch, just lay there staring. I was just completely gone. She said I was shaking.

What bothered me the most was that I thought she loved me, and if she did, why was she pressuring me? Why did I give in when I knew how I would feel? Saying no is just hard. Now I don't really have sex outside of relationships. Anytime I do give oral sex, it's with a girlfriend who understands and cares about me and wouldn't want me to put myself through something traumatic.

Sometimes after I've been intimate, I get that feeling that a lot of us survivors get, that you are dirty and disgusting and the fact that you've done it again makes you even more dirty and disgusting. God hates you. Everybody hates you because you do all these nasty things. Of course, there are things that I just cannot do sexually, and there are certain things that people do that make me have flash-backs. If you touch me in a certain place, I just can't take that. Before having sex, I tell the young lady that I don't like to be spanked, because I don't like to be touched there. You can understand why. I just don't like being touched there at all. It's very distressing when it happens.

At this point, I've told quite a few people about being abused. A lot of people who were part of a website where everyone was writing and posting diary entries, they all know. They just don't know who I am. It helped me to write about it. Posting my entries on the web-site ended up having a fringe benefit because there were a lot of sur-vivors there. It helped me to understand things, like not wanting to be alone and thinking that I was cursed to have a life that would be that way.

I've got a few male friends. My ex-roommate and I are pretty close. There's a group of us that went to college together who are still friends. They all know to varying degrees. I am more hesitant to tell male friends, for obvious reasons. I don't always feel it's good for me to be close to guys. I have guy friends around here that I grew up with, but none of them know. My cousin that I grew up with doesn't know, and I live with him. I have guy friends that I just flat out ain't telling.

Of my guy friends whom I have told, a lot of them said, "That's really messed up." One, who is Seventh-day Adventist, tries to give me a religious view on the whole thing. His coming at it from a spiritual perspective has been helpful. He explained to me that God didn't curse me to live through all these things, and that my life can be whatever I make it. These things that happened aren't going to define all that I am. I had a conversation with him the other day. When I said to him I suffered these things, he said, "No, you shouldn't think like that. You conquered these things." And I've been trying to feed off of that mindset.

He must know that there are a lot of people out there with depression and post-traumatic stress disorder who are just falling by the wayside, just falling apart. People who completely can't function or who have committed suicide, or turned to crime. He pointed out that I haven't done any of those things.

I told my aunt recently. That didn't help. She asked me why I hadn't said anything at the time and since I didn't have an answer, we never spoke about it again. I guess that added on to me feeling guilty about not having told my mother at all. I think everybody in my family has their own past hurt that they don't deal with, so I can't expect them to think one second about mine. One or two of my female friends have not responded very favorably. Their reaction was, "Just get over it."

Usually when I tell my female friends, a lot of them react with a "let me take care of you" attitude. "Let me help you through this." Maybe it's their motherly instinct. The reaction that has been most helpful for me is just basically listening and understanding. My female friends who are survivors, they're the best because they understand. Some of the most helpful things people have said: A, it wasn't your fault. B, get counseling. I hate to make it sound that cut-and-dry but it is.

I had been toying with the idea of getting counseling for about two years. But then I didn't want to relive what happened. I was thinking, maybe I can function properly without it, but then I realized I couldn't. I had problems at school. I had problems at work. Just the way I was conducting myself, my boss actually pulled me into his office and asked me if I was on drugs.

I decided that this just couldn't go on. I knew I had problems with how I approached different things like finances and relationships. I spent pretty much all of my mother's insurance money, going out to movies and going to dinner all the time. I had a lot of friends out of state so I had some high phone bills. I would be afraid to look at my bank statement. The first relationship that I had back in Baltimore, I was really, really, really insecure. Then I got into another relationship with another woman. I realized after a while that I was in it just because I needed to not be alone. I needed to keep my mind focused on something else. I realized that I was in it for all the wrong reasons. I realized that I was never, ever happy.

Sometimes I wasn't able to function at all. On some sad days, I would sleep like twelve hours so I didn't have to get out of the bed and face the world at all. I just decided this just couldn't go on anymore. I called the Black Mental Health Alliance, which is located here in Baltimore. They gave me a referral for the counselor that I have today. When I called, they asked what the issues were and I said child sex abuse. When they asked me what I was looking for, I said I wanted a woman. I preferred a woman counselor because I was raised around nothing but women, my mother, my aunts. It just feels more natural for me to share things with women. I just feel better letting myself be vulnerable with a woman.

My counselor is really, really nice. She's one of the very few people who's ever asked me what my dreams are, what my goals are. She actually said that she cares about my well-being, and that's good to know, that somebody cares.

When I started counseling, I was diagnosed as having clinical depression and post-traumatic stress disorder. I was surprised. I thought counseling would involve talking about your childhood and then you're going to be cured and that's it. It's definitely not like that. She wants to help me find healing, however that will come about. It's a holistic kind of thing. Being cured of the depression and the PTSD is good, but therapy is more about me trying to build a life, build my life the way I want it to be so that I can be happy.

Counseling is helping me in the sense that I don't always feel helpless about life. I used to feel hopeless and helpless. When something like this happens to you, it's easy to feel helpless. You feel like your power in part of your life has been taken from you. It's given me a different outlook on life.

In addition to getting past the abuse emotionally, I feel like I can do things now that I want to do. I made a decision that I want to do what's going to make me happy for the rest of my life. I don't know how to get there exactly but I really believe deep down writing and theater is what I was born to do.

Now I realize that I can follow my own path. I can go against the grain. I don't have to be anybody else. I don't have to hide from things that happened to me and I don't have to hide from what makes me happy. And of course, winning second place in a drama competition didn't hurt, because that tells me that I'm on the right path.

To male survivors, I would say no matter what happened to you as a child, it doesn't make you any less of a man. Once I decided to make decisions and think for myself and be more responsible, I realized I wasn't a boy anymore. I was there.

It's funny, my father actually considered me to be a man before I did. He would call me "boy" when I was younger. But around eighteen, nineteen, he just started saying, "What's up, man," and saying that making decisions for myself and determining how I want my life to be, that that's what men do. Another thing that lets me know I've become a man, after everything that happened, I've cried but I've never, ever broken down completely. No matter how weak I think I am, I'm still here, and I'm still kicking. That's what men do. And that is what women do too.

The way we have treated some of our brothers and sisters who have been through these things is really atrocious. I know that there are a lot of guys running around who have been through these things, who think that there's something really wrong with them. Lots of them feel in some way, maybe in a big way, that they have to be an outcast or that they have to be ashamed of what they've been through. And that's not good. It's definitely not good to live your life with that kind of weight on your shoulders. It's just not healthy and, to be honest, it's just not fair.

As for families, if one of your loved ones says that they've been a victim of abuse, get educated on it. We have to get educated on it. We can't just rely on antiquated ideas about these things. We have to come into this day and be supportive. We've got to be less judgmental because that's definitely not helping.

And to the significant others of male survivors, you have to be more understanding. You have to realize that to be intimate with a male survivor, you have to have a different view about sex. It just can't be about getting off every single time. You have to be more caring. That doesn't necessarily mean you always have to be gentle, because there might be guys out there who like it rough. You just have to understand what he's been through, and that there might be things that you just can't do. You have to understand that there might be things he's not going to want to do, and it's okay. That's just how it is. This is some really traumatic stuff. If he has a flashback, that's okay, too. It doesn't make him any less of a man. It makes him human.

Marta's Story

The trust shattered by acquaintance rape led to even more abuse for Marta during her teenage years. Silence and isolation caused by myths about rape prevented her for years from getting the support she needed. But through her passion for truth, she is trailblazing a path of healing for her entire family. She has also challenged her church to embrace uncomfortable truths about sexual violence and minister to survivors with a heightened level of compassion and love.

My mother is an African American from Queens. My great-grandparents on my father's side of the family were all born in Jamaica and immigrated to Panama, where my grandparents were born. My parents met in New York and settled in Panama, where I grew up. My home life was pretty much a mixture of the cultures that I was around. My grandmother's house was very West Indian. The doors stayed open to all the rooms. Rice and peas on Sunday. I went to a West Indian Baptist church, where I really enjoyed singing in the choir.

My dad has eight brothers and sisters, so I was always around lots of extended family. As a child, I was closest to a female cousin who is seven years older than I am. I also spent a lot of time with two cousins who are sisters. They and an older male cousin lived with my grandmother, who I have always adored. She is so kind and has a lot of positive energy. You know that if she's thinking of you, everything is going to be okay.

My mother was really busy when I was growing up. She had a job and was working on her Ph.D. most of the time, so I wasn't really close to her. But my father and I always talked about everything. He used to say that I was brutally honest, always speaking about what I believe in and jumping to people's defense if I saw something going wrong.

I must have been in about fifth or sixth grade when one of my best friends confided to me that she had been molested. I told my father. He apparently didn't think it was his place to mention it to the girl's family.

Years later, right before I was raped, I heard about a girl in the neighborhood where my grandmother's house is. She was gang-raped by a group of guys she knew, one of whom she had had a crush on. Hearing the reactions to her having these guys put in jail really dictated how I dealt with my rape. One cousin said that everyone knew that the girl had a crush on the guy, so she didn't understand why she had him put in jail. And I recall my father saying, "She probably let these guys run a train on her, and then afterwards felt bad and changed up her story." I didn't feel comfortable with that, but I didn't say much. My father doesn't remember making that statement.

When I was sixteen, the day before Christmas Eve, I was going to choir practice and I went out to the bus stop like I usually did. It was near the house of a guy I had a crush on. He saw me and offered me a ride.

My dad had warned me against him. The only reason he could give was that the guy's father had been kind of crazy. I do not judge people by their family because I know that I'm very different from all of my family. So I didn't think that was a valid reason.

I remember we were driving along and we saw his aunt walking a baby. We waved at her. Then we drove past the canal and up the hill. There's a wooded area and this little road that I had never noticed before that day. He turned off there and I asked him where he was going. He didn't answer me. Then he stopped the car. Immediately, he reached across me—this man was taller than six feet—and locked the door on my side. I was fearful of him hurting me. If he was disregarding what I wanted to the extent of locking me in the car, I wasn't sure what he would do to me. He raped me. Afterward, he immediately switched up and was all sunny again. Then he drove to the church.

It was dark and no one was inside. I didn't know whether the practice had been canceled or whether so much time had passed that everyone had left. I walked to the homes of several people I knew who lived nearby but no one was home. The loneliness I felt was like God wasn't there. It was like the whole world had stopped.

I would have told someone immediately if I hadn't had time to think about it. I figured I probably would hear from my parents that I wasn't supposed to be with him anyway so obviously I was to blame and why did I even get in the car. I went back to my grandmother's house. Having already been unable to defend myself during the rape, I wasn't sure I was ready to try to defend myself by explaining what had happened to my family. So I sat there on the floor with my head in the chair in my grandmother's room.

In the days that followed, suddenly I was sleeping very well and having these wonderful dreams with angels coming to me, telling me to protect this child. One day I ate breakfast—scrambled eggs and bacon and toast—got up from the table after everyone had finished, went in the kitchen and cooked myself some hot dogs and baked beans. At this point I'm eating strange things and a lot of it.

My mom asked me, "Have you been having sex with your boyfriend?" We had had sex before but we always used protection. She went and got a cup and told me to pee in it. Then she took it from me and slammed the door in my face. A little while later, she came to my room and threw this pregnancy test at me. It was positive. I said that

I needed to think about what I was going to do, and she told me there's nothing to think about. That meant I had no decision in the matter, that she was going to make sure that I got rid of the baby.

My mom scheduled the abortion for the day I was supposed to sing in a church choir festival. She was very concerned with people finding out about the pregnancy, so we flew to Miami. I remember we ran into one of her friends in the airport, and she said we were going to Miami to go shopping.

I had never even had a Pap smear before, so they decided that they were going to put me under to carry out the procedure. When I started to wake up after it was done, I was hearing this woman crying, screaming at the top of her lungs for her baby. I wasn't even fully conscious before I realized that it was me. The nurse was asking me why I had gone through with it if I didn't want to. I told her how I had been raped and nobody knew. She said, "Don't you think you should tell your mother?" Because I was still drugged up, I did. At the time, nothing more was said about it.

A few months later my parents cornered me to get me to tell them the whole story. After the abortion, I hadn't really been speaking to either of them. During that time, once when my mother and I were having a disagreement, I went outside just to be alone for a minute. She yelled out of the window, "You don't listen, that's why that thing happened to you." So there was a lot of distance there. I didn't feel like they would be the ones to help me. I really didn't feel like anybody could help me through what I was going through. I just acted like everything was normal, but things were getting even worse.

The first person to happen upon me at my grandmother's house the day I was raped was my male cousin, who from the moment I started growing breasts had tried numerous times to feel me up. When I was younger, sleeping in my grandmother's bed, I remember feeling someone's hands on my chest and then in the morning waking up and not really knowing if it had happened or if I had been dreaming.

Being at my grandmother's house was so different from being

alone with my parents in a far-off neighborhood. I need to be around people. I wanted to be near my grandmother. So I didn't tell anyone about my cousin bothering me because I felt like I would mess up the balance, disturb the peace in that home. I didn't want there to be any discomfort. And I thought that I could just deal with the situation on my own.

I remember I asked two of my female cousins who lived there if he'd ever tried anything like that with them. They said no and didn't believe what I was saying about him. Then one day we were laying there watching TV, and he started rubbing on my butt. They were just like, "Wow, that's weird." They didn't really say anything else. So I figured it was just my problem. If they had said that he was doing the same thing to them, I would have probably stood up for them at least.

After the rape, my cousin was getting more insistent. Up to that point I had always said, "Look, you're not going to touch me. You're never going to be able to." Really standing up for myself. And then when the rape happened, I got to a space where I couldn't fight for myself. I didn't even care to. It was a space where my body was just not my own. I gave up trying to fight him off. He forced sex on me. This went on until I went to college in the United States.

I thought that maybe I could get my cousin and the guy who had raped me to kill each other. So I tried telling each about the other. But they didn't care about anybody in this world except themselves. Definitely not about me. If anything, they would have used it as a defense: "If you tell anybody what I did to her, I'll tell them what you did to her."

At that point, I operated under the notion that people you trust and love can hurt you. People you don't trust and don't love cannot hurt you. So I began having sex with random people I was mildly attracted to. It was safe that way, because I knew they wouldn't be able to hurt me. They didn't know me. I didn't trust them. It was my decision what I did.

Off at college, my roommate and I went to a basketball game. Afterward when the crowd was rushing out, some guy tried to grab on me. I went off on him and I told him not to touch me. So he went off on me, called me a bitch, you know, the usual. My roommate goes, "You're going to get yourself into trouble doing that." As if I don't have a right to speak up for myself.

When someone backs me into a corner, my temper is horrible. I will defend myself. For instance, when I was still in college, this guy slapped me on the butt in a club and I grabbed him by his throat and threw him up on a wall. I held him there until he clearly stated that he understood that he's never allowed to touch me without my permission. Then I let him go. Now I refuse to physically retaliate to defend myself. I feel bad afterward because I'm bringing myself to their level with some kind of physical defense.

During college I had a few more relationships that were purely physical but I also had two long-term relationships, both were emotionally unhealthy and ended badly.

I always told whomever I was in a relationship with what happened to me. I thought that they needed to know what I'd been through so that they could understand me, understand why sometimes in the middle of sex I would just start crying.

I don't have difficulties with sex now. My boyfriend and I were friends for a long time before we started dating, so I am able to trust him in a way that I've never trusted anyone before. What I used to do so that I wouldn't cry during sex was distance myself. It seemed like most guys were just trying to get where they were going. My boyfriend sat me down one day and said, "Maybe we're just not compatible." He didn't want to have sex with me if I wasn't getting anything out of it. I was amazed that he was aware that I wasn't present, and so from there, fireworks. I responded by showing him that we were compatible.

When I had told a previous boyfriend about what I'd been through, he suggested I call my parents and tell them about my cousin. I had never really thought about it. He said, "Don't you think he's doing it to other people?" I did tell them. I thought they heard me, but they hadn't.

I got a job translating documents a month after I finished college. Ten months later I took volunteer training at a rape crisis center, but I didn't end up volunteering. I ended up going to work at a different crisis center as the multicultural outreach coordinator.

Through training it sunk in for me that these guys who sexually victimize people don't just stop. And so I called my parents again and said, "I really need you to call my aunt and tell her to be careful because I don't want the same thing that happened to me to happen to my little cousin."

Months went by without them calling. Finally I called myself. Immediately my aunt knew what I wanted to tell her. She said thanks for calling. That was it. I didn't have to go into details and she didn't question me.

About a year after graduating, I felt like my parents still weren't really hearing what I was saying to them about my cousin molesting me. Right before I started law school, I went home and tried again. I finally sat down with them in person and made sure that they heard everything in terms of how I felt about how they handled my pregnancy, just feeling like I'd been dealing with everything by myself.

I also talked to them about my cousin. I watched their faces change as if they'd never heard it before. They were terrified. They asked me if he'd had sex with me and I said yes. It was an incredible disappointment for my dad because he had treated him almost like a son. It was a shock to them, just really hard. They both started crying.

This time they were open to hearing what I had to say. It seemed like they were in awe of the way I was handling everything. They were like, "Wow, thanks for leading the way to dealing with it." That made me feel good.

I told my parents that we really needed to tell the rest of the family. By the time my father called everyone, everybody knew already, but nobody was talking about it. The cousin had tried something with at least two other cousins, and their parents had isolated them from him. He can't operate in anything but silence. If the family had been talking about this from the beginning, it would not have continued to happen.

Up until recently I felt a lot of distance from my family because we didn't talk about it. Even my cousin that I was closest to—I don't think she knows about the rape, she just knows about my cousin. And I just told her that part recently. She responded by saying, "We just spent a week at the beach and you didn't tell me." When do you tell someone that? Do you tell them on the beach? Do you tell them at dinner? Do you tell them by the pool? Before going to sleep? It's just never the perfect moment to tell someone something like that.

I also felt like, "It's my problem and I don't want to put it on anyone else." But people should always be able to rely on family and friends. The isolation that I felt was almost self-imposed, but in a way it wasn't because you hear so much about victim blaming. The myths about rape floating around in my family and community prevented me from speaking sooner.

I didn't really start dealing with the rape or the abuse for a long time. I didn't want to think about it. I first got counseling my freshman year of college for roommate issues. I was asked if I wanted to talk about the sexual assault or being molested, and I said no. I got counseling again my junior year because of the abusive relationship I was in. I finally got counseling for the rape and abuse after college because of my mother.

That year between undergrad and law school, I finally told her that I needed her to talk to a counselor. I said, "I feel like I haven't gotten appropriate responses from you and I need for you to know how to talk to me about this. I feel like I've been going through this alone."

She went. She told me what they had said, and that it felt good to talk about these things finally. She realized that there were things that she needed to learn. Both of my parents, from the point where I started asking for their help, started being there for me and were willing to look at how they were thinking and to hear my point of view.

The lady she'd talked to told her about EMDR (Eye Movement Desensitization and Reprocessing), a kind of therapy that helps people heal from trauma. My mom bought me a book on it. It sounded like a great way to work through things. So I went to a counselor for EMDR and we worked on issues regarding my cousin. I was having trouble every time I saw men about his complexion, height, and build—I would be on guard. I also told her I was having trouble sleeping and that was the main thing I wanted to work on. Through the EMDR, I was able to start getting good sleep.

Since coming to law school, I have learned how important it is to use caution when choosing a counselor. Going to counseling is a really big step for a lot of survivors. It's important to look for a counselor who has had training specifically in sexual assault, who is aware of the issues and won't come out with any myths. That's the last thing a survivor needs to hear when she finally gets up the nerve to go to counseling. You have to be your own advocate. A good way to find a counselor who won't respond to you based on myths or racial prejudices is to ask friends and associates for referrals.

I didn't go to church for a long time. I don't think anyone in my church at home knew what happened to me until recently. I wasn't ever comfortable enough to tell them. I also felt distanced because of little things you see in church that shouldn't be happening, like people talking about other people. I don't like the judgment that's passed. I think more understanding should come out of church.

I was on my way to church when I was raped. Society is so convincing with its messages that whatever you were doing at the time you were assaulted, you shouldn't have been doing—somehow it made me not want to go to church anymore. I felt a general distance from everyone and everything that I had been associated with before the rape happened. I've always been spiritual. I know everything in this world is connected. But in terms of being able to go to church and be peaceful, I kept trying but it's just not something that I could do for a while.

What is helping me heal from the abuse and the rape is painting, although I started for another reason. My senior year of college, I had gained some weight. My parents, who are very weight-conscious, were nagging me about it. So many media images tell us that a woman who is beautiful is so skinny her body looks more like a twelve-year-old. Women do not come in one size. So I sat down and painted this voluptuous woman. Really the woman is me but bigger. She's round with big arms. She's reaching for the sky because she can pretty much do anything.

I needed to do something for myself. I sketched a lot when I was young, but I had never painted before. I bought two big sheets of paper, tempera, and a brush. No big expense. I just wanted to see if I could paint and I found that I could. So I moved up and bought some oil paint and poster board. That was the second painting I did, "Change." It's a woman stepping forward, she has the world on one fingertip and she's blowing on it, like she's changing the world. She's pregnant. Pregnancy represents hope in my paintings.

I've completed nearly twenty paintings, and all of them have helped me heal because they tell my story without me having to speak. The second one is of a rooftop where the woman is crying and looking up at the moon. That's where I used to go, up on the roof of my parent's house. I'd sit, look at the moon, and just be by myself and cry a lot. That was my safe space. I was able to paint things that I really couldn't talk to people about. Now I can.

There is safety in painting. Nobody's going to argue with a painting. Nobody's going to take it personally. They're not going to tell you, "That's not how it really happened." They're not going to say, "What did you have on?" A lot of people, even if they haven't been sexually assaulted, look at my paintings and say they see what I felt.

I put together a website, www.hightrance.com, showing my paintings because this summer I've been taking time for me. I didn't even try to look for a legal job. I realized that I can sell my paintings. I also make things like wind chimes, candleholders, and postcards.

I set up a stand at the mall. I haven't sold a lot of things—I'm not really focused on making money—but it feels really great to just be out there talking to people. So many people come up to me and share their experiences. I'm meeting a lot of people that I hope to work with. One lady said she wants me to read some poems—which I started writing a few months ago for the same reason I paint—to girls at her church. I told her that I would definitely love to do that. Maybe that's a way to get back to going to church.

For survivors, there's so much I want to say to you. There is so much love in this world. Don't let anyone else's wrongdoings become a reflection of you. It's not you. It's outside of you. Hold tight to yourself. Find someone to talk to or some outlet to express how you're feeling. There's no need to hold things inside. I know what silence does to people's bodies. That energy has to go somewhere and if you hold it inside, it just attacks you. It will make you sick. That's what my painting "Silence Kills" is about. After the professor incident, the more I just sat there and thought about it—before I acted to make sure the situation was handled—the worse I began to feel. She's so much thinner than all the other women I paint because I found myself suffering physically and emotionally from a recent assault. One of the most emotionally draining aspects of the current situation was that, unlike other times in my life, I reached out for help immediately. I thought I had made contact with people who would act as my advocates. Instead, I found that I had to advocate for myself. The good thing to come out of this situation is that I'm forced to discover the very reliable support system of my friends and family. My phone bill is huge but my heart and soul are much happier.

Everybody should be able to find someone to talk to. You can call crisis hotlines anonymously, there's just no reason that people should have to deal with sexual assault or abuse by themselves. There are plenty of people out there who want to help you. It's a question of finding that person when you're ready to talk. I don't want to press anybody to talk about things if they're not comfortable, because you need to do it in your own time. Every survivor is different.

Another thing, we women need to use each other as a resource and not isolate each other, not put other women down, not allow others to put other women down. The moment you allow someone to call a woman a whore or a bitch, you are providing justification for someone else deciding you are a whore or a bitch, treating you with the same disrespect.

I just don't feel like there's any difference between me and the next woman. How am I going to help other people if I think that in some way I'm better than them? It's okay for it to happen to a certain type of woman but just not me? That's a major problem.

And to the families, there's nothing more important than being supportive and believing a survivor. "I'm sorry that happened" is a good thing to hear. "If you need anything, I'm here. If you want to talk about it, I'm here. Whenever."

Silent help is the best thing sometimes. People can feel this need to know what's wrong. Just let the survivor know: "I'm here for you. I don't necessarily need to know what's bothering you, but I just want you to know I'm here." Those can be the best words in the world.

Recently, I went back home to Panama. On the plane I felt a nagging urge to talk to the women at my church. Not understanding how I would specifically get the women together on such late notice (I was home for less than a week), I called the pastor of my church. His wife invited me to a women's program that was going on that evening. I took it as a clear sign and drove to the church to speak to her immediately. I cannot explain how relieved I was to talk to her. Mrs. Toppin gave me so much support, was so kind and so understanding. I feared so many responses from the church as a whole and received none of them. Later that evening I stood before the group of women and a few men and told them about my rape. I asked them to please stop passing judgment when they hear about situations like mine, and to hold people accountable when they make mistakes. I explained that rape does not happen because of a mistake the survivor makes, but because of a perpetrator's decision to rape. I asked them to please love and support one another.

Although no one was in the church the day I was raped, I was so grateful that they were present when I was truly ready to talk and ask for their help, their support and their love. They gave me all of these things and many hugs. Even better, Mrs. Toppin gave me a verse to read everyday, Isaiah 58:1. She said, "That is for you." And, it really is for me: "Cry aloud, spare not, lift up thy voice like a trumpet, and shew my people their transgression, and the house of Jacob their sins . . . "

She is right. It is really for all of us. We must find a way to communicate injustice any way we can—through art, poetry, music or books. Do a dance, write a play, advocate. We must show others the way things affect us. Otherwise they will not be able to do their part to prevent sexual violence or address past wrongdoings.

I am so grateful that my family, my friends and my church are behind me and help me make my voice heard. They support, love and nurture me. They give me the strength that I need to keep moving forward. This is all I need and it is exactly what every survivor deserves. I hope that each and every one of you will reach out for your support system and that you will find that it is just as solid. Until you are ready to do so, I hope you will trust yourself and give yourself the love and the time you need to heal. I am grateful for love and life.

AUDREE'S STORY

Audree is a single mother of three children and the full-time caretaker of her niece. The night a rapist invaded her home and attacked Audree, her children were all younger than age ten. Two of them were in the room with her throughout the assault. With no other family members living in her state, Audree struggled for years after the assault to provide a stable home for her family. Once she surrounded herself with positive, encouraging Black women, the professional counseling and spiritual teaching she needed to heal became readily available. Those resources, in addition to her writing exercises and voracious reading of self-help books, have produced in Audree a profound healing.

I'm from Anthony, a small, rural town in Florida. If horse farming or low-paying administrative jobs had been my speed, I might have stayed there my whole life. But I've always been a go-getter, so deciding to move wasn't hard.

An outgoing, open-minded sister, back in those days, I would strike up a conversation with anyone, from a politician to a homeless person. Upbeat and just happy to be on the planet, my personality would serve me well, I figured, in a much bigger town. I left in 1988, at age thirty, in search of new professional, cultural, and educational experiences for my kids and me. I found what I was looking for in Atlanta.

Two years later, I found myself living in the Wheat Street Garden Apartments in Atlanta's historic Sweet Auburn neighborhood. You could see the famous Wheat Street Baptist Church from my ground floor apartment window, and I worked about a block away at the Early Learning Center of the Martin Luther King Jr. Center for Non-Violent Social Change. A secretary and part-time teacher there, I was only a few weeks away from a new position as an intake counselor for a local welfare office, when a nightmare would ravage me and change my life forever.

One warm spring night, I left my kitchen window cracked after smelling gas. While my daughter and niece slept in one bedroom and I slept with my two other children, a man crawled in that window, picked up a knife from my kitchen, and found his way to my bed.

I tried to think my way out at first. I asked to go to the bathroom, where I figured I'd find something to throw in his eyes and disable him long enough to get to safety. But not only did my near-hysterical son cling to my leg, my assailant followed me to the bathroom. After cursing us, threatening my son with the knife, and trying to rape me on the floor of my girls' bedroom, I, at least, got this monster back to my room.

Fearing for the lives of my children, and for my own, I did what I had to do to survive. I simultaneously had to calm my son and the criminal who invaded our home. Then, I was raped while my baby girl slept and my two-year-old son cried facedown at my side.

I wish I could say the difficult journey back to wholeness started right away. Even though I have now reached a deep peace of mind and spirit, my ordeal didn't end with the rapist leaving my home.

I called the police immediately. Along with an officer, three emergency medical technicians showed up. I described the assailant by comparing his complexion and height to one of the technicians, the only Black person who'd come. He at once put his hands up and said,

"Don't look at me! It wasn't me," provoking rousing laughter from his colleagues. I was shocked—in an instant, the most horrendous trauma of my life had been transformed into the butt of a joke. It wouldn't be the last insensitivity I'd suffer.

The only family I've ever had in Atlanta were my children, who at the time ranged from one to nine years old. The next morning, I tried my best to carry on with my routine, somehow getting the children to school and day care, and getting myself to work. But I wasn't fooling anyone but myself. Co-workers kept asking what was wrong. It took a few hours before I finally broke down and told what had happened. Fortunately, I worked with some compassionate people, my first adopted family.

Between trying to forget what happened and assuming no authorities would care about the rape of a Black woman, especially one that lived in a low-income neighborhood, I hadn't planned on reporting my assault. But my co-workers insisted. One accompanied me to Grady Memorial Hospital's rape crisis center where a sympathetic woman doctor examined me. I had demanded a female doctor. A staff person had told me that I would have to see whomever was on duty, even if it was a man. I said, "I've just been raped by a man. Do you expect me now to let a man examine me?" It was by the grace of God that a woman doctor was on duty. If not, I would not have gone through with the exam.

Then my co-worker went with me to the police station. Now that was a fiasco. It was a Friday, around four o'clock in the afternoon. Someone informed a Black male detective that he needed to take my report. Right in front of me, he responded, "Aw man, why I gotta do this one? I'm ready to go home. It's the weekend!"

He picked the wrong sister to mess with that day. "You mother fucker, let me tell you what I just went through. I literally had to consent to a rape so this guy would not kill my son or kill me or my other children, and all you can think about is partying? I just lost half my soul this morning!" After I cussed him out good, I turned to storm out of the station.

I ranted and raved to my co-worker who'd been waiting, explaining what the detective had said, that that's what Black women are worth to society. "This is the kind of shit I'm talking about," I fumed. "Let's just drop it and go."

I don't know what she said to that detective, but he came out about ten minutes later and apologized. Still, as far as I was concerned, the damage was already done. He ended up leaving anyway and another detective took my statement. But before leaving, he had the nerve to tell me he would come to my apartment Monday morning to get more details. "What kind of fool do you think I am? Do you honestly think that I'm going to stay in this apartment over the weekend, knowing that this guy is still walking around out there?" I said in disgust.

That original detective was still assigned to my case, and we never got along. I didn't trust him to investigate my assault adequately, so I didn't leave it up to him. I started asking people around the neighborhood if they knew of anyone who fit the rapist's description. It didn't take very long to find someone who did.

A friend who used to baby-sit my children not only knew whom I was describing by name, she'd had him in her house before visiting her boyfriend. She also told me he had just gotten out of jail for killing his girlfriend, who had three kids. As a matter of fact, she said, I resembled that girlfriend!

Of course, I immediately told the detective what I'd heard, including that my assailant was probably living in a high-rise senior citizen's home. I warned him not to just bust up in there and ask everybody about this guy, because since it was against the regulations of the building, no one would admit to putting him up. But he goes down there and asks straight out. Needless to say, the man who raped me was never caught.

Detective work aside, I tried to go on with my life and take care of my family as best I could. I decided to try to handle everything alone. I didn't get counseling back then, although it was offered to me at the hospital's rape crisis center.

Truthfully, even though we lived only a few blocks from Grady, I was too scared to go. The counseling sessions would have me coming home after dark, and I couldn't handle that. One of the lasting effects of being assaulted for me is a continuing fear of being out at night, especially alone. It's a little ironic since I was raped in my home, but I was attacked at one o'clock in the morning, and I guess I haven't gotten over my dread of darkness.

In those early years after the rape, going out during the day could be an ordeal too. I would be looking over my shoulder, wondering if this person was still somewhere looking and peeking and hiding.

Even locked in my room, for the longest time I woke up at 1 A.M. every night. I must have been walking around sleep deprived. No matter how much sleep I got, I functioned in a daze. It was like I couldn't think clearly. Things I used to be able to do quickly without much effort had become complicated, time-consuming tasks. Before I had a routine, cooking dinner, getting the kids to bed. But after being raped, boiling hot dogs and giving the kids potato chips and punch became a two-hour process.

While I was struggling to care for my family at home, I tried to put on a brave face at work. I was doing pretty good in my new job— my responsibilities were easy. Emotionally, I stayed between anger and fear. Sometimes I would go to the bathroom and be okay, then all of a sudden just start crying, not able to stop. So I'd be in a stall, somebody would walk in the bathroom, and I found myself trying to muffle my cries because I didn't want anybody to ask me what was wrong. I didn't want to have to explain.

My new boss at the welfare office didn't help anything. She seemed to have personal problems with some of my co-workers and me. She was a controlling person and would belittle us. Had I not been raped, I think I would have ignored things she said. But every time I felt she was attacking me, I felt I had to defend myself. So we clashed. My attitude had a lot to do with me getting fired. I never told her what happened to me because I'd seen her betray the confidence of someone else in the office. I worked at the welfare office for only five or six months before she fired me.

Fortunately I soon got into an Urban League training program. My family survived on the program's stipend and my unemployment benefits. For about ten months I was there learning computer skills to help me land a better job.

One of the most difficult struggles I had after the assault was finding a stable place to live. My kids and I bounced around to different homes for the next few years. The friend who'd taken me to the hospital and the police station owned a boarding house, which became our first new home. The children and I stayed in one room. It was there that I started propping chairs or heavy furniture against the door at night. I also started sleeping with a knife under my pillow and a bat by my bed, habits I'd keep for years, trying to feel safe enough to sleep.

Mine were the only kids in the house, and it soon became apparent that my friend had little tolerance for them. So after a few months I found my own two-bedroom apartment. I rented one room to a friend and her little girl, and again I slept in a room with my kids. We lived there about six months before my friend moved out and I lost my job. Truth be told, I was also just too scared to stay there without another adult.

Next I moved in with a friend and her boyfriend. Even though their two-bedroom apartment had an alarm, I was still propping the door shut each night. About six months later they decided to move and yet another friend took us in, this time in a house. That lasted for several months before the woman who owned the first boarding house sold it to the residents and left town. They invited me back.

I felt like my healing process really began once I moved in the house with them. All women, the residents called themselves the Ajanaku family, a grassroots group committed to civic and community activism on behalf of African-American children. The sisters there really helped me out. They nurtured me and talked to me a lot. When they saw I was breaking apart, they'd come and give me a hug, tell me things were going to be all right. At times, if they saw I wasn't able to function, they would move in and take care of the kids.

My new job also helped jump-start my healing. Around the same time I moved in with the Ajanaku sisters, I started working at Spelman, the famous all-women's historically Black college. I was moved around to several temporary positions before getting a permanent job as the assistant to the director of the Women's Research and Resource Center on campus. Being exposed to so many positive Black women, many of whom encouraged me, slowly but surely started giving me more and more self-confidence.

It was after I'd begun to adapt to these new comforting environments that one friend in particular encouraged me to write out my thoughts and feelings about what happened to me. She produces videos and documentary films, so it's not surprising that she suggested I write a screenplay. Not that I should be concerned about structure, but that I should just write as a form of healing. Just let it flow, she said. And that's what I did.

I came up with a screenplay about the African-American community coming to grips with its own social ills. That's what I feel is important even to this day, that we can't look for outside help with our garbage. We need to do it ourselves.

Around that time, I had gone to a few events sponsored by the Black Women's Health Project, an organization that provides health information for African Americans. They had a publication called *Vital Signs*, which accepted submissions. When they had an issue coming up about violence against Black women, someone suggested that I write about my experience. I realized how freed up I felt after writing the screenplay, so I submitted an article that was published in the spring of 1994.

Once the article came out, I even passed it out on campus. I gave it basically to everybody I saw. When the word was out, a lot of people just approached me and said very supportive things. Some told me the same thing happened to them years ago, but they'd never told anyone. Many thanked me. When people asked if I was embarrassed, I would tell them, "No! I'm not ashamed of anything. I didn't do anything wrong."

I think that reading my article, and interacting with me and seeing that I really was not ashamed, made them feel better. Maybe they couldn't open up themselves, but because I represented some of the things that they had gone through and I had the kind of attitude I had, that helped them in their healing process.

Two incidents that hit close to home threatened to undo all the emotional progress I had made. Two administrative assistants at Spelman were killed by their partners. The first, Carrie Searcy, was murdered in February 1996. Vanessa Sanderson was shot dead in front of her five-year-old son in February, two years later. I knew them both but was especially tight with Vanessa.

I felt some of the same emotions I had felt after the rape. I didn't know whether I was coming or going. I knew I was having a nervous breakdown, and I wasn't the only one who thought so. People were worried about me because I walked around again in a daze, crying a lot, asking God why. I was so bad off, this time I decided to go to counseling. Through my job I had access to mental health care. I was referred to a Black woman psychotherapist, a Spelman grad as a matter of fact, who really helped me.

Dr. McDaniel-Ashe was a very supportive sister. She gave me some really good advice. She knew exactly where I was, like she was really thinking ahead of me sometimes. And she knew exactly what I needed when I needed it. I just basically did what she told me to do.

After my first few visits to Dr. McDaniel-Ashe, she began suggesting I go to a worship service, whatever my faith was. I had heard a lot of positive things about Hillside Truth Center, a church down the block from my house. Hillside was such a positive experience that I didn't feel the need to go back to my psychotherapist.

It's a very laid back, metaphysical, Christian church that welcomes all regardless of sexuality, race, or religious background. People don't frown at you if you don't wear your Sunday best. You can wear pants, shorts, whatever you want. Most importantly, it has helped me deal with all the negativity I've experienced in my life. I've learned not to put my energy into the stuff that's going on around me, but to put it into myself, get somewhere quiet, meditate, concentrate on my connection with the Higher Source.

Going to church is advice my mother had been giving me for years. She was the only family member I told about the rape, and I didn't tell her until a year after it happened. I was hesitant about telling her because I didn't want her to pity me or be sad for me. But after I told her over the phone, she was always supportive and encouraging.

What I also kept in my mind was that I was standing on the shoulders of other powerful Black women who have gone through slavery and all of its abuses. I thought about Sojourner Truth, Harriet Tubman, all of these great Black women who had been through ordeals that were even worse. I went through this one time. They went through it maybe all their lives. And if they can regroup and do what they did for the world, then I've got to regroup. That's empowered me a lot too.

Another major hurdle I've worked hard to overcome after the rape has been my anger toward Black men. In addition to being raped by a Black man, and mistreated by a Black ambulance worker and police detective, I revealed to my psychotherapist that I remember being molested once as a child, and that someone unsuccessfully attempted to rape me years earlier. I also knew that my sister had been raped. In my anger, sometimes I felt like I wanted to line them up and shoot them all.

I also had to deal with the issue of intimacy. That was very hard for a number of years. After I started to heal, I thought I really would like to find a nice brother. It was like being trapped in a love-hate relationship. You want to be with them, but you hate their guts. And to me that was an awful place to be. Through counseling and spiritual study, I've been able to work through many of these feelings and release much of my anger.

I've been seeing someone for eleven years now. I feel like we have a good relationship. He's very understanding and very open-minded. It's just been good that I found somebody like this. I can testify that there are some decent men left!

For a while it was very awkward to get intimate. But this person was very patient. He never pressured me, never even brought up the subject of sex. Sometimes being intimate now can still be a challenge. After having gone through a rape, it's hard for me to just let loose and let go and enjoy the whole sexual act between two loving people. When you've had a flashback, you don't want to tell somebody that you're trying to be intimate but that you just thought of the guy who was attacking you. But that happens less and less.

What's so strange is I never talked to my kids about the rape. I was already overbearing with my children. I didn't want to instill the same fear that I was feeling into them. Really, I've made up excuses not to address it. The rape definitely affected the way I've raised my kids. I feel like I hinder their independence. I have a daughter who's going to be on her own soon and I find myself still treating her like she's younger. If she wants to ride home on the bus alone, I'll insist on picking her up. That's something I still have to work on.

I am planning on taking self-defense and martial arts classes with my daughter. I also want to learn to use a handgun and eventually purchase one. Otherwise I don't know how I'll ever feel safe enough to move around at night.

Even though I love Spelman, most recently, I decided to go to college full-time. I am now studying at Georgia State University. I'm majoring in film and video, my passion.

Now that many people know what happened to me, I'm going to do whatever I can for sisters who come to me and need help. I try my best to walk them through things they can do to help themselves. The main thing I tell them is that in order to heal—and you've got to heal—they have to know that they are not at fault. They must not blame themselves regardless of what the situation was. You have to go on and understand what spiritual lesson can be learned from your trauma. Because if you walk around and hold on to that garbage, anger and other negative emotions, it's going to kill you one way or the other, physically, mentally, or spiritually. I'm not trying to die on any of those levels, especially spiritually. If I die spiritually, I don't need to be here.

I think just by getting the spiritual self in order and being happy and at peace with yourself, even if everything that's going on around you is in chaos, you will feel in balance. When I get to that spiritual level, I believe everything will just automatically flow. I think I'm well on my way.

In Conclusion

What a painful issue. Sexual violence is an insidious, persistent reality in the world, in our country, and in the African-American community. But there are so many strides being made against this tragedy all the time. There are individual triumphs of healing. There are victories by community activists and organizations. There is sanity. There is courage. There is love. There is life. There is transformation.

Second only to healing from rape, writing *I Will Survive* has been my greatest emotional challenge. It has been part of my healing journey, something I certainly never considered when starting this project. I envisioned this book as a healing tool for communities and for survivors, and I hope it serves this purpose. If it enlightens someone who believed the rape myths they'd always heard, or it gives someone the inspiration they need to find a therapist, or it teaches the loved one of a victim how to be supportive, it will have been worth the effort.

The messages I most want readers to come away with are:

- Sexual assault and abuse are never the victim's fault.
- Anyone, no matter what the trauma, can experience profound healing.

• Because of the painful, often brutally violent, history of oppression of both Black women and men, the Black community has an even harder time than others debunking myths about rape, which prevents survivors from getting help and prevents the entire community from addressing the issue in a productive way. This can change. Ordinary people can make it happen.

As a rape victim, I was blessed with family and friends who acknowledged the devastation caused by my assault, and at the same time seemed to always have the expectation that I would heal. My friend Sherri Roberts Lumpkin wrote the following poem—dated June 13, 1995, less than a month after my rape—using my middle name in the title.

What is Sasai

What is this beautiful Sasai, a flower
Who is she this companion of my soul
She is blossoms of power that transcend strength
A strength full of spirit and purity
But it appears that the spirit has been broken, blossoms wilted
Watering her with my tears of love does not quench her
Sasai blossoms have fallen
Feeding her with my words of wisdom does not nourish her
Only God's purist star, the sun, untouched by man,
can shine on her and penetrate her soul
This will bring back her spirit
For her purity, like the sun's, has never been touched
Both star and Sasai protected by God
New buds are sprouting, an inner peace unfolds
What is this beautiful Sasai, she is God's flower
And my soul's companion

I believe that the words of Sherri's prophetic poem have manifested. Just as my supporters ahd confidence that I could be restored to a state of well-being and peace. I am completely convinced that the same is possible for all survivors and for our community. We ahve already come so far. Let's keep striving until the threat of sexual violence no longer exists for any girl, woman, man or boy.

RESOURCES

Hotlines

National Sexual Assault Hotline
800-656-HOPE (800-656-4673)
www.rainn.org, info@rainn.org

National Domestic Violence Hotline
800-799-SAFE (800-799-7233)
www.ndvh.org, ndvh@ndvh.org
TTY: 800-787-3224, deafhelp@ndvh.org

Child Abuse Hotline
800-4-A-CHILD (800-422-4453)
www.childhelpusa.org

National STD/HIV Hotline
800-227-8922

National Hopeline Network
800-SUICIDE (800-784-2433)
www.hopeline.com

Resources by Chapter

Chapter 1

Centers for Disease Control and Prevention National STD/HIV Hotline
See listing under Hotlines above.

Child Advocacy Center
334-432-1101
A multi-agency facility in Mobile, Alabama, that provides comprehensive
services for children and teens who have been sexually or physically abused.

Child and Adolescent Protection Center
202-884-4950
Provides physical and mental health services for children. Located at Children's National Medical Center in Washington, D.C.

Child and Adolescent Sexual Abuse Resource Center
415-206-8386
Provides rape crisis services, including SANE exams, for children and youth up to 17 years old. Located at San Francisco General Hospital.

Children's Hospital Boston - Division of Emergency Medicine
617-355-6637
One of the largest emergency/trauma centers in New England.

Emergency Contraception Hotline
888-NOT-2-LATE (800-668-2528)
www.not-2-late.com
Provides information on emergency contraception and a national list of doctors and health care organizations that prescribe emergency contraception.

Grady Rape Crisis Center
404-616-4861
Provides rape crisis services, including forensic exams, for adults. Located at Grady Memorial Hospital in Atlanta.

Planned Parenthood Federation of America
800-230-PLAN (800-230-7526)
www.plannedparenthood.org
Through its more than 850 health centers in 49 states and Washington, D.C., offers low-cost women's health care, including emergency contraception and treatment of sexually transmitted diseases.

Rosa Parks Sexual Assault Crisis Center
323-751-9383

Provides counseling, advocacy, and other services for children and adults. Located in Inglewood, California.

Chapter 2

American Red Cross
877-272-7337
www.redcross.org
Primarily a disaster relief organization, provides various types of assistance to people in response to emergencies.

Justice for Children
800-733-0059
www.jfcadvocacy.org
info@jfcadvocacy.org
Provides legal advocacy for abused children, court watching, and community resource referrals. Intervenes on behalf of abused children when child protection agencies and courts fail to protect them. The book *Long and Mature Considerations: A Legal Guide for Adult Survivors of Child Sexual Abuse* is available for purchase by calling the Washington, D.C., chapter at 202-462-4688.

National Crime Victim Bar Association
202-467-8753
www.victimbar.org
victimbar@ncvc.org
A network of attorneys and allied professionals dedicated to facilitating civil actions brought by crime victims. Refers crime victims to civil attorneys in their local area.

National Organization for Victim Assistance
202-232-6682
800-TRY-NOVA (800-879-6682)
www.try-nova.org
Provides referrals to state compensation boards, state bar associations, crisis intervention, and sexual assault programs.

National Organization for Women (NOW) Legal Defense and Education Fund
212-925-6635
www.nowldef.org, lir@nowldef.org
The Public Education and Outreach Help Line is open weekdays between 9:30
a.m. and 1:00 p.m. (EST) to answer questions about your rights. Legal Resource
Kits available online or by phone include: *Guide to Court Watching in Domestic Violence and Sexual Assault Cases*, *How to Find a Lawyer*, *Violence Against Women*, and
Incest and Child Sexual Abuse, which contains a directory of attorneys by state.

Office for Victims of Crime Resource Center
800-627-6872
TTY: 877-712-9279
www.ojp.usdoj.gov/ovc/ovcres/welcome.html
askovc@ojp.usdoj.gov
An information clearinghouse for victimization issues that provides referrals to
victim assistance and compensation programs by state.

Rape Crisis Advocacy Project
434-244-2630
A student organization at the University of Virginia School of Law in Charlottesville, Virginia, that provides legal advice for survivors.

Chapter 3

American Academy of Medical Acupuncture
323-937-5514
www.medicalacupuncture.org
JDOWDEN@prodigy.net
Provides referrals to medical doctors who practice acupuncture.

American Art Therapy Association
888-290-0878
www.arttherapy.org
info@arttherapy.org

Refers you to the association's chapter in your state, which will provide the names of local therapists.

American Association of Oriental Medicine
888-500-7999
www.aaom.org
hq@aaom.org
Provides referrals and an online list of acupuncturists by state or zip code.

American Association of Pastoral Counselors
703-385-6967
www.aapc.org
info@aapc.org
Provides online listing of pastoral counseling centers accredited by the association that offer counseling and psychotherapy services. Also gives phone referrals to pastoral counselors in private practice and other settings.

American Dance Therapy Association
410-997-4040
www.adta.org
info@adta.org
Provides information on dance therapists.

American Music Therapy Association
301-589-3300
www.musictherapy.org
info@musictherapy.org
Provides referrals to music therapists.

American Society of Clinical Hypnosis
630-980-4740
www.asch.net
info@asch.net
140 North Bloomingdale Road, Bloomingdale, IL 60108

Provides an online listing of referrals by location and/or specialty. Will send a list of clinicians in your state if you send a self-addressed stamped envelope.

Association of Black Psychologists
202-722-0808
www.abpsi.org, admin@abpsi.org
Primarily a professional membership organization, provides referrals to African-American psychologists.

Bellevue/NYU Program for Survivors of Torture
212-683-7446
www.survivorsoftorture.org
Provides multidisciplinary treatment and rehabilitative services to survivors of political torture and their families.

Biofeedback Certification Institute of America
303-420-2902
www.bcia.org
bcia@resourcecenter.com
Provides referrals to certified practitioners.

Daily Thoughts from the Hill
404-758-6811
www.hillsidechapel.org
A monthly daily devotional guide.

Daily Word
800-669-0282
www.unityworldhq.org
A monthly inspirational mini-magazine.

EMDR (Eye Movement Desensitization and Reprocessing) Institute
831-372-3900
www.emdr.com

referrals@emdr.com
Provides referrals to clinicians in your area who have completed EMDR
Institute training.

International Association of Reiki Professionals
603-827-3290
www.iarp.org
info@iarp.org
Provides an online listing of reiki practitioners by state.

National Association for Drama Therapy
202-966-7409
www.nadt.org
nadt@dmg-dc.com
Provides a listing of drama therapists.

National Association for Holistic Aromatherapy
888-ASK-NAHA (888-275-6242)
www.naha.org
info@naha.org
Refers you to the association's branch in your area, which will provide the names
of local therapists.

National Association for Poetry Therapy
866-844-NAPT (866-844-6278)
www.poetrytherapy.org
info@poetrytherapy.org
Provides referrals to poetry therapists.

National Center for Victims of Crime
800-FYI-CALL (800-394-2255)
TTY: 800-211-7996
www.ncvc.org
gethelp@ncvc.org

Provides sustained victim advocacy support, referrals, and information for emotional, physical and financial concerns, legal assistance, safety planning, and shelter.

National Certification Commission for Acupuncture and Oriental Medicine
703-548-9004
www.nccaom.org
Provides referrals to an acupuncturist in your area.

National Mental Health Association Resource Center
800-969-NMHA (800-969-6642)
TTY: 800-433-595
www.nmha.org
infoctr@nmha.org
Not a crisis line, gives referrals to community mental health services and provides information about medications, treatments, and consumer rights. Website features an online help desk through which you can submit specific questions or request a referral.

National Organization for Victim Assistance
See listing under Chapter 2.

National Organization on Male Sexual Victimization
800-738-4181
www.nomsv.org
Not a crisis line, provides a listing of clinicians by state. A book list and information on the organization's annual retreat for survivors in recovery can be accessed on the website.

Office for Victims of Crime Resource Center
See listing under Chapter 2.

Reiki Alliance
208-783-3535

www.reikialliance.com

internationaloffice@reikialliance.com

Provides an online listing of reiki practitioners by state as well as in other countries.

Yoga Journal

www.yogajournal.com

The magazine *Yoga Journal* provides a list of teachers in each December issue and an online listing year round.

YWCA Greater Los Angeles Sexual Assault Crisis Program

310-764-1403

www.ywcagla.org

A rape crisis center providing counseling, advocacy, prevention education and other services.

Chapter 6

The Black Church and Domestic Violence Institute

770-909-0715

www.bcdvi.org

bcdvorg@aol.com

An educational ministry that trains pastoral leaders and other professionals to prevent and respond to domestic violence. Also provides workshops for congregations and holds an annual conference open to women and men of all faiths.

WomanSpace: A Sacred Space for God's Professional Woman

616-767-9706

www.geocities.com/womanspace2003/

WTWMI99@aol.com

A sanctuary for today's professional woman in order to assist in deveoping her fullest divine potential. Provides spiritual direction, seminars for successful living, and business strategies for both networking and community outreach.

Chapter 7

Black Church Initiative's National Black Religious Summit on Sexuality
202-628-7700
www.rcrc.org/bci
www.rcrc.org
Helps African-American clergy and laity address sexual education and other reproductive health issues within the context of African-American culture and religion. Holds annual summit in Washington, D.C., and provides faith-based sexuality education curricula for adults and teens.

Dove Center
202-638-0875
A private, spirituality-centered healing practice featuring psychotherapy, reiki, aromatherapy, and reflexology, located in Washington, D.C.

Fernwood United Methodist Church
773-445-7100
Organizing base for Operation Defense, a grassroots program created to protect Black women in the wake of serial rapes that occurred on Chicago's South Side.

Gadohi Usquanigodi Native American Spiritual Center of Chicago
773-233-8235
www.gadohi.org
Pursues cultural and spiritual harmony between all peoples through the traditional spiritual and healing teachings of North American Indigenous nations.

The Generations Center
856-667-3033
A mental health facility that meets the holistic needs of men of color and all women, in Cherry Hill, New Jersey.

God Can Ministries
312-746-8458

Godcan1@aol.com
A church of the United Church of Christ denomination in Ford Heights, Illinois.

Jemima Ministries
425-687-5815
jemimaministries@aol.com
Helps women develop self-esteem. Located in King County, Washington.

Sisters of Tamar Ministry
202-332-9567
sistersoftamar250@msn.com
A ministry for survivors of sexual abuse and sexual violence.

Time of Refreshing Women's Support Group
561-882-9323
Gives safe haven and emotional and spiritual aid to women in crisis. Located in
West Palm Beach, Florida.

Trinity African Methodist Episcopal Church
913-621-2306
A church of the historic African Methodist Episcopal denomination located in
Kansas City, Kansas.

Chapter 8

The Dinah Project
615-726-3876
www.metropolitanfrc.com/dinah_project.asp
metrofrc@aol.com
Educates about sexuality, violence, and appropriate relationships to prevent violence in the Black community.

A Long Walk Home: A Story of a Rape Survivor
617-491-2302

www.alongwalkhome.com

info@alongwalkhome.com

A multimedia performance that documents the journey from trauma victim to survivor. Through poetry, music, photography, West African, and modern dance, artists educate about sexual violence through workshops, lecture series, exhibitions, and community education programs nationwide.

Los Angeles Commission on Assaults Against Women

213-955-9090

TDD: 213-955-9095

www.lacaaw.org

info@lacaaw.org

A community-based sexual assault, domestic violence, youth violence, and child abuse prevention center. Also provides counseling and has produced excellent awareness campaign materials and a teen curriculum.

Men Overcoming Violence

415-626-MOVE (415-626-6683)

www.menovercomingviolence.org

A progressive, pro-feminist, social change organization in San Francisco dedicated to ending young and adult men's violence in their relationships.

Men Stopping Violence

404-688-1376

www.menstoppingviolence.org

msv@menstoppingviolence.org

A social change organization in Atlanta dedicated to ending men's violence against women.

National Advisory Council on Violence Against Women

http://toolkit.ncjrs.org

Provides guidance to communities, policy leaders, and individuals engaged in activities to end violence against women. With 16 chapters focused on a particular audience or environment, their Toolkit to End Violence against Women includes recommendations for strengthening prevention efforts and advocacy. Can be downloaded from the website.

National Organization for Women
202-628-8669
TTY: 202-331-9002
www.now.org
now@now.org
A feminist membership organization with chapters nationwide. Addresses violence against women in a variety of ways, including championing legislation, advocating for survivors of rape, sexual harassment, and sex discrimination, and sponsoring annual Take Back the Night rallies.

National Organization for Women Legal Defense and Education Fund
See listing under Chapter 2.

National Sexual Violence Resource Center
877-739-3895
www.nsvrc.org
resources@nsvrc.org
Principal clearinghouse of resources and research for survivors, healing professionals, and educators.

Oakwood Center of the Palm Beaches
DrMAJones@aol.com
561-844-9741
Provides education and training through its Sexual Violence Awareness and Prevention Program in West Palm Beach, Florida.

Todos Institute
510-444-6448
todos@igc.org
Offers anti-violence programs and workshops for youth and adults.

Women Organized Against Rape
215-985-3315
24-hour hotline: 215-985-3333
www.woar.org
Located in Philadelphia, provides comprehensive sexual assault counseling and advocacy services, as well as community education.

Chapter 9

Center for the Prevention of Sexual and Domestic Violence
206-634-1903
www.cpsdv.org
cpsdv@cpsdv.org
An interfaith educational resource center addressing sexual and domestic violence. Offers many publications and videos, including "Love—All That and More," a multicultural video series for youth on healthy relationships.

Cleveland Rape Crisis Center
216-619-6194
24-hour hotline: 216-619-6192
www.clevelandrapecrisis.org
crcc@core.com
Serves all survivors and those supporting them at any point following sexual violence through advocacy, education, training, and activism.

Committee for Children
800-634-4449
www.cfchildren.org
info@cfchildren.org
Dedicated to promoting the safety, well-being, and social development of children. Develops and publishes research-based curricula to prevent bullying, child abuse, and youth violence, and to encourage social and emotional literacy. Also develops programs for family and parent education.

Contact Mobile
251-431-5100
Help line: 251-431-5111
helpline@mobilecan.org
A rape crisis program providing counseling, advocacy, prevention education, and other services.

The Empower Program
202-232-8200
www.empowered.org
empower@empowered.org
Teaches youth in the Washington, D.C. metropolitan area to prevent violence, and trains educators at schools, hospitals, and other sites nationwide to implement its curricula for boys and girls.

Family Violence Prevention Fund
888-RX-ABUSE (888-792-2873)
www.endabuse.org
Works to prevent domestic violence and help women and children whose lives are devastated by abuse. Call for a community action kit designed to help African Americans prevent domestic violence. Also offers the public education campaign "Coach Boys into Men."

The Good Knight Campaign Child Empowerment Network
301-595-8989
www.goodknight.org
contactus@goodknight.org
A national crime and violence prevention coalition, provides child safety programs for groups. Offers the Family Security Kit, including a 45-minute video and an activity book, and other educational products.

Hays-Caldwell Women's Center
512-396-3404
www.hcwc.org

Housed at Southwest Texas State University in San Marcos, Texas, offers counseling, advocacy, a shelter, and educational outreach for women, children, and men.

Men Can Stop Rape
202-265-6530
www.mencanstoprape.org
info@mencanstoprape.org
Empowers male youth and the institutions that serve them to help prevent rape and other forms of men's violence through community projects, workshops, and clubs. Posters and postcards from its powerful educational campaign "My Strength is Not for Hurting" are available.

Men Stopping Violence
See listing under Chapter 8.

National Black Women's Health Project
202-548-4000
www.blackwomenshealth.org
A health education, research, advocacy, and leadership development institution. Offers "Tell Me What's Going On . . . My Body, My Self, My Life," a video for parents and teen daughters.

National Coalition Against Domestic Violence
303-839-1852
www.ncadv.org
Committed to the elimination of personal and societal violence in the lives of battered women and their children. Provides a wide range of services, including the development of public policy, educational materials, and awareness campaigns, including teen dating violence information.

National Crime Prevention Council
202-466-6272
www.ncpc.org
An educational organization helping individuals, communities, and governments

reduce crime. Offers resources for violence prevention training and community programs, and information on personal and family safety.

National Sexual Violence Resource Center
See listing under Chapter 8.

Black Church Initiative
See listing under Chapter 7.

Safer Society Foundation
802-247-3132
www.safersociety.org
ssfi@sover.net
A national research, advocacy, and referral center for the prevention and treatment of sexual abuse. Gives nationwide referrals for abuse-reactive children and juvenile and adult sex offenders.

San Francisco Women Against Rape
415-861-2024
24-hour crisis hotline: 415-647-RAPE (415-647-7273)
www.sfwar.org
info@sfwar.org
A rape crisis center providing counseling, advocacy, and prevention education.

SEX, ETC.
732-445-7929
www.sxetc.org
A sexuality and health newsletter written by teens for teens. Offers an educational manual, "Teaching with SEX, ETC.: Articles & Activities," for educators. Schools and organizations can order the SEX, ETC. newsletter for free. More than 200 articles are available on the website.

Sexuality Information and Education Council of the United States
212-819-9770

www.siecus.org

siecus@siecus.org

www.familiesaretalking.org

Promotes comprehensive education about sexuality. Has launched the Family Project to help parents and caregivers talk to children about sexuality-related issues. Provides online lists of books, fact sheets, and other resources about sexuality. Materials can also be ordered.

Chapter 10

Black Women's Leadership Roundtable

773-752-6772

www.stoptheassaults.com

info@stoptheassaults.com

An evolving collective of Black women community leaders formed to focus attention on a serial rape crisis in Chicago. A multifaceted communications network that performs court advocacy for the serial rape survivors, presents a traveling forum, offers experts for media interviews, and advises other communities of color.

Columbus Urban League

614-257-6300

www.cul.org

This community service organization's rape prevention initiative provides public awareness programs, cultural sensitivity training, intervention, and support to reduce sexual violence. The CUL also offers services for domestic violence survivors and other crime victims.

Fernwood United Methodist Church

See listing under Chapter 7.

Gadohi Usquanigodi Native American Spiritual Center of Chicago

See listing under Chapter 7.

Houston Area Women's Center
713-528-6789
www.hawc.org

Sexual assault hotline: 713-528-7273
Domestic violence hotline: 713-528-2121
Provides shelter and comprehensive support services to survivors of domestic
and sexual violence. Educates youth and the community at large to prevent
and eliminate the causes of domestic and sexual violence.

Incite! Women of Color Against Violence
www.incite-national.org
415-553-3837
National activist organization of radical feminists of color mobilizing to end all
forms of violence against women of color and our communities. Offers Activist
Institutes and conferences in various locations.

National Center for Human Rights Education
404-344-9629
www.nchre.org
nchre@nchre.org
Dedicated to building a human rights movement, provides educational programs for community groups, nonprofit organizations, schools, and universities.

ADDITIONAL RESOURCES

Advocacy/Research

National Violence Against Women Prevention Research Center
843-792-2945
www.vawprevention.org
Sponsored by the Centers for Disease Control and Prevention, provides general information, research, advocacy, public policy education, and training for scientists, practitioners, advocates, grassroots organizations, and any other professional or lay person interested in current topics related to violence against women.

National Youth Violence Prevention Resource Center
866-SAFEYOUTH (866-723-3968)
TTY: 800-243-7012
www.safeyouth.org
A central point of access to federal information on prevention and intervention programs, publications, research, and statistics on violence committed by and against children and teens. The resource center is a collaboration between the Centers for Disease Control and Prevention and other federal agencies.

Rape, Abuse, and Incest National Network (RAINN)
800.656.4673
www.rainn.org
info@rainn.org
The nation's largest anti-sexual assault organization, it operates the National Sexual Assault Hotline and serves as a resource for statistics and other information for the media, policymakers, and the public.

Stop Prisoner Rape
323-653-STOP (323-653-7867)
www.spr.org
info@spr.org

A human rights organization that seeks to end sexual violence against men, women, and youth in all forms of detention.

Violence Against Women Online Resources
www.vaw.umn.edu
Provides up-to-date information on interventions to stop violence against women for criminal justice practitioners, advocates, and social service professionals with the latest in research and promising practices regarding issues of domestic violence, stalking, batterer intervention, child custody and protection, sexual assault, and welfare reform.

Violence Against Women Website
www.4women.gov/violence/index.cfm
The federal government's National Women's Health Information Center created the Violence Against Women site to provide resources and information for abused women, their loved ones, and service providers.

Domestic Violence

Baitul Salaam Network
800-285-9489 pin #00
404-366-6610
http://alnisaa1.hypermart.net
haleem1@aol.com
An Islamic organization that works to eradicate spousal abuse. Provides counseling, shelter for battered women, temporary financial assistance, employment assistance, and other services.

Battered Women's Justice Project
www.bwjp.org
800-903-0111
Works to enhance justice for battered women in civil court and provides technical assistance to battered women charged with crimes committed in self-defense and in other circumstances, and their defense attorneys and advocates.

Family Violence Department
800-527-3223
www.nationalcouncilfvd.org
famvio@ncjfcj.unr.edu
A department of the National Council of Juvenile and Family Court Judges dedicated to improving the way courts, law enforcement, agencies, and others respond to family violence, with the ultimate goal of improving the lives of domestic violence victims and their children.

Institute on Domestic Violence in the African American Community
www.dvinstitute.org
877-NIDVAAC (877-643-8222)
Raises community awareness of the impact of violence in the African-American community. Sponsors local and national conferences and trainings.

Multi-level Interfaith Church Domestic Violence Project (Project MIC)
206-324-5530
www.cara-seattle.org/bpp_faith.html
Educates church leaders about domestic and youth violence, sexual assault, and substance abuse prevention and awareness. Provides culturally sensitive support to batterers taking responsibility for their actions.

National Association of Black Law Enforcement Executives
703-658-1529
www.noblenatl.org
noble@noblenatl.org
Works to ensure equity in the administration of justice. Offers resources for police departments and communities on responding to family violence.

Healing

www.brokenspirits.com
An online community and support group aiding current and past victims of child abuse, sexual abuse, and domestic violence.

National Center for Post-Traumatic Stress Disorder
617-232-9500
www.ncptsd.org
Only military veterans and their eligible dependents can be treated at this center, located at the Veteran's Administration Boston Healthcare System. The Women's Health Sciences Division (ext. 4145) provides mental health services for female survivors and the Behavioral Sciences Division (ext. 4143) provides mental health services for male survivors.

To find a rape crisis center or other healing resources near you, contact the National Sexual Assault Hotline (800-656-HOPE) or one of the state organizations listed below for referrals.

Alabama Coalition Against Rape
PO Box 4091
Montgomery, AL 36102
Ph: (334) 264-0123
Toll-free: (888) 725-7273
Fax: (334) 264-0128
www.acar.org, acar@acar.org

Alaska Network on Domestic Violence and Sexual Assault
130 Seward Street, Ste. 209
Juneau, AK 99801
Ph: (907) 586-3650
Toll-free: (800) 520-2666
Fax: (907) 463-4493
andvsa@hotmail.com

Arkansas Coalition Against Sexual Assault
200 South University, Ste. 202
Little Rock, AR 72205
Ph: (501) 663-7300
Toll-free: (866) 63-ACASA (866) 632-2272

Fax: (501) 663-0596

www.acasa.ws

Arizona Sexual Assault Network

77 East Thomas Road, Ste. 110

Phoenix, AZ 85012

Ph: (602) 258-1195

Fax: (602) 258-7390

info@azsan.org

California Coalition Against Sexual Assault

1215 K Street, Ste. 1100

Sacramento, CA 95814

Ph: (916) 446-2520

Fax: (916) 446-8166

www.calcasa.org, info@calcasa.org

Colorado Coalition Against Sexual Assault

PO Box 300398

Denver, CO 80203

Ph: (303) 861-7033

Fax: (303) 832-7067

www.ccasa.org, info@ccasa.org

Connecticut Sexual Assault Crisis Services, Inc.

96 Pitkin Street

East Hartford, CT 06108

Ph: (860) 282-9881

Fax: (860) 291-9335

www.connsacs.org, info@connsacs.org

Contact Delaware, Inc.

PO Box 9525

Wilmington, DE 19809

Ph: (302) 761-9800
Fax: (302) 761-4280
www.contactdelaware.org

D.C. Rape Crisis Center
PO Box 34125
Washington, DC 20043
Ph: (202) 232-0789
Fax: (202) 387-3812
www.dcrcc.org, dcrcc@dcrcc.org

Florida Council Against Sexual Violence
1311-A Paul Russell Road
Tallahassee, FL 32301
Ph: (850) 297-2000
Toll-free: (888) 956-7273
Fax: (850) 297-2002
information@fcasv.org

Georgia Network to End Sexual Assault
619 Edgewood Avenue SE, Ste. 104
Atlanta, GA 30312
Ph: (678) 701-2700
Fax: (678) 701-2709
manderson@gnesa.org

Guam Healing Arts Crisis Center
790 Gov. Carlos G. Camacho Road
Tamuning, GU 96911
Ph: (671) 647-5351
Toll-free: (800) 711-4826
Fax: (671) 647-6948
csmau@mail.gov.gu

Hawaii Coalition Against Sexual Assault
741A Sunset Avenue
Honolulu, HI 96816
Ph: (808) 733-9038
Fax: (808) 733-9032
(contact info will be changing in 2003, do not have a website)

Sex Abuse Treatment Center
55 Merchant Street, 22nd Floor
Honolulu, HI 96813
Ph: (808) 535-6730
www.kapiolani.org

Idaho Coalition Against Sexual and Domestic Violence
815 Park Boulevard, Ste. 140
Boise, ID 83712
Ph: (208) 384-0419
Toll-free: (888) 293-6118
Fax: (208) 331-0687
domvio@mindspring.com

Illinois Coalition Against Sexual Assault
100 North 16th St.
Springfield, IL 62703
Ph: (217) 753-4117
Fax: (217) 753-8229
icasa@icasa.org

Indiana Coalition Against Sexual Assault
55 Monument Circle, Ste. 1224
Indianapolis, IN 46204
Ph: (317) 423-0233
Toll-free: (800) 691-2272

Fax: (317) 423-0237
incasa@incasa.org

Iowa Coalition Against Sexual Assault
2603 Bell Avenue
Des Moines, IA 50321
Ph: (515) 244-7424
Fax: (515) 244-7417
www.iowacasa.org

Kansas Coalition Against Sexual Assault and Domestic Violence
220 SW 33rd Street, Ste. 100
Topeka, KS 66611
Ph: (785) 232-9784
Fax: (785) 266-1874
www.kcsdv.org, coalition@kcsdv.org

Kentucky Association of Sexual Assault Programs, Inc.
106-A St. James Court
Frankfort, KY 40601
Ph: (502) 226-2704
Fax: (502) 226-2725
www.kasap.org

Louisiana Foundation Against Sexual Assault
PO Box 40
Independence, LA 70443
Ph: (985) 345-5995
Fax: (985) 345-5592
lafasa@i-55.com

Maine Coalition Against Sexual Assault
83 Western Avenue, Ste. 2

Augusta, ME 04330
Ph: (207) 626-0034
Toll-free: (800) 871-7741
Fax: (207) 626-5503
www.mecasa.org, info@mecasa.org

Maryland Coalition Against Sexual Assault
1517 Ritchie Highway, Ste. 207
Arnold, MD 21012
Ph: (410) 974-4507
Toll-free: (800) 983-7273
Fax: (410) 757-4770
www.mcasa.org, info@mcasa.org

Massachusetts Coalition Against Sexual Assault and Domestic Violence - Jane
Doe Inc.
14 Beacon Street, Ste. 507
Boston, MA 02108
Ph: (617) 248-0922
Fax: (617) 248-0902
www.janedoe.org

Michigan Coalition Against Domestic and Sexual Violence
3893 Okemos Road, Ste. B2
Okemos, MI 48864
Ph: (517) 347-7000
Fax: (517) 347-1377
www.mcadsv.org, general@mcadsv.org

Minnesota Coalition Against Sexual Assault
420 N. 5th Street, Ste. 690
Minneapolis, MN 55401
Ph: (612) 313-2797
Toll-free: (800) 964-8847

Fax: (612) 313-2799
www.mncasa.org, info@mncasa.org

Mississippi Coalition Against Sexual Assault
PO Box 4172
Jackson, MS 39296
Ph: (601) 987-9011
Toll-free: (888) 987-9011
Fax: (601) 987-9166
www.mcasa.net

Missouri Coalition Against Sexual Assault
PO Box 104866
Jefferson City, MO 65110
Ph: (573) 636-8776
Fax: (573) 636-6613
Mocasajc@aol.com

Montana Coalition Against Domestic and Sexual Violence
PO Box 644
Helena, MT 59624
Ph: (406) 443-7794
Fax: (406) 443-7818
mcadsv@mt.net

Nebraska Domestic Violence Sexual Assault Coalition
825 M Street, Ste. 404
Lincoln, NE 68508
Ph: (402) 476-6256
Fax: (402) 476-6806
www.ndvsac.org, info@ndvsac.org

Nevada Coalition Against Sexual Violence
3027 E. Sunset Road, Ste. 101

Henderson, NV 89120
Ph: (702) 940-2033
Fax: (702) 940-2032
www.ncasv.org, regina@ncasv.org

New Hampshire Coalition Against Domestic and Sexual Violence
PO Box 353
Concord, NH 03302
Ph: (603) 224-8893
Fax: (603) 228-6096
www.nhcadsv.org

New Jersey Coalition Against Sexual Assault
1 Edinburg Road
Trenton, NJ 08619
Ph: (609) 631-4450
Toll-free hotline: (800) 601-7200
Fax: (609) 631-4453
www.njcasa.org

New Mexico Coalition of Sexual Assault Programs
4004 Carlisle NE, Ste. D
Albuquerque, NM 87107
Ph: (505) 883-8020
Toll-free: (888) 883-8020
Fax: (505) 883-7530
www.swcp.com/nmcaas/, nmcsaas@swcp.com

New York State Coalition Against Sexual Assault
63 Colvin Avenue
Albany, NY 12206
Ph: (518) 482-4222
Fax: (518) 482-4248
www.nyscasa.org, info@nyscasa.org

New York City Alliance Against Sexual Assault
c/o St. Luke Roosevelt Hospital CVTC
411 West 114th Street, Ste. 6D
New York, NY 10025
Ph: (212) 523-4185
Fax: (212) 523-4429
www.nycagainstrape.org, Contact-us@nycagainstrape.org

North Carolina Coalition Against Sexual Assault (NCCASA)
4426 Louisburg Road, Ste. 100
Raleigh, NC 27616
Ph: (919) 431-0995
Toll-free: (888) 737-2272
Fax: (919) 431-0996
www.nccasa.org, info@nccasa.org

North Dakota Coalition Against Sexual Assault
418 East Rousser, Ste. 320
Bismarck, ND 58501
Ph: (701) 255-6240
Toll-free: (888) 255-6240
Fax: (701) 255-1904
www.ndcaws.org, ndcaws@ndcaws.org

Ohio Coalition On Sexual Assault (OCOSA)
933 High Street, Ste. 120B
Worthington, OH 43085
Ph: (614) 781-1902
Fax: (614) 781-1933
ohiocoalition@aol.com

Oklahoma Coalition Against Domestic Violence and Sexual Assault
2525 NW Express Way, Ste. 101
Oklahoma City, OK 73112

Ph: (405) 848-1815
Fax: (405) 848-3469
www.ocadv.org

Oregon Coalition Against Domestic and Sexual Violence
115 Mission Street SE, Ste. 100
Salem, OR 97302
Ph: (503) 365-9644
Toll-free: (800) 622-3782
Fax: (503) 566-7870
www.ocadsv.com, info@ocadsv.com

Pennsylvania Coalition Against Rape
125 N. Enola Drive
Enola, PA 17025
Ph: (717) 728-9740
Toll-free: (800) 692-7445
Fax: (717) 728-9781
www.pcar.org, stop@pcar.org

Puerto Rico Rape Crisis
Centro de Ayuda Victimas de Violacion - Departamento de Salud
PO Box 70184
San Juan, PR 00913
Ph: (787) 756-0910
Fax: (787) 765-7840

Rhode Island Sexual Assault Coalition
300 Richmond Street, Ste. 205
Providence, RI 02903
Ph: (401) 421-4100
Fax: (401) 454-5565
www.satrc.org, info@satrc.org

South Carolina Coalition Against Domestic Violence and Sexual Assault
PO Box 7776
Columbia, SC 29202
Ph: (803) 256-2900
Toll-free: (800) 260-9293
Fax: (803) 256-1030
www.sccadvasa.org

South Dakota Coalition Against Domestic Violence and Sexual Assault
PO Box 141
Pierre, SD 57501
Ph: (605) 945-0869
Toll-free: (800) 572-9196
Fax: (605) 945-0870
www.southdakotacoalition.org

Tennessee Coalition Against Domestic and Sexual Violence
PO Box 120972
Nashville, TN 37212
Ph: (615) 386-9406
Statewide crisis line: (800) 356-6767
Fax: (615) 383-2967
www.tcadsv.org, Tcadsv@tcadsv.org

Texas Association Against Sexual Assault
7701 N. Lamar Blvd., Ste. 200
Austin, TX 78752
Ph: (512) 474-7190
Toll-free: (888) 918-2272
Fax: (512) 474-6490
www.taasa.org

Utah Coalition Against Sexual Assault
220 East 3900 South, Ste. 1

Salt Lake City, UT 84107
Ph: (801) 266-5094
Fax: (801) 266-5187
www.ucasa.org

Vermont Network Against Domestic Violence and Sexual Assault
PO Box 405
Montpelier, VT 05601
Ph: (802) 223-1302
Fax: (802) 223-6943
www.vtnetwork.org, vtnetwork@vtnetwork.org

Virginians Aligned Against Sexual Assault
508 Dale Avenue, Ste. B
Charlottesville, VA 22903
Ph: (434) 979-9002
Fax: (434) 979-9003
www.vaasa.org

Women's Coalition of St. Croix
PO Box 222734
Christiansted-St. Croix, USVI 00822
Ph: (340) 773-9272
Fax: (340) 773-9062
wcscstx@attglobal.net

Washington Coalition of Sexual Assault Programs
2415 Pacific Avenue SE
Olympia, WA 98501
Ph: (360) 754-7583
Fax: (360) 786-8707
www.wcsap.org

West Virginia Foundation for Rape Information and Services, Inc.
112 Braddock Street
Fairmont, WV 26554
Ph: (304) 366-9500
Fax: (304) 366-9501
www.fris.org/fris.html

Wisconsin Coalition Against Sexual Assault
600 Williamson Street
Madison, WI 53703
Ph/TTY: (608) 257-1516
Fax: (608) 257-2150
wcasa@wcasa.org

Wyoming Coalition Against Domestic Violence and Sexual Assault
PO Box 236
Laramie, WY 82073
Ph: (307) 755-5481
Toll-free: (800) 990-3877
Fax: (307) 755-5482
www.wcadvsa.vcn.com

Help for Offenders

Association for the Treatment of Sexual Abusers
503-643-1023
www.atsa.com
atsa@atsa.com
An interdisciplinary, membership organization founded to foster research, facilitate information exchange, and further professional education, standards, and practices for those who treat offenders. Its goals are the protection of communities through responsible and ethical treatment of sex offenders, and the elimination of sexual victimization.

Center for Sex Offender Management
301-589-9383
www.csom.org
AskCSOM@CSOM.org
National project that aims to enhance public safety by preventing further victimizations. It supports state and local jurisdictions in the effective management of sex offenders under community supervision.

Sex Criminals Website
www.sexcriminals.com
Provides news articles, statistics, links to sex offender registries nationwide, and other resources.

Stop It Now!
888-PREVENT (888-773-8368)
413-268-3096
www.stopitnow.org
info@stopitnow.org
Calls on all abusers and potential abusers to stop and seek help, educates adults about ways to stop sexual abuse, and increases public awareness of the trauma of child sexual abuse. Offers a helpline for adult abusers and those at risk of sexually abusing a child, for friends and family members of sexual abusers or victims, and for parents of children with sexual behavior problems.

Prevention—Organizations

Breaking the Cycle/The Public Training Institute
317-745-6946
www.breakingthecycleinc.com
www.publictraining.com
Publictraining@aol.com
Offers domestic violence and sexual assault seminars and workshops for criminal justice systems, social service agencies, health care professionals, mental health professionals, community organizations, and the business community.

Center for the Study of Sport in Society—Mentors in Violence Prevention
Program
617-373-7651
www.sportinsociety.org
j.o'brien@neu.edu
This multiracial, mixed-gender program motivates student-athletes and student leaders to play a central role in solving problems that have historically been considered "women's issues": rape, battering, and sexual harassment. Empowers students to confront abusive peers.

Communities Against Rape and Abuse
www.cara-seattle.org
info@cara-seattle.org
206-322-4856
A social justice organization focused on anti-rape activism in Seattle. Its Black People's Project encourages new strategies for addressing sexual violence in culturally relevant ways.

National Black Police Association
202-986-2070
mbpanatofc@worldnet@att.net
www.blackpolice.org
Available to help communities develop crime prevention programs, education programs, provide workshops and trainings around crime-related issues and public safety.

National Center for the Health of Men, Boys, and Society
510-444-7738
www.preventioninstitute.org/boysguide.html
prevent@preventioninstitute.org
A project of the Prevention Institute. An Oakland-based advocacy organization, it address men's health from the perspective that their health-related beliefs and behaviors influence the well-being of women, girls, other men and boys, and the communities in which they live. Offers the resource guide "Young Men, Gender Socialization and Violence Prevention."

National Organization for Men Against Sexism

303-666-7043

www.nomas.org

info@nomas.org

The oldest pro-feminist men's group in the country, NOMAS is a progressive network of activist men and women. Its Ending Men's Violence Network provides an umbrella organization to support domestic violence, sexual assault, and victim assistance groups in local communities.

No More: The National Organization of Men's Outreach for Rape Education

757-221-2322

www.nomorerape.org

nomore@wm.edu

An organization of men and women that educates men about rape using the most effective methods shown by scientific research studies. Offers "The Men's Program," an all-male peer education program.

V-Day

www.vday.org

info@vday.org

This global movement distributes funds to grassroots, national, and international organizations and programs working to stop violence against women and girls. Local volunteers and college students produce benefit performances of the award-winning play "The Vagina Monologues" to raise money and awareness for antiviolence groups within their own communities. V-Day itself stages large-scale benefits and promotes innovative gatherings and programs to change social attitudes toward violence against women.

Prevention—Independent Male Educators

Nefera Amen

510-268-1284

neferaamen@yahoo.com

Founder of Enlighten Communications, Amen is available for speaking engagements, train-the-trainer programs, facilitator training, and program development.

Antonio Arrendel
617-354-4603
anarrendel@mail.com
Facilitates trainings and workshops on masculinity, gender issues, and violence prevention for boys and men age 13 and up.

Kenya Black
740-788-0306
mhacapp@hotmail.com
Coordinator of the Prevent Assault & Violence Education (PAVE) program at the Mental Health Association of Licking County, Black facilitates anger management support groups for men.

Daryl Fort
dfort44@yahoo.com
Works with male and mixed-gender groups in anti-gender violence trainings, orientations, and discussion groups focusing on potential bystander intervention.

Byron Hurt
617-482-3593
www.bhurt.com
bhurt@optonline.net
An anti-sexist activist and documentary filmmaker, Hurt is available for multimedia presentations and Q&A sessions.

Jackson Katz
562-997-3953
562-997-7804
www.jacksonkatz.com
Co-founder of the Mentors in Violence Prevention Model for gender violence

prevention and current founding director of MVP Strategies, Katz runs educational programs, gives lectures, holds trainings, writes curricula and articles, and makes educational films.

Kitwana Tyhimba
510-663-2185
kitwana007@hotmail.com
Founder of Tyhimba Consulting, Tyhimba conducts trainings and facilitates support groups and individual support sessions for men's issues including battering, child witnesses of domestic violence, child and adult survivors of physical or sexual violence, anger management, and parenting.

Paul Kivel
510-654-3015
pkivel@mindspring.com
www.paulkivel.com
Provides workshops, traingings, and curricula on men's violence against women and youth violence prevention.

Quentin Walcott
212-683-0015 ext. 225
qwalcott@connectnyc.org
www.urbanjustice.org
Facilitates domestic violence groups for male batterers, trains facilitators, develops curriculum for family violence programs, and provides community workshops and forums on battering intervention through the Community Empowerment Program of the Urban Justice Center.

Self-Defense

American Women's Self-Defense Association
888-STOP-RAPE (888-786-7727)
www.awsda.org
awsda@nvbb.net

Offers rape prevention courses for groups and rape awareness courses for high schools and colleges in the New York metro area. Gives referrals to self-defense training facilities, rape crisis centers, counselors, and support groups nationwide.

Arming Women Against Rape and Endangerment (AWARE)
781-893-0500
877-67-AWARE (877-672-9273)
www.aware.org
info@aware.org
Offers training, information, and support for organizations and individuals, primarily women, in New England. Teaches self-protection and self-defense skills that can enable women to avoid, resist, and survive various types of attack.

Sexuality Education and Healing

American Association of Sex Educators, Counselors, and Therapists
www.aasect.org
aasect@aasect.org
Provides professional education and certification of sex educators, counselors, and therapists and encourages research related to sex education, counseling, and therapy. Supports the Healthy Sex website (www.healthysex.com), an educational site developed by Wendy Maltz, an author and sex therapist in private practice in Eugene, Oregon, to promote healthy sexuality based on caring, respect, and safety.

The Sexual Health Network
203-924-4623
www.sexualhealth.com
Provides access to sexuality information, education, support, counseling, healthcare, products, and other resources for people with disabilities, illness or physical changes throughout the lifecycle and those who love them or care for them.

I Will Survive

Videos

Boys Will Be Men
A documentary film examining contemporary masculine identity and its development.
Available from Bullfrog Films
800-543-3764
www.bullfrogfilms.com
info@bullfrogfilms.com

I Am A Man
A documentary film on how racism, sexism, homophobia, and the threat of violence help shape Black masculine identity in contemporary American culture.
Available from God Bless the Child Productions, Inc.
631-234-1719
www.bhurt.com
bhurt@optonline.net

No! The Rape Documentary
A feature-length documentary exposing the Black community's collective silence about the sexual violation of women and girls.
215-735-7372
afrolez@aol.com

The Preachers: Working to End Sexual and Domestic Violence
Featuring sermons by ordained clergy who have survived partner violence.
Available from The Black Church and Domestic Violence Institute
770-909-0715
www.bcdvi.org
bcdvorg@aol.com

Rape Is . . .
A documentary exploring the meaning and consequences of rape.
Available from Cambridge Documentary Films
617-484-3993

www.cambridgedocumentaryfilms.org
cdf@shore.net
Relearning Touch: Healing Techniques for Couples
Partners in Healing: Couples Overcoming the Sexual Repercussions of
Incest
Available from Independent Video Services
800-678-3455

Sister, I'm Sorry
An hour-long video depicting Black men apologizing to Black women for the
social, emotional, psychological, and physical wrongs they have inflicted. Featuring Blair Underwood and other celebrities, it is designed to spark open dialogue and healing between men and women with an emphasis on creating a
healthier environment for children. Staff members are available for workshops
and seminars nationwide.
800-291-8561
www.sisterimsorry.com
sisterimsorry@aol.com

Tough Guise: Violence, Media, and the Crisis in Masculinity and
Wrestling With Manhood: Boys, Bullying, and Battering
Available from Media Education Foundation
800-897-0089
www.mediaed.org

Books

Healing
Angelou, Maya. *I Know Why the Caged Bird Sings*. New York: Bantam Books,
    1983.
Angus, W.A. *Anger Management Workbook*. Point Roberts, Wa.: PsychTest.com,
    2001.
Aranow, Vicki and Monique Land. *Journey to Wholeness: Healing from the
    Trauma of Rape*. Holmes Beach, FL: Learning Publications, 2000.

Bass, Ellen and Laura Davis. *Beginning to Heal: A First Book for Survivors of Child Sexual Abuse.* New York: HarperCollins, 1993.

Bass, Ellen and Laura Davis. *The Courage to Heal: A Guide for Women Survivors of Child Sexual Abuse.* New York: HarperPerennial, 1994.

Benedict, Helen. *Recovery: How to Survive Sexual Assault for Women, Men, Teenagers, Their Friends and Families.* New York: Columbia University Press, 1994.

Gandy, Debrena Jackson. *Sacred Pampering Principles: An African-American Woman's Guide to Self-Care and Inner Renewal.* New York: Quill, 1998.

Herman, Judith. *Trauma and Recovery.* New York: Basic Books, 1997.

Hollies, Linda H. *Jesus and Those Bodacious Women: Life Lessons from One Sister to Another.* Cleveland: United Church Press, 1998.

Lauer, Teresa M. *The Truth About Rape.* RapeRecovery.com, 2002.

Ledray, Linda E. *Recovering from Rape.* New York: Owlet Books, 1994.

Levine, Peter A. *Waking the Tiger: Healing Trauma: The Innate Capacity to Transform Overwhelming Experiences.* Berkeley: North Atlantic Books, 1997.

Lew, Mike. *Leaping upon the Mountains: Men Proclaiming Victory over Sexual Child Abuse.* Berkeley: North Atlantic Books, 2000.

Lew, Mike. *Victims No Longer: Men Recovering from Incest and Other Sexual Child Abuse.* New York: HarperCollins, 1990.

Mather, Cynthia L. *How Long Does It Hurt? A Guide for Recovering from Incest and Sexual Abuse for Teenagers, Their Friends and Their Families.* San Francisco: Jossey-Bass, 1994.

Matsakis, Aphrodite. *I Can't Get Over It: A Handbook for Trauma Survivors.* Oakland: New Harbinger, 1996.

Matsakis, Aphrodite. *Trust After Trauma: A Guide to Relationships for Survivors and Those Who Love Them.* Oakland: New Harbinger, 1998.

Schitaldi, Glenn R. *Post-Traumatic Stress Disorder Sourcebook.* Chicago: McGraw-Hill/Contemporary Books, 2000.

Vanzant, Iyanla. *Acts of Faith: Daily Meditations for People of Color.* New York: Fireside, 1993.

Vermilyea, Elizabeth G. *Growing Beyond Survival: A Self-Help Toolkit for Managing Traumatic Stress.* Towson, MD: Sidran Press, 2000.

West, Carolyn M., ed. *Violence in the Lives of Black Women: Battered, Black, and Blue.* Binghampton: The Haworth Press, 2002.

Domestic/Dating Violence

Betancourt, Marian. *What to Do When Love Turns Violent: A Practical Resource for Women in Abusive Relationships.* New York: Harper Perennial, 1997.

Davidson, Sue and Ginny NiCarthy. *You Can Be Free: An Easy-to-Read Handbook for Abused Women.* Seattle: Seal Press, 1997.

Gaddis, Patricia Riddle. *Dangerous Dating: Helping Young Women Say No to Abusive Relationships.* Colorado Springs: Shaw Books, 2000.

Levy, Barrie, ed. *Dating Violence: Young Women in Danger.* Seattle: Seal Press, 1998.

Levy, Barrie. *In Love and In Danger: A Teen's Guide to Breaking Free of Abusive Relationships.* Seattle: Seal Press, 1998.

Milano, Susan Murphy. *Defending Our Lives: Getting Away from Domestic Violence and Staying Safe.* New York: Anchor Books, 1996.

NiCarthy, Ginny. *Getting Free: You Can End Abuse and Take Back Your Life.* Seattle: Seal Press, 1997.

Statman, Jan Berliner. *The Battered Woman's Survival Guide.* Dallas: Taylor Publishing, 1995.

White, Evelyn C. *Chain Chain Change: For Black Women in Abusive Relationships.* Seattle: Seal Press, 1995.

Sexual Education and Health

Berman, Jennifer and Laura Berman. *For Women Only: A Revolutionary Guide to Overcoming Sexual Dysfunction and Reclaiming Your Sex Life.* New York: Henry Holt & Company, 2001.

Boston Women's Health Book Collective. *Our Bodies, Ourselves: For the New Century.* Carmichael, CA: Touchstone Books, 1998.

Boyd, Julia A. *Embracing the Fire: Sisters Talk About Sex and Relationships.* New York: Dutton Books, 1997.

Federation of Feminist Women's Health Centers. *A New View of a Woman's Body.* New York: Simon & Schuster, 1981.

Foley, Sallie, Sally A. Kope and Dennis P. Sugrue. *Sex Matters for Women: A Complete Guide to Taking Care of Your Sexual Self.* New York: Guilford Press, 2002.

Gordon, Sol. *Girls Are Girls and Boys Are Boys—So What's the Difference?* Amherst, NY: Prometheus Books, 1991.

Gordon, Sol and Judith Gordon. *Did the Sun Shine Before You Were Born?* Amherst, NY: Prometheus Books, 1992.

Haffner, Debra W. and Alyssa Haffner Tartaglione. *Beyond the Big Talk: Every Parent's Guide to Raising Sexually Healthy Teens—From Middle School to College.* New York: Newmarket Press, 2001.

Hutcherson, Hilda. *What Your Mother Never Told You About Sex.* New York: Putnam Pub Group, 2002.

Madaras, Lynda with Area Madaras. *The What's Happening to My Body? Book for Girls: A Growing-Up Guide for Parents and Daughters.* New York: Newmarket Press, 2000.

Maltz, Wendy. *Passionate Hearts: The Poetry of Sexual Love.* Novato, CA: New World Library, 2000.

Maltz, Wendy. *The Sexual Healing Journey: A Guide for Survivors of Sexual Abuse.* New York: Quill, 2001.

Miron, Amy G. and Charles D. Miron. *How to Talk With Teens About Love, Relationships, and S-E-X: A Guide for Parents.* Minneapolis: Free Spirit Publishing, 2002.

Newman, Susan. *Oh God! A Black Woman's Guide to Sex and Spirituality.* New York: One World, 2002.

Stewart, Elizabeth G. *The V Book: A Doctor's Guide to Complete Vulvovaginal Health.* New York: Bantam Doubleday Dell, 2002.

Wilson, Pamela. *When Sex Is the Subject: Attitudes and Answers for Young Children.* Hunt Valley, MD: Network Publications, 1991.

Wyatt, Gail Elizabeth. *Stolen Women: Reclaiming Our Sexuality, Taking Back Our Lives.* Hoboken, NJ: John Wiley & Sons, 1997.

Books for Loved Ones of Survivors

Cameron, Grant. *What About Me? A Guide for Men Helping Female Partners Deal with Childhood Sexual Abuse.* Carp, Ontario: Creative Bound, 1994.

Davis, Laura. *Allies in Healing: When the Person You Love Was Sexually Abused as a Child.* New York: HarperPerennial, 1991.

Graber, Ken. *Ghosts in the Bedroom: A Guide for Partners of Incest Survivors.* Deerfield Beach, FL: Health Communications, 1991.

Hagans, Kathryn B. and Joyce Case. *When Your Child Has Been Molested: A Parent's Guide to Healing and Recovery.* San Francisco: Jossey-Bass, 1998.

Levine, Peter A. *It Won't Hurt Forever: Guiding Your Child Through Trauma.* Louisville: Sounds True Inc., 2001.

Levine, Robert Barry. *When You Are the Partner of a Rape or Incest Survivor: A Workbook for You.* San Jose, CA: Resource Publications, 1996.

Myers, John E. B. *A Mother's Nightmare—Incest: A Practical Legal Guide for Parents and Professionals.* Thousand Oaks, CA: Sage Publications, 1997.

Prevention and Education

Creighton, Allan. *Helping Teens Stop Violence: A Practical Guide for Educators, Counselors, and Parents.* Alameda, CA: Hunter House, 1992.

Creighton, Allan and Paul Kivel. *Men's Work: How to Stop the Violence that Tears Our Lives Apart.* New York: Ballantine Books, 1992.

Davis, Angela. *Violence Against Women and the Ongoing Challenge to Racism.* New York: Kitchen Table/Women of Color, 1988.

Davis, Angela. *Women, Race and Class.* New York: Random House, 1983.

Gordon, Sol and Judith Gordon. *A Better Safe Than Sorry Book: A Family Guide for Sexual Assault Prevention.* Amherst, NY: Prometheus Books, 1992.

Hine, Darlene Clark, ed. *Black Women in America: An Historical Encyclopedia.* Pittsburgh: Carlson Publications, 1993.

Hunter, Tera W. *To Joy My Freedom: Southern Black Women's Lives and Labors After the Civil War.* Cambridge: Harvard University Press, 1998.

Kivel, Paul. *I Can Make My World a Safer Place: A Kid's Book About Stopping Violence.* Alameda, CA: Hunter House, 2001.

Lerner, Gerda, ed. *Black Women in White America: A Documentary History.* New York: Vintage Books, 1992.

Lindquist, Scott. *The Date Rape Prevention Book.* Naperville, IL: Sourcebooks, 2000.

Miedzian, Myriam. *Boys Will Be Boys: Breaking the Link Between Masculinity and Violence.* New York: Doubleday, 1991.

Nelson, Terry Spahr. *For Love of Country: Confronting Rape and Sexual*

Harassment in the U.S. Military. Binghamton, NY: Haworth Maltreatment & Trauma Press, 2002.

Sanford, Linda Tschirhart. *The Silent Children: A Parent's Guide to the Prevention of Child Sexual Abuse*. New York: McGraw-Hill, 1985.

Smith, George Edmond. *Walking Proud: Black Men Living Beyond the Stereotypes*. New York: Kensington Publishing Corporation, 2001.

Vanzant, Iyanla and Almasi Wilcots. *Don't Give It Away! A Workbook of Self-Awareness and Self-Affirmations for Young Women*. New York: Fireside, 1999.

ABOUT THE AUTHOR

Lori S. Robinson, a rape survivor herself, is a journalist and educator. Most recently, she taught media at Universidad San Francisco de Quito in Quito, Ecuador. A former editor and columnist at *Emerge: Black America's News Magazine,* her honors and awards include the National Association of Black Journalist awards, the Unity Award in Media, and the International Black Women's Congress Inspirational Award. Her work has appeared in the *Crisis, Source, Essence,* and the *Washington Post.* She lives in Silver Spring, Maryland.

Julia A. Boyd is a Seattle-based psychotherapist and the author of *In the Company of My Sisters: Black Women and Self Esteem* and *Can I Get a Witness: Black Women and Depression.* She has worked with sexual and domestic abuse survivors for over twenty years.

Index

patriarchy, 228–29

pepper spray, 188

perpetrators

　(*see also* rapists)

　Black men protected by Black
　　women, xviii, 31–32, 31–32,
　　229

　Blacks treated differently than
　　Whites, xviii, 27, 228

　child sexual abuse, 18, 196–97

　criminal prosecution of (see
　　civil litigation; criminal pros-
　　ecution)

　HIV testing of, 14–15

　identifying, 33

　known to victims, xix, 18, 174

　myths, 176

　profile, xviii–xix

　recidivism, 32

Peru, xxi

Phelps, Dr. Jamie T., 147, 148

phobias, 65, 81, 110

physical examination. See medical
　examination

Planned Parenthood, 12, 14, 15

police

　African American aversion to,
　　31

　insensitivity, 32–33

　notifying, 32–35

post-traumatic stress disorder
　(PTSD)

　biofeedback, 80

　child sexual abuse, 106

　hypnotherapy, 81

　sexual violence, 62, 69, 108,
　　109, 110

"Prayer and Chant" (Hall), 150

"Prayer for Church Empower-
　ment" (Simpson), 170 n.7

"Prayer for Church Empowerment
　to Stant Up and Speak Out
　Against Domestic Violence, A"
　(Simpson), 152–54

"Prayer for Incest Survivors"
　(Huggins), 143–44

"Prayer for Peace" (Gardner),
　161–62, 171 n-11

"Prayer for Spiritual Healing, A"
　(Simons), 169–70

"Prayer of Unending Praise!"
　(Hollies), 145

prayers, 139–62, 169–70

"Preacher's Prayer for the Sisters
　and the Brothers, A" (Sampson),
　155–56

pregnancy, 12

prisons, xx, 107, 108, 176

promiscuity, 66

prostitution, 37

　child sexual abuse, 106, 107, 175

"Protective Presence, A"
　(Newman), 140–41

Public Health Service, 15

race

　criminal justice, 27, 38, 227–28

　rape, xviii, 31

　sexism, 180, 228

racism, 62, 177

　in criminal justice system, 27,
　　38, 227–28

　rape culture, xviii, 228

　sexism, 180, 228

Selected Titles from Seal Press

The Black Women's Health Book: Speaking for Ourselves edited by Evelyn C. White. $16.95, 1-878067-40-0. A pioneering anthology addressing the health issues facing today's black woman. Features Alice Walker, bell hooks, Toni Morrison, Byllye Y. Avery, Audre Lorde, Faye Wattleton, Jewelle L. Gomez, Marian Wright Edelman, and many others.

Chain Chain Change by Evelyn C. White. $12.95, 1-878067-60-5. This invaluable guide for black women suffering from domestic violence offers words of advice and solace for black women who are victims of abuse.

Dating Violence: Young Women in Danger edited by Barrie Levy, M.S.W. $20.95, 1-58005-001-8. Written for counselors, social workers, and parents, this comprehensive resource includes stories from teens in abusive relationships, information from researchers, and perspectives from activists working in schools and communities.

In Love and In Danger: A Teen's Guide to Breaking Free of Abusive Relationships by Barrie Levy, M.S.W. $10.95, 1-58005-002-6. *In Love and In Danger* helps teens recognize and end abusive dating relationships. This new edition includes an updated resource list, in addition to testimonies, checklists, charts, and helpful advice that provide at-a-glance information. Also available in Spanish language edition, *Jóvenes, Enamorados y en Peligro*.

Getting Free: You Can End Abuse and Take Back Your Life by Ginny NiCarthy, M.S.W. $16.95, 1-878067-92-3. This important self-help book covers issues such as defining physically and emotionally abusive relationships; getting emergency help; deciding to leave or stay; the economics of single life; and how to be your own counselor.

You Can Be Free: An Easy-to-Read Handbook for Abused Women by Ginny NiCarthy, M.S.W. and Sue Davidson. $10.95, 1-878067-06-0. This simplified version of *Getting Free: You Can Be Free* is written in an accessible style for the woman in crisis. It covers a range of topic designed to help women leave abusive relationships.

To Be an Anchor in the Storm: A Guide for Families and Friends of Abused Women by Susan Brewster, M.S.W. $12.95, 1-58005-037-9. Here is the first practical guide for those who want to assist a friend or loved one in her struggle to escape from an abusive relationship.

Seal Press publishes many books of fiction and nonfiction by women writers. Please visit our website at **www.sealpress.com**.